DISTRIBUTED OPEN SYSTEMS

DISTRIBUTED OPEN SYSTEMS

F.M.T. Brazier and D. Johansen

IEEE Computer Society Press
Los Alamitos, California

Washington • Brussels • Tokyo

Library of Congress Cataloging-in-Publication Data

Distributed open systems / [edited by] F.M.T. Brazier and D. Johansen.
    p. cm.
    Includes papers presented at a EurOpen conference held in Tromsø,
Norway in 1991, in addition to a number of new papers.
    "IEEE catalog number EH0373-1" — T.p. verso.
    Includes bibliographical references.
    ISBN 0-8186-4292-0. — ISBN 0-8186-4291-2 (microfiche).
    1. Electronic data processing — Distributed processing.
I. Brazier, F.M.T. (Frances M.T.) II. Johansen, D. (Dag)
QA76.9.D5D5563   1994
004'.36 — dc20   93-29386
                                                                                         CIP

Published by the
IEEE Computer Society Press
10662 Los Vaqueros Circle
P.O. Box 3014
Los Alamitos, CA 90720-1264

© 1994 by the Institute of Electrical and Electronics Engineers, Inc. All rights reserved.

Copyright and Reprint Permissions: Abstracting is permitted with credit to the source. Libraries are permitted to photocopy beyond the limits of US copyright law, for private use of patrons, those articles in this volume that carry a code at the bottom of the first page, provided that the per-copy fee indicated in the code is paid through the Copyright Clearance Center, 27 Congress Street, Salem, MA 01970. For other copying, reprint, or republication permission, write to IEEE Copyrights Manager, IEEE Service Center, 445 Hoes Lane, P.O. Box 1331, Piscataway, NJ 08855-1331.

IEEE Computer Society Press Order Number 4292-03
Library of Congress Number 93-29386
IEEE Catalog Number EH0373-1
ISBN 0-8186-4292-0 (case)
ISBN 0-8186-4291-2 (microfiche)

Additional copies can be ordered from

IEEE Computer Society Press	IEEE Service Center	IEEE Computer Society	IEEE Computer Society
Customer Service Center	445 Hoes Lane	13, avenue de l'Aquilon	Ooshima Building
10662 Los Vaqueros Circle	P.O. Box 1331	B-1200 Brussels	2-19-1 Minami-Aoyama
P.O. Box 3014	Piscataway, NJ 08855-1331	BELGIUM	Minato-ku, Tokyo 107
Los Alamitos, CA 90720-1264	Tel: (908) 981-1393	Tel: +32-2-770-2198	JAPAN
Tel: (714) 821-8380	Fax: (908) 981-9667	Fax: +32-2-770-8505	Tel: +81-3-3408-3118
Fax: (714) 821-4641			Fax: +81-3-3408-3553
Email: cs.books@computer.org			

Technical Editor: Felipe Cabrera
Production Editor: Edna Straub
Cover: Joe Daigle / Schenk-Daigle Studios
Printed in the United States of America by Braun-Brumfield, Inc.

The Institute of Electrical and Electronics Engineers, Inc.

Preface

Distributed Open Systems was the theme of a very successful EurOpen conference in Tromsø, Norway, in 1991. The most relevant papers presented at that conference have been revised for this book, and new papers have been added.

Without Bruce Shriver this volume would not have been produced; he was the initiator of this endeavour, for which we are most appreciative. We would also like to thank Hans Strack-Zimmerman and Ernst Janich for their valuable input; the IEEE Computer Society's representatives, Henry Ayling and Luis Felipe Cabrera, for their assistance in the realisation of this manuscript; and the IEEE Computer Society's production editor, Edna Straub, for proving that, with a little patience, distributed processing of a manuscript can be successfully achieved across both oceans and time zones.

And finally, we are sincerely grateful to the authors, all of whom have not only revised their original papers, but have also graciously provided their texts in different formats for different purposes, upon request.

Frances Brazier
Vrije Universiteit Amsterdam, the Netherlands

Dag Johansen
University of Tromsø, Norway

About This Book

Dag Johansen and Frances Brazier

Considerable progress has been made in the design and implementation of distributed systems and distributed applications over the last decade. The purpose of this book is to present some of these developments.

The first paper gives a brief introduction to distributed computing, presenting an architecture for distributed systems. This architecture contains a kernel layer, a service layer, a distributed programming support layer, and an application layer. The rest of the book is structured around this architecture, presenting real experience with actual systems and applications.

The kernel layer is represented by three different papers. The first reports on the Amoeba microkernel, emphasizing interprocess communication. Interprocess communication is the glue that binds the different components of a distributed system together. The functionality of the mechanism decides how to do this, and the performance of the mechanism indicates how well this is done. The second kernel paper reports on the Chorus approach to providing a microkernel-based UNIX system. Clearly, there is a large computing community that wants to achieve the benefits normally provided by a distributed system. Simultaneously, there is a strong interest in keeping the well-known functionality of UNIX. The Chorus/Mix microkernel-based distributed system is binary-compatible with UNIX. Plan 9 from AT&T is the subject of the third kernel paper. The Plan 9 approach is orthogonal to many of the distributed systems being built. The minimalistic microkernel approach has not been adopted because the Plan 9 kernel provides most of the operating system's functionality. Alternative approaches implement a limited set of frequently used services in the kernel. The rest of the functionality is implemented in user space as separate servers.

The kernel layer provides the basic services of a distributed system. Additional services are normally needed to provide a complete environment for application programs. These services are located in the service layer of our architecture. The paper on the OSF framework for a distributed computing environment reports on an approach to provide this. The paper also deals with security issues. Authentication is vital in securing a distributed system. Authentication means that communicating parties can be identified across insecure networks. The paper on the evolution of the Kerberos authentication service presents details on a widely adopted authentication service. Reliability and availability are considered important attributes of a distributed system. Replication techniques frequently utilize the fault-tolerance potential found in a distributed system running on several nodes. This is also the approach taken in the ISIS system, a system that provides tools to support the construction of reliable distributed software. ISIS is based on the process group approach to achieve increased reliability and availability. The ISIS paper in this book reports on the new version currently under development.

Management is an important task of a distributed system. The Meta toolkit, built on top of ISIS to provide tools for monitoring and controlling distributed applications, is the subject of the next paper. Meta assists in the construction and execution of reactive systems by instrumenting applications with sensors and actuators for management purposes.

The distributed programming support layer is the third layer of our architecture. The next paper in this volume has as its topic the concept of objects in a distributed environment. It presents requirements for adding distribution to the object concept. The paper following that addresses a comparative study of five parallel programming languages. This study is based on actual programming experience with multiple languages.

The application layer is the highest layer in our architecture. Currently, this layer is dominated by traditional sequential applications taking advantage of a virtual machine in a distributed environment. The paper on the StormCast approach shows that applications created for distribution should be structured as truly distributed applications. An architecture for distributed monitoring applications with distributed application derivatives is presented in the paper.

The final paper briefly summarizes benefits of distributed systems. It is illustrated with some of the approaches presented in the rest of the book.

Table of Contents

Preface v
Frances Brazier and Dag Johansen

About this Book vi
Dag Johansen and Frances Brazier

Software Structures for Supporting Distributed Computing 1
D. Johansen and R. van Renesse

The Amoeba Microkernel 11
A.S. Tanenbaum and M.F. Kaashoek

A New Look at Microkernel-Based UNIX Operating Systems: Lessons in Performance and Compatibility 31
A. Bricker, M. Gien, M. Guillemont, J. Lipkis, D. Orr, and M. Rozier (first published as "Architectural Issues in Microkernel-Based Operating Systems: The CHORUS Experience," in *Computer Communications*, Vol. 14, No. 6, July/August 1991, pages 347–357)

Plan 9: A Distributed System 49
D. Presotto, R. Pike, K. Thompson, H. Trickey, and P. Winterbottom

A Distributed Computing Environment Framework: An OSF Perspective 57
B.C. Johnson (an Open Software Foundation technical report)

The Evolution of the Kerberos Authentication Service 78
J.T. Kohl, B.C. Neuman, and T.Y. Ts'o

Fault-Tolerant Programming Using Process Groups 96
R. van Renesse and K. Birman

Tools for Monitoring and Controlling Distributed Applications 113
K. Marzullo and M.D. Wood

Distributing Objects 123
A. Herbert

A Comparative Study of Five Parallel Programming Languages 134
H.E. Bal

StormCast: Yet Another Exercise in Distributed Computing 152
D. Johansen

Distributed Systems in Perspective 175
D. Johansen and R. van Renesse

About the Authors 181

Software Structures for Supporting Distributed Computing

Dag Johansen
Dept. of Computer Science
University of Tromsø
Tromsø, Norway
<dag@cs.uit.no>

Robbert van Renesse
Dept. of Computer Science
Cornell University
Ithaca, NY, USA
<rvr@cs.cornell.edu>

Abstract

This paper gives a brief introduction to distributed systems. A layered architecture of distributed systems is presented with details on models and abstractions at the different layers.

1 Towards distributed computing

Advances in computer technology over the past few years include faster, cheaper computers delivering more power at lower cost. Fast computer networks also enable communication between the different computers, both in local area and wide area network configurations. The spread of computer systems into all aspects of society also adds pressure for more sophisticated applications. Driven by these technological advances, computer systems are being constructed that span several computers.

In this new environment, a configuration with a network of high-performance graphical workstations and servers typically provides the framework for what we call distributed computing. Distributed computing is a term used when a set of communicating processes usually located at different nodes, cooperate to solve a common problem.

This network of workstations and servers can be viewed as a single, time-shared computer with extra functionality, including the ability to hide the presence and the location of the components. A system providing such a transparent virtual machine is called a distributed system.

Distributed system was one of the computer buzzwords of the 80s. Unfortunately, no universally converging agreement exists on the concept. Our approach is the same as taken by Tanenbaum and van Renesse [Tane85] where a distributed system is equivalent with a distributed operating system. This distributed system is built on top of a hardware layer containing a set of physically separated computers which fail independently. Each computer has at least one processor, local main memory and a local clock, and may contain disks.

In this paper we identify three layers in distributed systems: the kernel layer, the service layer, and the language layer. In particular, for each layer, we will discuss some popular models and abstractions that deal with distribution at that layer. It is our intention to provide the reader, through these layers, with a basic understanding of how distributed systems are organized.

The remainder of the paper is organized as follows. Section 2 presents some of the main problems with distribution. Section 3 presents a layered architecture of distributed systems. Sections 4, 5 and 6 detail the three main layers. Finally, Section 7 summarizes the paper.

2 Main problems with distribution

There are several major difficulties in building a distributed system on top of separate hardware components. Heterogeneity, lack of a common clock, no common address space, network delays, network malfunctions, and nondeterministic behavior of communicating concurrent processes are some of the problems that have to be dealt with in such environments.

A first problem to solve is related to how to name entities in a distributed system. It is important that a global naming scheme is used where the same name can be used throughout the entire distributed system independent of the actual location of the named entity.

A second problem is related to how to access services provided by a distributed system. It is vital that a service can be requested independent of where the service provider or providers are located. A global access mechanism must allow a process on one node to contact processes on remote nodes as if they were located locally.

A third problem is related to management of distributed systems. Distributed systems scaling to thousands of nodes can be commonplace in the near future. Distributed systems are already spanning both local area networks, organizations and even countries. Monitoring and controlling such systems are a challenge.

Global scheduling problems have to be solved to meet user demands. Distributed systems can be running a diverse set of computation-intensive applications, complex applications with hard timing constraints, and applications with high reliability requirements. These applications have to be scheduled in an efficient manner.

Obtaining security in distributed systems is a challenge compared to centralized computer systems installed in a single room. It is recognized that a centralized computer system has potential security flaws already present. Additionally, a distributed environment creates new security threats through the network interface. Global security must provide the same authentication and access control mechanisms everywhere. Privacy and integrity must also be ensured by securing networks.

New problems can also be caused as a side-effect of other solutions in distributed systems. One example is consistency problems caused by replication techniques used to increase availability and reliability in distributed systems. Another is the demand for disconnected operability for mobile users.

Last, but not least, performance is a main consideration in the design and implementation of any system, and distributed systems in particular.

3 Layered architecture of distributed systems

It is often desirable to hide network details for application programmers in networking environments. One approach to achieve this is taken at the operating system level by extending the functionality normally provided by a set of monolithic operating systems. For example, global naming, addressing and location mechanisms can be used to provide a location-independent way of connecting the different parts of the distributed system.

The other approach taken is language oriented. Programming languages especially designed for distributed programming can express, for instance, parallelism, communication and synchronization between programming entities at a high level. More details on the language approach can be found in Bal et al. [Bal89] [Bal90]. Figure 1 illustrates the two different approaches with the language approach at right. The operating system support for the language approach can be traditional operating systems such as the UNIX[*] system.

---
[*] UNIX is a registered trademark of AT&T Bell Laboratories.

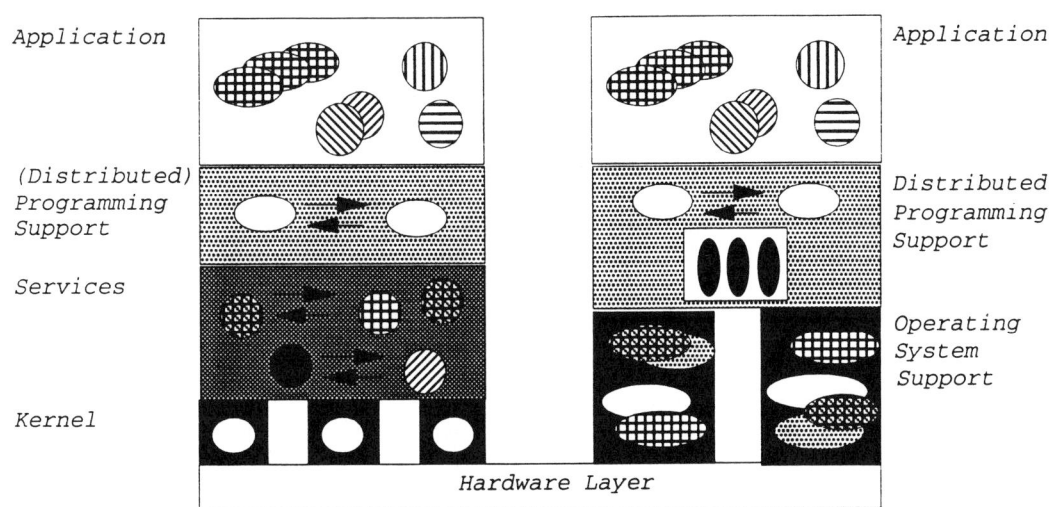

Figure 1. A distributed system architecture and a distributed programming support architecture.

An architecture for the distributed system approach is shown on the left side of Figure 1. This four layer architecture has a kernel layer in the bottom, then a service layer, a distributed programming support layer and an application layer at the top. The kernel layer is above a hardware layer which can be similar in both approaches. This hardware layer often provides hardware abstractions through an assembly language interface. The rest of this paper focuses on the distributed system approach. Examples of distributed systems include Amoeba [Tane90], Chorus [Rozi88] and Mach [Acce86].

Distributed system software components are normally structured as either kernel or user space modules. A set of kernels running on each node in the distributed system provides general low-level services in kernel mode with extra hardware protection. Regular users can only access a local kernel through its defined interface, but cannot modify the kernel itself. The rest of the distributed system functionality is built outside the kernels in user space.

4 The kernel layer

The kernel layer in the architecture provides basic operating system services often structured as micro-kernels such as the V-kernel [Cher88], Amoeba, Chorus and Mach. Each node in the distributed system runs the same micro-kernel. The term micro refers to functionality, rather than amount of code. For example, although the Plan 9 kernel [Pres91] is small, it contains most of the operating system's functionality. As such it is not a micro-kernel.

Little transparency is provided by the kernel layer itself, as each user often knows which kernel and node he is using when additional software is loaded and run. The control of each kernel is also local. Location transparency and global control are normally provided at higher layers in the architecture. Indeed, the job of the kernel is to operate the local machine; by definition it cannot be distributed.

4.1 Kernel layer models

A typical distributed system configuration includes a communication subsystem as a local area network to which a collection of nodes are connected. A distributed system is often based on the workstation model or processor pool model. Each node in both models basically runs a replica of the same operating system kernel. Hybrid models also exist combining features from the two other models.

4.1.1 The workstation model

The workstation model consists of a set of workstations interconnected by one or more local area networks, typically with a transfer rate of 10 Mbit/s. The workstations are active as nodes in the system running software locally. Specialized server computers are added to this configuration to provide extra services or better quality of services. Chorus and Mach are distributed systems based on the workstation model. Figure 2 illustrates the workstation model.

For instance, a workstation can provide a programming environment running a window system and an editor, a specialized compute server located elsewhere can be used for compilations, and a specialized storage server can be used for data storage and retrieval.

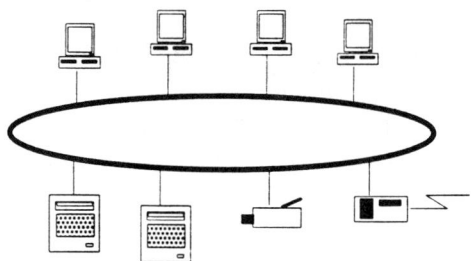

Figure 2. The workstation model.

4.1.2 The processor pool model

The basic idea behind the processor pool model is to access a processor pool through terminals interconnected by a local area network. This processor pool functions as a dedicated processing server. Together with other specialized servers, it provides services off-loading work normally done locally as in the workstation model. The Cambridge Distributed Computing System [Need82] was based on the processor pool model where terminals shared pools of minicomputers. Amoeba is also a distributed system based on this model with terminals or later workstations sharing a rack-mounted pool of processors. The operating system Plan 9 is also based on this model. Figure 3 illustrates the processor pool model.

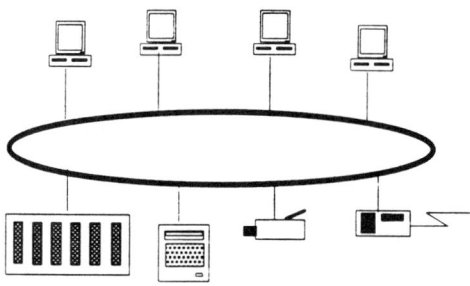

Figure 3. The processor pool model.

Terminals or workstations can be seen as the front-end to the accessible servers elsewhere in the system. Such servers include compute servers as a rack-mounted pool of processors in Amoeba or multiprocessors in Plan 9. The processor pool model differs basically from the workstation model by running little if any computations on the workstation itself, although the distinction may be small.

4.2 Kernel layer abstractions

At the kernel layer in a distributed system, a basic abstraction for a program in execution must be provided. In the Amoeba system, the term process denotes a computer program in execution with its registers, program counter and stack. This is similar to the task concept in Mach and actor concept in Chorus. A related key abstraction is a block of memory, in Amoeba a segment, in Mach a memory object.

Another key abstraction in the kernel layer is needed for communication and synchronization. The Amoeba and Chorus abstraction is a message which can be sent between processes located at the same or different nodes. Mach only provides local communication at the kernel layer.

An abstraction for addressing of senders and receivers can be the port abstraction as in Amoeba, Mach and Chorus. A port is used to address the destination of a message as well as the sender when a reply is required. Port groups as found in Chorus is also a basic addressing abstraction to be used when the same message should be sent to a set of receivers at the same time.

An additional task of the kernel is to manage local devices, such as disks. However, the kernel itself does not provide an abstraction for such devices. Instead these will be provided by higher-level services.

5 The service layer

Operating system services not provided by the lowest layer must be provided at the service layer. In this case, library routines are called rather than actual kernel calls. The library routines may communicate with server processes, which may be remote, or run on the same machine.

These services are implemented as user-space servers that use low-level services provided by the kernel. The service layer unifies the different nodes running a kernel replica into a single, location transparent virtual machine. Together with the kernel layer, the service layer often contains the operating system software needed to provide an operating system interface.

For example, distributed file systems are often implemented at this layer, even if performance might suffer. Advantages by having the file servers as well as other servers running in user space is a smaller kernel, a more structured system for maintenance and potential coexistence of different servers. This also gives a well-defined separation between mechanisms implemented in the kernel layer and policies implemented in the service layer.

5.1 Service layer models

The client-server model is a common paradigm for structuring distributed systems. In this model, one or a set of servers is responsible for the provision of a service. This service can be requested by clients who have the permission and knowledge to use it. This service is defined and accessed via an interface made known to its environment.

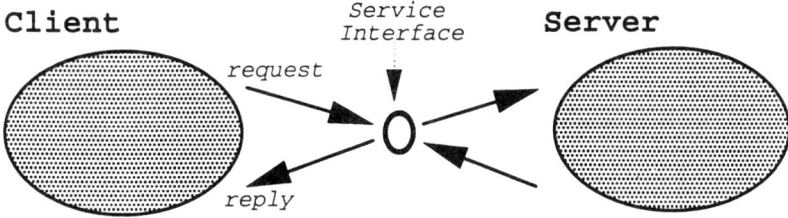

Figure 4. The client-server model.

The concept client-server is widely used. The service model is a similar concept, "service" indicating that clients request a service, not a particular server. In distributed systems, this gives a higher level of transparency since a service can be implemented by several servers. Yet, only one server normally responds to a single request. The client-server model is illustrated in Figure 4.

Another model is the group model. The group model is characterized by a set of group members forming a group which is addressed as one entity. This is illustrated in Figure 5.

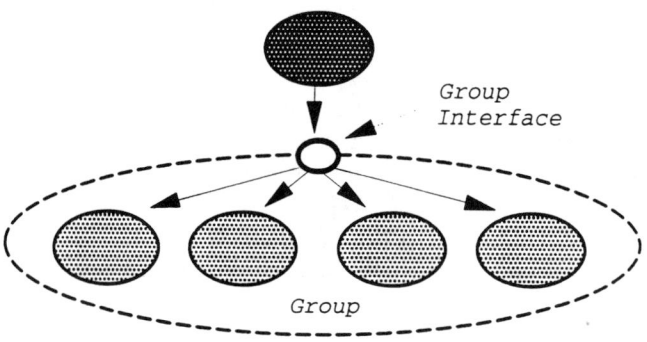

Figure 5. The group model.

5.2 Service layer abstractions

The service layer contains abstractions for the loci of control as well as the communication between them. These map directly down to the fundamental abstractions in the kernel layer. A thread as in Mach, Chorus or Amoeba is a common abstraction describing the loci of control at the service layer. A thread is running in the address space provided by kernel abstractions as a task, process or actor. Multiple threads may coexist sharing the same program code and global data, but with private registers, program counter and stack. This is typically used to implement servers handling several requests at the same time. One thread might for instance have to block until some input is received. Then, another thread might be activated handling another request to the same server. This is illustrated in Figure 6.

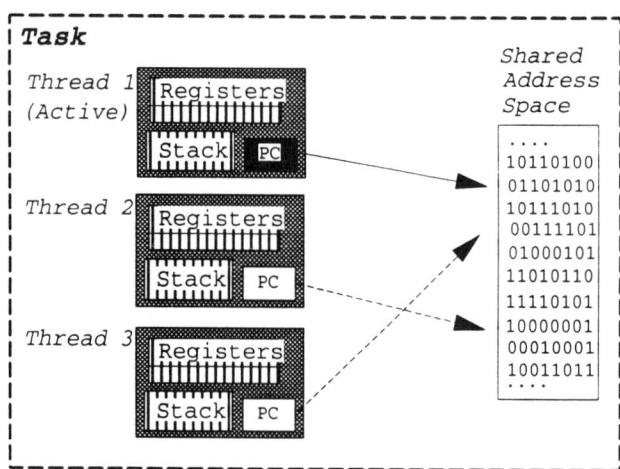

Figure 6. Multiple threads in one task.

Communication is provided by some kind of structured message interface. The majority of interaction in distributed systems today is formed by *client/server* interactions, consisting of a request message sent by a client process to a server process, and the server responding with a reply message after it serviced the request. An common example is a file service, where clients send read and write requests to a particular server that holds the relevant file.

Process groups as found in ISIS [Birm87] provide a convenient abstraction for distributed application programmers. The basic idea is to enable sending of a message to several receivers simultaneously. ISIS group communication abstractions can also ensure a total ordering of messages sent to a group, and deal with failures of the members in a group. Thus the abstraction is both a communication and management paradigm. Process groups have also been implemented at the kernel layer in distributed systems as V [Cher85] and Amoeba. A port group in Chorus also allows such grouping.

6 Distributed programming support — the language layer

The kernel and service layers provide an environment for user applications, be they regular sequential applications as found in uniprocessor systems, or distributed applications. A distributed application is structured as a set of modules cooperating to achieve a common goal. Examples of distributed applications include distributed banking and distributed monitoring applications [Joha91].

As Figure 1 shows, programming languages providing parallel and distributed execution can be used to support the building of distributed applications. Nevertheless, an application programmer on a distributed system often uses existing sequential languages with library extensions for distributed system services. Application programs are then executed as client processes requesting distributed system services mostly by a synchronous RPC interface. Application modules can also interact with other modules at the application layer through the RPC interface provided.

6.1 Language layer models

Imperative languages as C with focus on variables and values are commonly used for programming applications to be run on distributed systems. Applications are then structured as cooperating sequential processes.

The object-oriented paradigm has also become popular. This paradigm models distributed applications as a set of objects where the focus is on the behavior of each object. An object is an instance of a certain class and encapsulates data and its operations, the operations defining the interface of the object. Data can only be modified by these local operations, which are invoked through the interface of the object. Interactions between objects can still be in a client-server style, but variables and values as found in imperative programming languages are hidden inside each object. It is obvious that this model maps well to a distributed environment, where operations on objects may be invoked remotely through the use of RPC.

Yet another paradigm, the functional model, allows no data to be modified, but just the manipulation of values. As there are no side-effects of function calls in such a model, arguments to functions may be evaluated in parallel. Furthermore, in the case of failures, functions may be re-evaluated without any problems. Although parallelism is easily extracted from functional languages, it is hard to divide the tasks over distributed components as the granularity of the parallel activities is often very small.

6.2 Language layer abstractions

To express parallelism, languages often provide a procedural interface to threads at the service layer. Other languages may provide parallel execution abstracts, like cobegin/coend blocks, to allow users to specify parallelism explicitly. Yet other languages, especially functional and data flow languages, may detect independent blocks themselves and hide the parallelism from the users altogether.

Remote procedure calls [Birr84] dominate the interaction mechanisms found at the language layer in distributed systems. The idea is to have a method of accessing both local and remote procedures resembling the semantics and syntax of normal procedure calls as found in high-level programming languages. An RPC interaction is basically a client/server interaction, where the client is blocked until a reply is received or a timeout occurs. RPC often provides location transparency, especially in a local area network environment. The run time system of an RPC facility handles the mapping between the high-level location transparent RPC interface and the low level underlying network protocols. This includes locating a server implementing the service, marshalling arguments at the client side, sending them over the network, unmarshalling the arguments at the server node, and sending them to the local server who does the actual work that was requested. A reply is sent back to the client in a similar fashion.

Stubs provide presentation transparency. First, the stub, a computer-generated language procedure, is responsible for the binding between a naming and location mechanism. A third-party name server or binder can be contacted replying with the mapping between a server and its network address. All servers available must register with this name server. Then, the stub marshals the argument of the call and sends it over the network using lower layer protocols. The server stub unmarshals the arguments and sends a local request to the server. The client-stub operates on behalf of the server at the other side of the connection and the server-stub operates on behalf of the client. This is illustrated in Figure 7. Consequently, the client stub and the server stub hide network details for the RPC programmer.

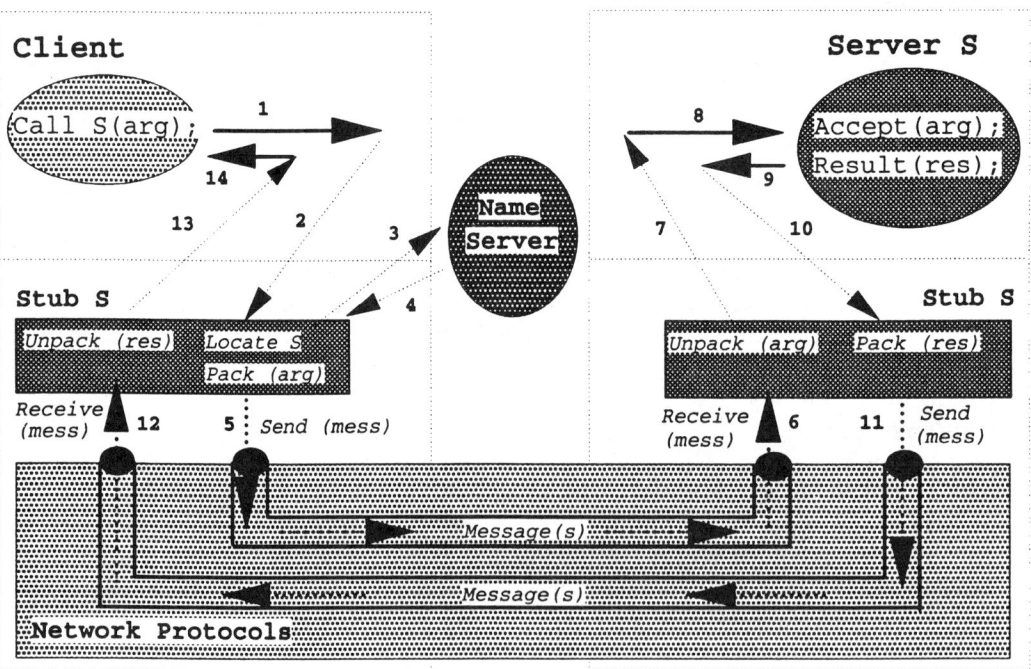

Figure 7. RPC with stubs.

7 Summary

Advances in computer technology combined with more sophisticated user needs have resulted in an increasing interest in distributed computing. Normal users are interested in applications only, and a distributed system should provide a transparent virtual machine for these users.

We can structure a distributed system into a hierarchical architecture with a kernel layer above the general hardware layer and a service layer above the kernel layer. A distributed programming support layer can be located on top of the service layer with the application layer on top.

A distributed system must provide basic abstractions as, for instance, processes, memory segments, messages and ports. Basic services built around these abstractions must also be provided. Examples include process management, memory management and inter-process communication. Such services are provided at different layers in the distributed system architecture. In distributed systems, basic operating system services are often provided by so-called micro-kernels. These are often small, highly optimized kernels designed and implemented to contain minimal overhead and functionality. Operating system services not found in the kernel layer are implemented in user space as dedicated server processes.

Micro-kernels have been around in research laboratories for over two decades and are now growing into the marketplace. Such kernels do not form a distributed system by themselves, but provide an open platform where a set of operating system services can be implemented to coexist on the same platform.

Acknowledgments

We would like to thank Mike Schroeder for helpful discussions and comments on earlier drafts of this paper.

References

Acce86   M. Accetta, R. Baron, W. Bolosky, D. Golub, R. Rashid, A. Tevanian, and M. Young, "Mach: A New Kernel Foundation for UNIX Development," *Proc. USENIX 1986 Summer Conference*, July 1986, pp. 93-113.

Bal89   H.E. Bal, J.G. Steiner, and A.S. Tanenbaum, "Programming Languages for Distributed Computing Systems," *ACM Computing Surveys*, Vol. 21, No. 3, Sept. 1989, pp. 261-322.

Bal90   H.E. Bal, *Programming Distributed Systems*, Silicon Press, Summit, NJ, 1990, (also published by Prentice Hall Int'l, 1991).

Birm87   K. P. Birman, and T. A. Joseph, "Exploiting Virtual Synchrony in Distributed Systems," *Proc. of the 11th ACM Symp. on Operating Systems Principles*, Austin, Texas, Nov. 1987, pp. 123-138.

Birr84   A.D. Birrell and B.J. Nelson, "Implementing Remote Procedure Calls," *ACM Trans. Computer Systems*, Vol. 2, Feb. 1984, pp. 39-59.

Cher85   D.R. Cheriton, and W. Zwaenepoel, "Distributed Process Groups in the V-Kernel," *ACM Trans. Computer Systems*, Vol. 3, No. 2, May 1985, pp. 77-107.

Cher88   D.R. Cheriton, "The V Distributed System," *Comm. ACM*, Vol. 31, No. 3, Mar 1988, pp. 314 - 333.

Joha91   D. Johansen, and G. Hartvigsen, "StormCast — A Distributed Application," *Proc. EurOpen Autumn '91*, Sept. 1991, pp. 273-286.

Need82   R.M. Needham, and A.J. Herbert, *The Cambridge Distributed Computing System*, Addison-Wesley, Wokingham, England, 1982.

Pres91   D. Presotto, R. Pike, K. Thompson, and H. Trickey, "Plan 9, A Distributed System," *Proc. EurOpen Spring '91* (Tromsø, Norway), May 1991, pp. 43-50.

Rozi88 M. Rozier, V. Abrossimov, F. Armand, I. Boule, M. Gien, M. Guillemont, F. Herrmann, C. Kaiser, S. Langlois, P. Leonard, and W. Neuhauser, "CHORUS Distributed Operating Systems," *Computing Systems Journal* (The USENIX Association), Vol. 1, No. 4, Dec. 1988, pp. 305-370.

Tane85 A.S. Tanenbaum, and R. van Renesse, "Distributed Operating Systems," *ACM Computing Surveys*, Vol. 17, No. 4, Dec. 1985, pp. 419-470.

Tane90 A.S. Tanenbaum, R. van Renesse, H. van Staveren, G.J. Sharp, S.J. Mullender, A.J. Jansen, and G. van Rossum, "Experiences with the Amoeba Distributed Operating System," *Comm. ACM*, Vol. 33, No. 12, Dec. 1990, pp. 46-63.

The Amoeba Microkernel

Andrew S. Tanenbaum   M. Frans Kaashoek

Dept. of Mathematics and Computer Science
Vrije Universiteit
De Boelelaan 1081
1081 HV Amsterdam, The Netherlands
Internet: ast@cs.vu.nl, kaashoek@cs.vu.nl

Abstract

In this paper we will give an up-to-date overview of the Amoeba distributed operating system microkernel. We will examine process management, memory management, and the communication primitives, emphasizing the latter since these contain the most new ideas.

1 Introduction

Amoeba is a distributed operating system designed to connect together a large number of machines in a transparent way. Its goal is to make the entire system look to the users like a single computer. The system consists of two parts: a microkernel and server processes. In this paper we will describe the microkernel. For information about other aspects of Amoeba, see Mullender et al., 1990 and Tanenbaum et al., 1990.

An Amoeba system consists of several components, including a pool of processors (compute service, where most of the work is done), terminals (e.g., computers running the X window servers) that handle the user interface, and specialized servers (e.g., directory servers). All these machines normally run the same (micro)kernel.

The microkernel has four primary functions:

1. Manage processes and threads.
2. Provide low-level memory management support.
3. Support communication.
4. Handle low-level I/O.

Let us consider each of these in turn.

Like most operating systems, Amoeba supports the concept of a process. In addition, Amoeba also supports multiple threads of control within a single address space. A process with one thread is essentially the same as a process in UNIX. Such a process has a single address space, a set of registers, a program counter, and a stack.

In contrast, although a process with multiple threads still has a single address space shared by all threads, each thread logically has its own registers, its own program counter, and its own stack. In effect, a collection of threads in a process is similar to a collection of independent processes in UNIX, with the one exception that they all share a single common address space.

A typical use for multiple threads might be in a file server, in which every incoming request is assigned to a separate thread to work on. That thread might begin processing the request, then block waiting for the disk, then continue work. By splitting the server up into multiple threads, each thread can be purely sequential, even if it has to block waiting for I/O. Nevertheless, all the threads can, for example, have access to a single shared software cache. Threads can synchronize using semaphores or mutexes to prevent two threads from accessing the shared cache simultaneously.

The second task of the kernel is to provide low-level memory management. Threads can allocate and deallocate blocks of memory, called *segments*. These segments can be read and written, and can be mapped into and out of the address space of the process to which the calling thread belongs. A process must have at least one segment, but it may have many more of them. Segments can be used for text, data, stack, or any other purpose the process desires. The operating system does not enforce any particular pattern on segment usage. Normally, users do not think in terms of segments, but this facility could be used by libraries or language run-time systems.

The third job of the kernel is to handle interprocess communication. Two forms of communication are provided: point-to-point communication and group communication.

Point-to-point communication is based on the model of a client sending a message to a server, then blocking until the server has sent a reply back. This request/reply exchange is the basis on which almost everything else is built. The request/reply is usually packaged in library routine so the remote call looks like a local procedure call. This mechanism is generally known as remote procedure call (RPC), and is discussed in Birrell and Nelson (1984).

The other form of communication is group communication. It allows a message to be sent from one source to multiple destinations. Software protocols provide reliable, fault-tolerant group communication to user processes even with lost messages and other errors.

Both the point-to-point message system and the group communication make use of a specialized protocol called FLIP. This protocol is a network layer protocol, and has been specifically designed to meet the needs of distributed computing. It deals with both unicasting and multicasting on complex internetworks.

The fourth function of the kernel is to manage low-level I/O. For each I/O device attached to a machine, there is a device driver in the kernel. The driver manages all I/O for the device. Drivers are linked with the kernel, and cannot be loaded dynamically.

In the following sections we will discuss process management, memory management, and communication services and protocols provided by the Amoeba microkernel. However, since the concept of an object permeates the whole system, we will first briefly describe how objects fit into Amoeba.

2 Objects

Amoeba is organized as a collection of objects (essentially abstract data types), each with some number of operations that processes can perform on it. Objects are generally large, like files, rather than small, like integers, due to the overhead required in accessing an object. Each object is managed by an object server process. Operations on an object are performed by sending a message to the object's server.

When an object is created, the server returns a *capability* to the process creating it. The capability is used to address and protect the object. A typical capability is shown in Figure 1. The *Port* field identifies the server. The *Object* field tells which object is being referred to, since a server normally will manage thousands of objects. The *Rights* field specifies which operations are allowed (e.g., a capability for a file may be read-only). Since capabilities are managed in user

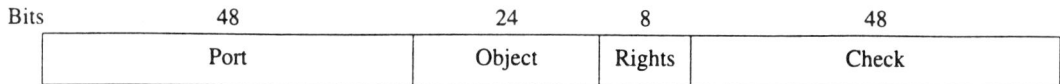

Figure 1. A typical capability.

space the *Check* field is needed to protect them cryptographically, to prevent users from tampering with them.

The basic algorithm used to protect objects is as follows (Tanenbaum et al., 1986). When an object is created, the server picks a random *Check* field and stores it both in the new capability and inside its own tables. All the rights bits in a new capability are initially on, and it is this **owner capability** that is returned to the client. When the capability is sent back to the server in a request to perform an operation, the *Check* field is verified.

To create a restricted capability, a client can pass a capability back to the server, along with a bit mask for the new rights. The server takes the original *Check* field from its tables, EXCLUSIVE ORs it with the new rights (which must be a subset of the rights in the capability), and then runs the result through a one-way function. Such a function, $y = f(x)$, has the property that given x it is easy to find y, but given only y, finding x requires an exhaustive search of all possible x values (Evans et al., 1974).

The server then creates a new capability, with the same value in the *Object* field, but the new rights bits in the *Rights* field and the output of the one-way function in the *Check* field. The new capability is then returned to the caller. In this way, processes can give other processes restricted access to their objects.

3 Process management in Amoeba

A process in Amoeba is basically an address space and a collection of threads that run in it. In this section we will explain how processes and threads work, and how they are implemented.

3.1 Processes

A process is an object in Amoeba. When a process is created, the parent process is given a capability for the child process, just as with any other newly created object. Using this capability, the child can be suspended, restarted, or destroyed.

Process creation in Amoeba is different from UNIX. The UNIX model of creating a child process by cloning the parent is inappropriate in a distributed system due to the potential overhead of first creating a copy somewhere (FORK) and almost immediately afterwards replacing the copy with a new program (EXEC). Instead, in Amoeba it is possible to create a new process on a specific processor with the intended memory image starting right at the beginning. The children, can, in turn, create their own children, leading to a tree of processes.

Process management is handled by calling kernel threads running on every machine. To create a process on a given machine, another process does an RPC with that machine's process server, providing it with the necessary information.

At a higher level, a user-level server, the *run* server, can be invoked to choose a machine and start the process there. The *run* server keeps track of the load on the various processors and chooses the most favorable machine based on CPU load and memory usage.

Some of the process management calls use a data structure called a *process descriptor* to provide information about a process to be run. It is used both for new processes and those that have run for a while and been suspended (e.g., by a debugger). One field in the process descriptor (see Figure 2) tells which CPU architecture the process can run on. In heterogeneous systems, this field is essential to make sure 386 binaries are not run on SPARCs, and so on.

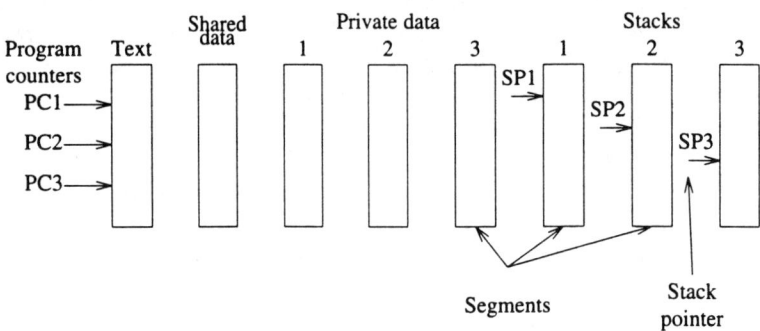

Figure 2. A process descriptor and the corresponding process. In this example, the process has one text segment, one data segment shared by all threads, three segments that are each private to one thread, and three stack segments.

Another field contains a capability for communicating the exit status to the owner. When the process terminates or is stunned (see below), RPCs will be done using this capability to report the event. It also contains descriptors for all the process' segments, which collectively define its address space.

Finally, the process descriptor also contains a descriptor for each thread in the process. The content of a thread descriptor is architecture dependent, but as a bare minimum, it contains the thread's program counter and stack pointer. It may also contain additional information necessary to run the thread, including other registers, the thread's state, and various flags.

The low-level process interface to the process management system consists of several procedures. Only three of these will concern us here. The first one, *exec*, is the most important. It has two input parameters, the capability for a process server and a process descriptor. Its function is to do an RPC with the specified process server asking it to run the process. If the call is successful, a capability for the new process is returned to the caller.

A second important procedure is *getload*. It returns information about the CPU speed, current load, and amount of memory free at the moment. It is used by the run server to determine the best place to execute a new process.

A third major procedure is *stun*. A process' parent can suspend it by *stunning* it. More commonly, the parent can give the process' capability to a debugger, which can stun it and later restart it for interactive debugging purposes. Two kinds of stuns are supported: normal and emergency. They differ with respect to what happens if the process is blocked on one or more RPCs at the time it is stunned. With a normal stun, the process sends a message to the server it is currently waiting for saying, in effect: "I have been stunned. Finish your work instantly and send me a reply." If the server is also blocked, waiting for another server, the message is propagated further, all the way down the line to the end, where it generates an interrupt. If the server at the end of the line catches the interrupt, it replies with a special error message. In this way, all the pending RPCs are terminated quickly in a clean way, with all of the servers finishing properly. The nesting structure is not violated, and no "long jumps" are needed. Processes that do not want to be interrupted can have their wish by simply not enabling handlers (the default is to ignore stuns). Then, the client process stays alive until it receives the reply from the server process.

An emergency stun stops the process instantly. It sends messages to servers that are currently working for the stunned process, but does not wait for the replies. The computations being done by the servers become orphans. When the servers finally finish and send replies, these replies are discarded.

3.2 Threads

Amoeba supports a simple threads model. When a process starts up, it has at least one thread and possibly more. The number of threads is dynamic. During execution, the process can create additional threads, and existing threads can terminate. When a new thread is created, the parameters to the call specify the procedure to run and the size of the initial stack.

Although all threads in a process share the same program text and global data, each thread has its own stack, its own stack pointer, and its own copy of the machine registers. In addition, if a thread wants to create and use variables that are global to all its procedures but invisible to other threads, library procedures are provided for that purpose. These variables are managed by the thread itself; the kernel does not intervene.

Three methods are provided for thread synchronization: signals, mutexes, and semaphores. Signals are asynchronous interrupts sent from one thread to another thread in the same process. They are conceptually similar to UNIX signals, except that they are between threads rather than between processes. Signals can be raised, caught, or ignored. Asynchronous interrupts between processes use the stun mechanism.

The second form of interthread communication is the mutex. A *mutex* is like a binary semaphore. It can be in one of two states, locked or unlocked. Trying to lock an unlocked mutex causes it to become locked. The calling thread continues. Trying to lock a mutex that is already locked causes the calling thread to block until another thread unlocks the mutex. If more than one thread is waiting on a mutex, when it is unlocked, exactly one thread is released. In addition to the calls to lock and unlock mutexes, there is also a call that tries to lock a mutex, but if it is unable to do so within a specified interval, it times out and returns an error code.

The third way threads can synchronize is by counting semaphores. These are slower than mutexes, but there are times when they are needed. They work in the usual way, except that here too an additional call is provided to allow a DOWN operation to time out if it is unable to succeed within a specified interval.

All threads are managed by the kernel. The advantage of this design is that when a thread does an RPC, the kernel can block that thread and schedule another one in the same process if one is ready. Thread scheduling is done using priorities, with kernel threads having higher priority than user threads. Within a user process, threads do not have priorities, and run nonpreemptively.

4 Memory management in Amoeba

Amoeba also has a simple memory model. A process can have any number of segments and they can be located wherever it wants in the process' virtual address space. Segments are not swapped or paged, so a process must be entirely memory resident to run. Since the hardware MMU is used, a segment can be located anywhere within the virtual address space. Each segment is stored contiguously in physical memory.

Although this design is perhaps somewhat unusual these days, it was done for three reasons: performance, simplicity, and economics. Having a process entirely in memory all the time makes RPC go faster. When a large block of data must be sent, the system knows that all of the data is contiguous not only in virtual memory, but also in physical memory. This knowledge saves having to check if all the pages containing the buffer happen to be around at the moment, and eliminates having to wait for them if they are not. Similarly, on input, the buffer is always in memory, so the incoming data can be placed there simply and without page faults. This design was one of the factors that allowed Amoeba to achieve high transfer rates for large RPCs (Tanenbaum et al., 1990).

The second reason for the design is simplicity. Not having paging or swapping makes the system considerably simpler and makes the kernel smaller and more manageable. However, it is the third reason that makes the first two feasible. Memory is becoming so cheap that within a few years, all Amoeba machines will probably have tens of megabytes of it. Such large memories will reduce the need for paging and swapping, namely, to fit large programs into small machines. Programs that do not fit in physical memory cannot be run on Amoeba.

Processes have several calls available to them for managing segments. Most important among these is the ability to create, destroy, read, and write segments. When a segment is created, the caller gets back a capability for it. This capability is used for all the other calls involving the segment.

Because segments can be read and written, it is possible to use them to construct a main memory file server. To start, the server creates a segment as large as it can, determining the maximum size by asking the kernel. This segment will be used as a simulated disk. The server then formats the segment as a file system, putting in whatever data structures it needs to keep track of files. After that, it is open for business, accepting and processing requests from clients.

Virtual address spaces in Amoeba are constructed by mapping segments into them. When a process is started, it must have at least one segment. Once it is running, a process can create additional segments and map them into its address space at any unused virtual address. Figure 3 shows a process with three memory segments currently mapped in.

A process can also unmap segments. Furthermore, a process can specify a range of virtual addresses and request that the range be unmapped, after which those addresses are no longer legal. When a segment or a range of addresses is unmapped, a capability is returned, so the segment may still be accessed, or even mapped back in again later, possibly at a different virtual address (on the same processor).

A segment may be mapped into the address space of two or more processes at the same time. This allows processes to operate on shared memory. For example, two processes can map the screen buffer or other hardware devices into their respective address spaces. Also, cooperating processes can share a buffer. Segments cannot be shared over a network.

5 Communication in Amoeba

Amoeba supports two forms of communication: RPC, which is based on point-to-point message passing, and group communication. At the lowest level, an RPC consists of a request message sent by a client to a server followed by a reply message from the server back to the client. Group communication uses hardware broadcasting or multicasting if it is available; otherwise it transparently simulates it with individual messages. In this section we will describe both RPC and group communication, and then discuss the underlying FLIP protocol that is used to support them.

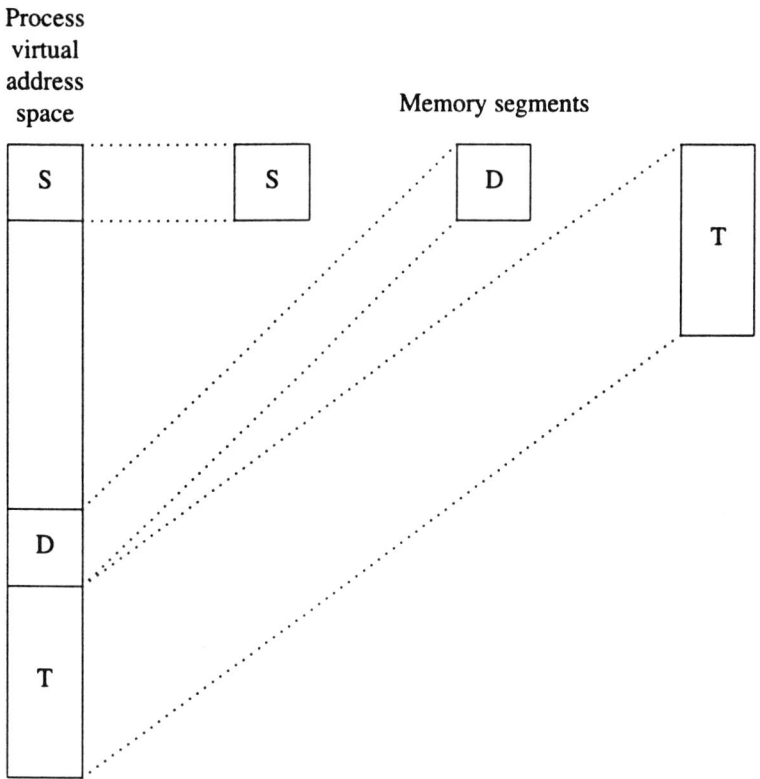

Figure 3. A process with three segments mapped into its virtual address space.

5.1 Remote procedure call

All point-to-point communication in Amoeba consists of a client sending a message to a server followed by the server sending a reply back to the client. It is not possible for a client to just send a message and then go do something else. The primitive that sends the request automatically blocks the caller until the reply comes back, thus forcing a certain amount of structure on programs. Separate *send* and *receive* primitives can be thought of as the distributed system's answer to the *goto* statement: parallel spaghetti programming.

Each standard server defines a procedural interface that clients can call. These library routines are stubs that pack the parameters into messages and invoke the kernel primitives to actually send the message. During message transmission, the stub, and hence the calling thread, is blocked. When the reply comes back, the stub returns the status and results to the client. Although the kernel-level primitives are closely related to the message passing, the use of stubs makes this mechanism look like RPC to the programmer, so we will refer to the basic communication primitives as RPC, rather than the slightly more precise "request/reply message exchange." Stubs can either be hand written or generated by a stub compiler.

In order for a client thread to do an RPC with a server thread, the client must know the server's address. Addressing is done by allowing any thread to choose a random 48-bit number, called a *port*, to be used as the address for messages sent to it. Different threads in a process may use different ports if they so desire. All messages are addressed from a sender to a destination port. A port is nothing more than a kind of logical thread address. There is no data structure and no storage associated with a port. It is similar to an IP address or an Ethernet address in that respect, except that it is not tied to any particular physical location. The first field in each capability gives the port of the server that manages the object.

5.1.1 RPC Primitives

The RPC mechanism makes use of three principal kernel primitives, as listed below. Programs (or more often, library procedures) can make these calls to send and receive messages.

1. get_request — indicates a server's willingness to listen on a port
2. put_reply — done by a server when it has a reply to send
3. trans — send a message from client to server and wait for the reply

The first two are used by servers. The third is used by clients to *transmit* a message and wait for a reply. All three are true system calls, that is, they do not work by sending a message to a communication server thread. Users access the calls through library procedures, as usual, however.

When a server wants to go to sleep waiting for an incoming request, it calls *get_request*. This procedure has three parameters, as follows:

get_request(&header, buffer, bytes)

The first parameter points to a message header, the second points to a data buffer, and the third tells how big the data buffer is. This call is analogous to

read(fd, buffer, bytes)

in UNIX in that the first parameter identifies what is being read, the second provides a buffer to put the data, and the third tells how big the buffer is. The analogy is not strict because the header contains multiple fields, some of which are filled in when the call returns.

When a request message is transmitted over the network, it contains a header and (optionally) a data buffer. The header is a fixed 32-byte structure and is shown in Figure 4. The first parameter of the *get_request* call tells the kernel where to put the incoming header. In addition, prior to making the *get_request* call, the server must initialize the header's *Port* field to contain the port it is listening to. This is how the kernel knows which server is listening to which port. The incoming header overwrites the one initialized by the server.

When a server is blocked on a *get_request* waiting for a message and one arrives, the server is unblocked. It normally first inspects the header to find out what the client wants. The *Signature* field is currently not in use, but is reserved for authentication purposes.

The remaining fields are not specified by the RPC protocol, so a server and client can agree to use them any way they want. The normal conventions are as follows. Most requests to servers contain a capability, to specify the object being operated on. Many replies also have a capability as a return value. The *Private* part is normally used to hold the rightmost three fields of the capability.

Most servers support multiple operations on their objects, such as reading, writing, and destroying. The *Command* field is conventionally used on requests to indicate which operation is needed. On replies it tells whether the operation was successful or not, and if not, it gives the reason for failure.

The last three fields hold parameters, if any. For example, when reading a segment or file, they can be used to indicate the offset within the object to begin reading at, and the number of bytes to read.

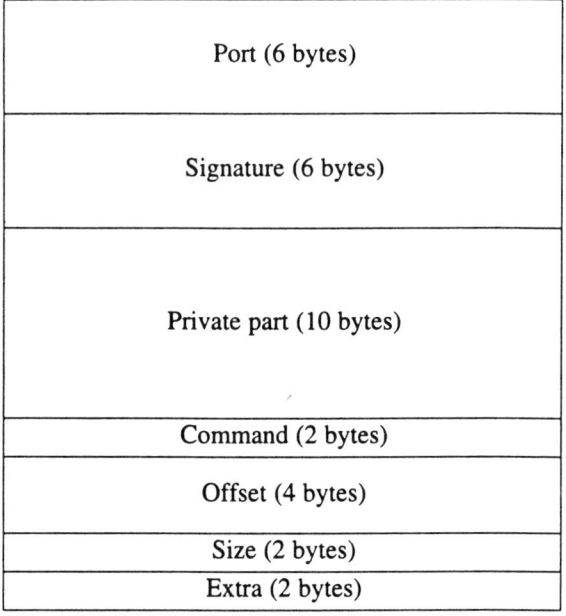

Figure 4. The header used on all Amoeba request and reply messages. The numbers in parentheses give the field sizes in bytes.

Note that for many operations, no buffer is needed or used. In the case of reading again, the object capability, the offset, and the size all fit in the header. When writing, the buffer contains the data to be written. On the other hand, the reply to a READ contains a buffer, whereas the reply to a WRITE does not.

After the server has completed its work, it makes a call

   put_reply(&header, buffer, bytes)

to send back the reply. The first parameter provides the header and the second provides the buffer. The third parameter tells how big the buffer is. If a server thread does a *put_reply* without having previously done an unmatched *get_request*, the *put_reply* fails with an error. Similarly, two consecutive *get_request* calls fail. The two calls must be paired in the correct way.

Now let us turn from the server to the client. To do an RPC, the client calls a stub which makes the following call:

   trans(&header_in, buffer_in, bytes_in, &header_out, buffer_out, bytes_out)

The first three parameters provide information about the header and buffer of the outgoing request. The last three provide the same information for the incoming reply. The *trans* call sends the request and blocks the client until the reply has come in. This design forces processes to stick closely to the client-server RPC communication paradigm, analogous to the way structured programming techniques prevent programmers from doing things that generally lead to poorly structured programs (such as using unconstrained GOTO statements).

If Amoeba actually worked as described above, it would be possible for an intruder to impersonate a server just by doing a *get_request* on the server's port. These ports are public after all, since clients must know them to contact the servers. Amoeba solves this problem cryptographically. Each port is actually a pair of ports: the *get-port*, which is private, only known to the server, and the *put-port*, which is known to the whole world. The two are related through a one-way function, *F*, according to the relation:

$$\text{put-port} = F(\text{get-port})$$

When a server does a *get_request*, the corresponding put-port is computed by the kernel and stored in a table of ports being listened to. All *trans* requests use put-ports, so when a packet arrives at a machine, the kernel compares the put-port in the header to the put-ports in its table to see if any match. Since get-ports never appear on the network and cannot be derived from the publicly known put-ports, the scheme is secure. It is illustrated in Figure 5 and described in more detail in (Tanenbaum et al., 1986).

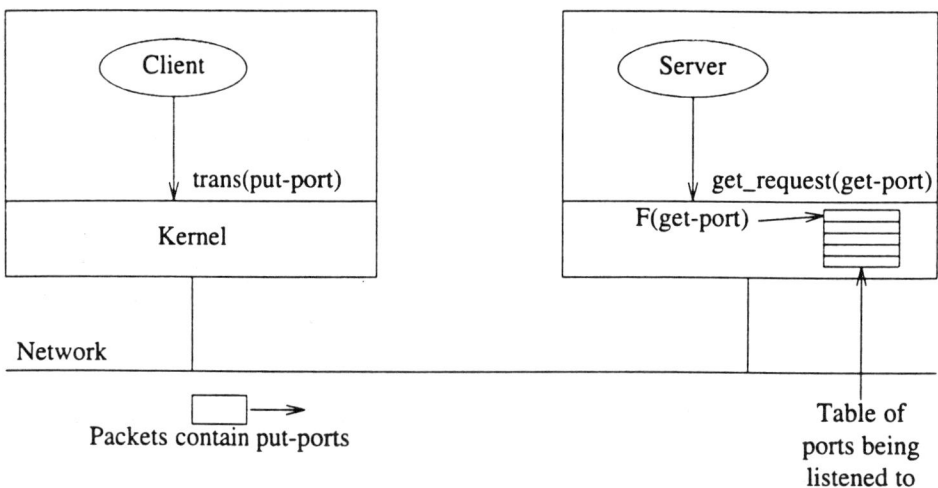

Figure 5. Relationship between get-ports and put-ports.

Amoeba RPC supports at-most-once semantics. In other words, when an RPC is done, the system guarantees that an RPC will never be carried out more than one time, even in the face of server crashes and rapid reboots.

5.2 Group communication in Amoeba

RPC is not the only form of communication supported by Amoeba. It also supports group communication. A group in Amoeba consists of one or more processes that are cooperating to carry out some task or provide some service. Processes can be members of several groups at the same time. Groups are closed. The usual way for a client to access a service provided by a group is to do an RPC with one of its members. That member then uses group communication within the group, if necessary, to determine who will do what.

5.2.1 Group Communication Primitives

The operations available for group communication in Amoeba are listed in Figure 6. *CreateGroup* creates a new group and returns a group identifier used in the other calls to identify which group is meant. The parameters specify various sizes and how much fault tolerance is required (how many failed members the group must be able to withstand and continue to function correctly).

Call	Description
CreateGroup	Create a new group and set its parameters
JoinGroup	Make the caller a member of a group
LeaveGroup	Remove the caller from a group
SendToGroup	Reliably send a message to all members of a group
ReceiveFromGroup	Block until a message arrives from a group member
ResetGroup	Initiate recovery after a process crash

Figure 6. Amoeba group communication primitives.

JoinGroup and *LeaveGroup* allow processes to enter and exit from existing groups. One of the parameters of *JoinGroup* is a small message that is sent to all group members to announce the presence of a newcomer. Similarly, one of the parameters of *LeaveGroup* is another small message sent to all members to say goodbye and wish them good luck in their future activities. The point of the little messages is to make it possible for all members to know who their comrades are, in case they are interested. When the last member of a group calls *LeaveGroup* the group is destroyed.

SendToGroup atomically broadcasts a message to all members of a specified group, in spite of lost messages, finite buffers, and processor crashes. If two processes call *SendToGroup* nearly simultaneously, the system ensures that all group members will receive the messages in the same order. This is guaranteed; programmers can count on it.

ReceiveFromGroup tries to get a message from a specified group. If no message is available (buffered by the kernel) the caller blocks until one is available. If a message has already arrived, the caller gets the message with no delay. The protocol insures that under no conditions are messages irretrievably lost.

The final call, *ResetGroup* is used to recover from crashes. It specifies how many members the new group must have as a minimum. If the kernel is able to establish contact with the requisite number of processes and rebuild the group, it returns the size of the new group. Otherwise, it fails.

5.2.2 The Amoeba reliable broadcast protocol

Let us now look at how Amoeba implements group communication. Amoeba works best on LANs that support either multicasting or broadcasting (or like Ethernet, both). For simplicity, we will just refer to broadcasting, although in fact the implementation uses multicasting when it can to avoid disturbing machines that are not interested in the message being sent. It is assumed that the hardware broadcast is good, but not perfect. In practice, lost packets are rare, but receiver overruns do happen occasionally. Since these errors can occur, the protocol has been designed to deal with them.

The key idea that forms the basis of the implementation of group communication is *reliable broadcasting*. By this we mean that when a user process broadcasts a message (e.g., with *SendToGroup*) the user-supplied message is correctly delivered to all members of the group, even though the hardware may lose packets. For simplicity, we will assume that each message fits into a single packet. For the moment, we will assume that processors do not crash. We will consider the case of unreliable processors afterwards. The description given below is just an outline. For more details, see (Kaashoek and Tanenbaum, 1991; and Kaashoek et al., 1989).

Other reliable broadcast protocols are discussed in (Birman and Joseph, 1987a; Chang and Maxemchuk, 1984; Garcia-Molina and Tseung, 1989).

The hardware/software configuration required for reliable broadcasting in Amoeba is shown in Figure 7. The hardware of all the machines is normally identical, and they all run exactly the same kernel. However, when the application starts up, one of the machines is elected as sequencer (like a committee electing a chairman). If the sequencer machine subsequently crashes, the remaining members elect a new one. Many election algorithms are known, such as choosing the process with the highest network address.

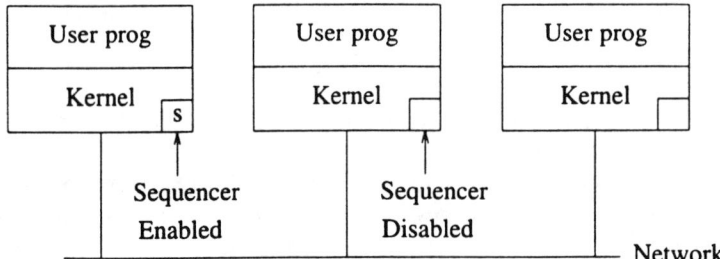

Figure 7. System structure for group communication in Amoeba.

One sequence of events that can be used to achieve reliable broadcasting can be summarized as follows.

1. The thread traps to the kernel.
2. The thread, now in kernel mode, adds a protocol header and sends the message to the sequencer using a point-to-point message.
3. When the sequencer gets the message, it allocates the next available sequence number, puts the sequence number in the protocol header, and broadcasts the message (and sequence number).
4. When the sending kernel sees the broadcast message, it unblocks the calling process to let it continue execution.

Let us now consider these steps in more detail. When an application process executes a broadcast primitive, such as *SendToGroup*, a trap to its kernel occurs. The calling thread switches to kernel mode and builds a message containing a kernel-supplied header and the application-supplied data. The header contains the message type (*Request for Broadcast* in this case), a unique message identifier (used to detect duplicates), the number of the next broadcast expected by the kernel and some other information.

The kernel sends the message to the sequencer using a normal point-to-point message, and simultaneously starts a timer. If the broadcast comes back before the timer runs out (normal case), the sending kernel stops the timer and returns control to the caller. In practice, this case happens well over 99% of the time, because LANs are highly reliable.

On the other hand, if the broadcast has not come back before the timer expires, the kernel assumes that either the message or the broadcast has been lost. Either way, it retransmits the message. If the original message was lost, no harm has been done, and the second (or subsequent) attempt will trigger the broadcast in the usual way. If the message got to the sequencer and was broadcast, but the sender missed the broadcast, the sequencer will detect the retransmission as a duplicate (from the message identifier) and just tell the sender that everything is all right. The message is not broadcast a second time.

A third possibility is that a broadcast comes back before the timer runs out, but it is the wrong broadcast. This situation arises when two processes attempt to broadcast simultaneously.

One of them, A, gets to the sequencer first, and its message is broadcast. A sees the broadcast and unblocks its application program. However its competitor, B, sees A's broadcast and realizes that it has failed to go first. Nevertheless, B knows that its message probably got to the sequencer (since lost messages are rare) where it will be queued, and broadcast next. Thus B accepts A's broadcast and continues to wait for its own broadcast to come back or its timer to expire.

Now consider what happens at the sequencer when a *Request for Broadcast* arrives there. First a check is made to see if the message is a retransmission, and if so, the sender is informed that the broadcast has already been done, as mentioned above. If the message is new (normal case), the next sequence number is assigned to it, and the sequencer counter is incremented by one. The message and its identifier are then stored in a *history buffer*, and the message is then broadcast. The message is also passed to the application running on the sequencer's machine (because the broadcast does not interrupt itself).

Finally, let us consider what happens when a kernel receives a broadcast. First, the sequence number is compared to the sequence number of the most recently received broadcast. If the new one is 1 higher (normal case), no broadcasts have been missed so the message is passed up to the application program, assuming that it is waiting. If it is not waiting, it is buffered until the program calls *ReceiveFromGroup*.

Suppose that the newly received broadcast has sequence number 25, while the previous one had number 23. The kernel is alerted to the fact that it has missed number 24, so it sends a point-to-point message to the sequencer asking for a private retransmission of the missing message. The sequencer fetches the missing message from its history buffer and sends it. When it arrives, the receiving kernel processes 24 and 25, passing them to the application program in numerical order. Thus the only effect of a lost message is a minor time delay. All application programs see all broadcasts in the same order, even if some messages are lost.

The reliable broadcast protocol is illustrated in Figure 8. Here the application program running on machine A passes a message, M, to its kernel for broadcasting. The kernel sends the message to the sequencer, where it is assigned sequence number 25. The message (containing the sequence number 25) is now broadcast to all machines and is also passed to the application running on the sequencer itself. This broadcast message is denoted by M25 in the figure.

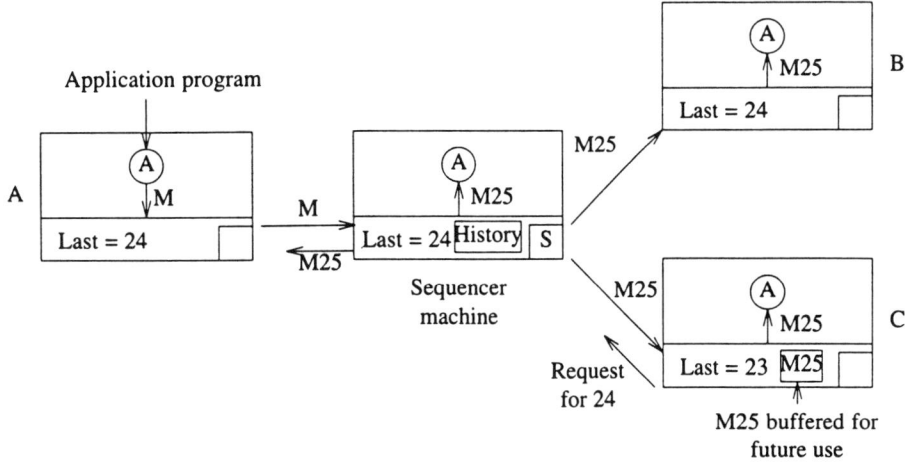

Figure 8. The application of machine *A* sends a message to the sequencer, which then adds a sequence number (25) and broadcasts it. At *B* it is accepted, but at *C* it is buffered until 24, which was missed, can be retrieved from the sequencer.

The *M25* message arrives at machines *B* and *C*. At machine *B* the kernel sees that it has already processed all broadcasts up to and including 24, so it immediately passes *M25* up to the application program. At *C*, however, the last message to arrive was 23 (24 must have been lost), so *M25* is buffered in the kernel, and a point-to-point message requesting 24 is sent to the sequencer. Only after the reply has come back and been given to the application program will *M25* be passed upwards as well.

Now let us look at the management of the history buffer. Unless something is done to prevent it, the history buffer will quickly fill up. However, if the sequencer knows that all machines have correctly received broadcasts, say, 0 through 23, it can delete these from its history buffer.

Several mechanisms are provided to allow the sequencer to discover this information. The basic one is that each *Request for Broadcast* message sent to the sequencer carries a piggybacked acknowledgment, k, meaning that all broadcasts up to and including $k-1$ have been correctly received and that it expects k next. This way, the sequencer can maintain a piggyback table, indexed by machine number, telling for each machine which broadcast was the last one received. Whenever the history buffer begins to fill up, the sequencer can make a pass through this table to find the smallest value. It can then safely discard all messages up to and including this value.

If a machine happens to be silent for a long period of time, the sequencer will not know what its status is. To inform the sequencer, it is required to send a short acknowledgment message when it has sent no broadcast messages for a certain period of time. Furthermore, the sequencer can broadcast a *Request for Status* message, which asks all other machines to send it a message giving the number of the highest broadcast received in sequence. In this way, the sequencer can update its piggyback table and then truncate its history buffer.

Although in practice *Request for Status* messages are rare, they do occur, and thus raise the mean number of messages required for a reliable broadcast slightly above 2, even when there are no lost messages. The effect increases slightly as the number of machines grows.

There is a subtle design point concerning this protocol that should be clarified. There are two ways to do the broadcast. In method 1 (described above), the user sends a point-to-point message to the sequencer, which then broadcasts it. In method 2, the user broadcasts the message, including a unique identifier. When the sequencer sees this, it broadcasts a special *Accept* message containing the unique identifier and its newly assigned sequence number. A broadcast is only "official" when the *Accept* message has been sent. The two methods are compared in Figure 9.

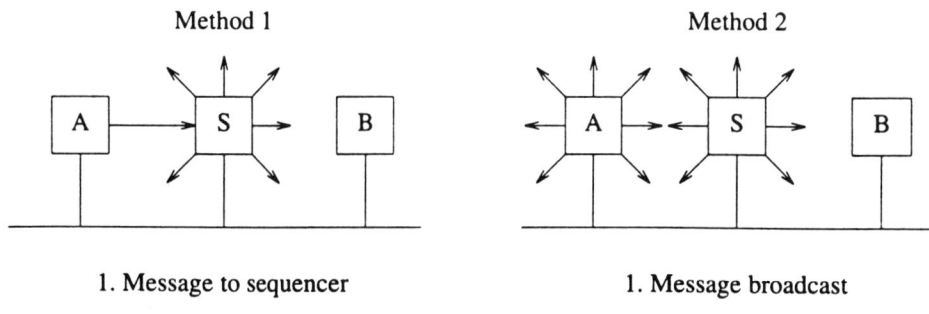

Figure 9. Two methods for doing reliable broadcasting.

These protocols are logically equivalent, but they have different performance characteristics. In method 1, each message appears in full on the network twice: once to the sequencer and once from the sequencer. Thus a message of length m bytes consumes $2m$ bytes worth of network bandwidth. However, only the second of these is broadcast, so each user machine is only interrupted once (for the second message).

In method 2, the full message only appears once on the network, plus a very short *Accept* message from the sequencer, so only half the bandwidth is consumed. On the other hand, every machine is interrupted twice, once for the message and once for the *Accept*. Thus method 1 wastes bandwidth to reduce interrupts compared to method 2. Depending on the average message size, one may be preferable to the other.

In summary, this protocol allows reliable broadcasting to be done on an unreliable network in just over two messages per reliable broadcast. Each broadcast is indivisible, and all applications receive all messages in the same order, no matter how many are lost. The worst that can happen is that a short delay is introduced when a message is lost, which rarely happens. If two processes attempt to broadcast at the same time, one of them will get to the sequencer first and win. The other will see a broadcast from its competitor coming back from the sequencer, and will realize that its request has been queued and will appear shortly, so it simply waits.

5.3 The Fast Local Internet Protocol (FLIP)

Amoeba uses a custom protocol called *FLIP* (*Fast Local Internet Protocol*) for actual message transmission (Kaashoek et al., 1991). This protocol supports both RPC and group communication and is below them in the protocol hierarchy. In OSI terms, FLIP is a network layer protocol, whereas RPC is more of a connectionless transport or session protocol (the exact location is arguable, since OSI was designed for connection-oriented networks). Conceptually, FLIP can be replaced by another network layer protocol, such as IP, although doing so would cause some of Amoeba's transparency to be lost. Although FLIP was designed in the context of Amoeba, it is intended to be useful in other operating systems as well. In this section we will describe its design and implementation.

5.3.1 Protocol requirements for distributed systems

Before getting into the details of FLIP, it is useful to understand something about why it was designed. After all, there are plenty of existing protocols, so the invention of a new one clearly has to be justified. In Figure 10 we list the principal requirements that a protocol for a distributed system should meet. First, the protocol must support both RPC and group communication efficiently. If the underlying network has hardware multicast or broadcast, as Ethernet does, for example, the protocol should use it for group communication. On the other hand, if the network does not have either of these features, group communication must still work exactly the same way, even though the implementation will have to be different.

Item	Description
RPC	The protocol should support RPC
Group communication	The protocol should support group communication
Process migration	Processes should be able to take their addresses with them
Security	Processes should not be able to impersonate other processes
Network management	Support should be provided for automatic reconfiguration
Wide-area networks	The protocol should work on wide-area networks

Figure 10. Desirable characteristics for a distributed system protocol.

A characteristic that is increasingly important is support for process migration. A process should be able to move from one machine to another, even to one in a different network, with nobody noticing. Protocols such as OSI, X.25, and TCP/IP that use machine addresses to identify processes make migration difficult, because a process cannot take its address with it when it moves.

Security is also an issue. Although the get-ports and put-ports provide security for Amoeba, a security mechanism should also be present in the packet protocol so it can be used with operating systems that do not have Amoeba-type cryptographically secure addresses.

Another point on which most existing protocols score badly is network management. It should not be necessary to have elaborate configuration tables telling which network is connected to which other network. Furthermore, if the configuration changes, due to routers (gateways) going down or coming back up, the protocol should adapt to the new configuration automatically.

Finally, the protocol should work on both local and wide-area networks. In particular, the same protocol should be usable on both.

5.3.2 The FLIP interface

The FLIP protocol and its associated architecture was designed to meet all these requirements, although when used on wide-area networks, it is best suited to a modest number of sites. A typical FLIP configuration is shown in Figure 11. Here we see five machines, two on an Ethernet and four on a token ring. Each machine has one user process, *A* through *E*. One of the machines is connected to both networks, and as such automatically functions as a router. Routers may also run clients and servers, just like other nodes.

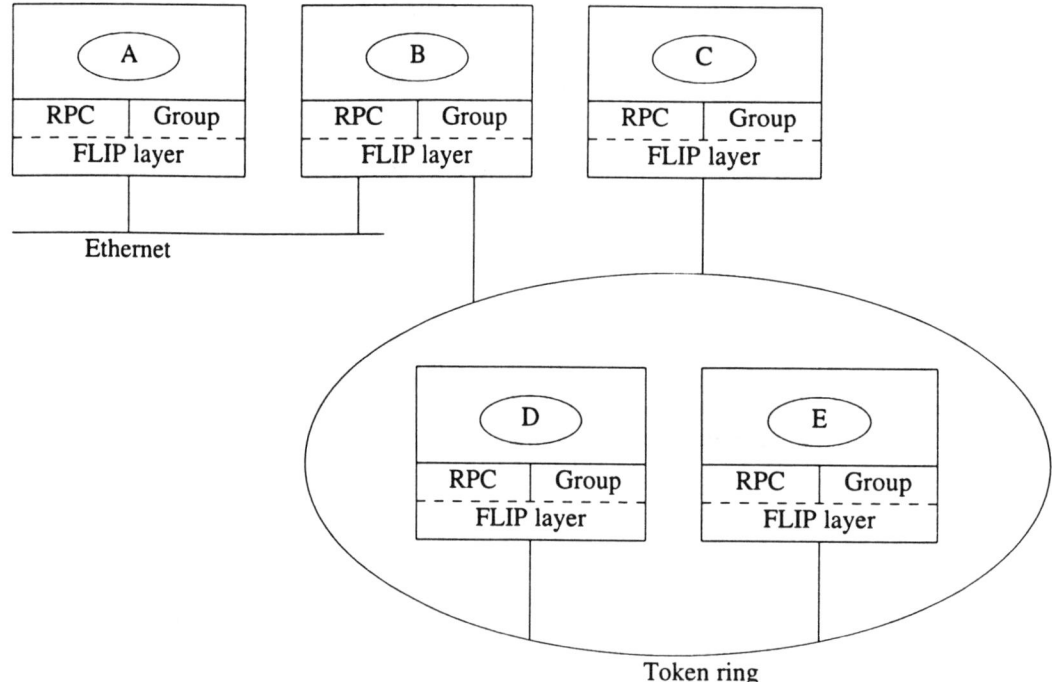

Figure 11. A FLIP system with five machines and two networks.

The software is structured as shown in Figure 11. The kernel contains two layers. The top layer handles calls from user processes for RPC or group communication services. The bottom layer handles the FLIP protocol. For example, when a client calls *trans*, it traps to the kernel. The RPC layer examines the header and buffer, builds a message from them, and passes the message down to the FLIP layer for transmission.

All low-level communication in Amoeba is based on *FLIP addresses*. Each process has one or more FLIP addresses: 64-bit random numbers chosen by the system when the process is created. If the process ever migrates, it takes its FLIP address with it. If the network is ever reconfigured, so that all machines are assigned new (hardware) network numbers or network addresses, the FLIP addresses still remain unchanged. It is the fact that a FLIP address uniquely identifies a process (or a group of processes), not a machine, that makes communication in Amoeba insensitive to changes in network topology and network addressing.

A FLIP address is really two addresses, a public-address and a private-address, related by

$$\text{Public-address} = DES(\text{private-address})$$

where DES is the Data Encryption Standard. To compute the public-address from the private one, the private-address is used as a DES key to encrypt a 64-bit block of 0s. Given a public address, finding the corresponding private address is computationally infeasible. Servers listen to private-addresses, but clients send to public-addresses, analogous to the way put-ports and get-ports work, but at a lower level.

FLIP has been designed to work not only with Amoeba, but also with other operating systems. A version for UNIX also exists, although for technical reasons it differs slightly from the Amoeba version. The security provided by the private-address, public-address scheme also works for UNIX to UNIX communication using FLIP, independent of Amoeba.

Furthermore, FLIP has been designed so that it can be built in hardware, for example, as part of the network interface chip. For this reason, a precise interface with the layer above it has been specified. The interface between the FLIP layer and the layer above it (which we will call the RPC layer) has nine primitives, seven for outgoing traffic and two for incoming traffic. Each one has a library procedure that invokes it. The nine calls are listed in Figure 12.

Call	Description	Direction
Init	Allocate a table slot	Down
End	Return a table slot	Down
Register	Listen to a FLIP address	Down
Unregister	Stop listening to a FLIP address	Down
Unicast	Send a point-to-point message	Down
Multicast	Send a multicast message	Down
Broadcast	Send a broadcast message	Down
Receive	Packet received	Up
Notdeliver	Undeliverable packet received	Up

Figure 12. The calls supported by the FLIP layer.

The first one, *init*, allows the RPC layer to allocate a table slot and initialize it with pointers to two procedures (or in a hardware implementation, two interrupt vectors). These procedures are the ones called when normal and undeliverable packets arrive, respectively. *End* deallocates the slot when the process is being shut down.

Register is invoked to register a process' FLIP address (or a group address) with the FLIP layer. It is called when the process starts up (or at least, on the first attempt at getting or sending a message). The FLIP layer immediately runs the private-address offered to it through the DES function, and stores the public-address in its tables. If an incoming packet is addressed to the public FLIP address, it will be passed to the RPC layer for delivery. The *unregister* call removes an entry from the FLIP layer's tables. The difference between *end* and *unregister* is that a process may use multiple FLIP addresses. *Unregister* removes one of these from the table, but leaves the others. When no more communication is needed, *end* is called to free the interface slot.

The next three calls are for sending point-to-point messages, multicast messages, and broadcast messages, respectively. None of these guarantee delivery. To make RPC reliable, acknowledgments are used. To make group communication reliable, even in the fact of lost packets, the sequencer protocol discussed above is used.

The last two calls are for incoming traffic. The first is for messages originating elsewhere and directed to this machine. The second is for messages sent by this machine but sent back as undeliverable.

5.3.3 Operation of the FLIP Layer

Packets passed by the RPC layer or group communication layer (see Figure 11) to the FLIP layer are addressed by FLIP addresses, so the FLIP layer must be able to convert these addresses to network addresses for actual transmission. In order to perform this function, the FLIP layer maintains the routing table shown in Figure 13. Currently this table is maintained in software, but future chip designers could implement it in hardware.

FLIP address	Network address	Hop count	Trusted bit	Age

Figure 13. The FLIP routing table.

Whenever an incoming packet arrives at any machine, it is first handled by the FLIP layer, which extracts from it the FLIP address and network address of the sender. The number of hops the packet has made is also recorded. Since the hop count is only incremented when a packet is forwarded by a router, the hop count tells how many routers the packet has passed through. The hop count is therefore a crude measure of how far away the source is. (Actually, things are slightly better than this, as slow networks count for multiple hops, with the weight a function of the network speed.) If the FLIP address is not presently in the routing table, it is entered. This entry can later be used to send packets to that FLIP address, since its network number and address are now known.

An additional bit present in each packet tells whether the path the packet has followed so far is entirely over trusted networks. It is managed by the routers. If the packet has gone through one or more untrusted networks, packets to the source address should be encrypted if absolute security is desired. With trusted networks, encryption is not needed.

The last field of each routing table entry gives the age of the routing table entry. It is reset to 0 whenever a packet is received from the corresponding FLIP address. Periodically, all the ages are incremented. This field allows the FLIP layer to find a suitable table entry to purge if the table fills up (large numbers indicate that there has been no traffic for a long time).

5.3.4 Locating put-ports

To see how FLIP works in the context of Amoeba, let us consider a simple example using the configuration of Figure 11. *A* is a client and *B* is a server. With FLIP, any machine having connections to two or more networks is automatically a router, so the fact that *B* happens to be running on a router machine is irrelevant.

When *B* is created, the RPC layer picks a new random FLIP address for it and registers it with the FLIP layer. After starting, *B* initializes itself and then does a *get_request* on its get-port, which causes a trap to the kernel. The RPC layer computes the put-port from the get-port and makes a note that a process is listening to that port. It then blocks until a request comes in.

Later, *A* does a *trans* on the put-port. Its RPC layer looks in its tables to see if it knows the FLIP address of the server process that listens to the put-port. Since it does not, the RPC layer sends a special broadcast packet to find it. This packet has a maximum hop count of 1 to make sure that the broadcast is confined to its own network. (When a router sees a packet whose current hop count is already equal to its maximum hop count, the packet is discarded instead of being forwarded.) If the broadcast fails, the sending RPC layer times out and tries again with a maximum hop count of 2, and so on, until it locates the server.

When the broadcast packet arrives at *B*'s machine, the RPC layer there sends back a reply announcing its get-port. This packet, like all incoming packets, causes *A*'s FLIP layer to make an entry for that FLIP address before passing the reply packet up to the RPC layer. The RPC layer now makes an entry in its own tables mapping the put-port onto the FLIP address. Then it sends the request to the server. Since the FLIP layer now has an entry for the server's FLIP address, it can build a packet containing the proper network address and send it without further ado. Subsequent requests to the server's put-port use the RPC layer's cache to find the FLIP address and the FLIP layer's routing table to find the network address. Thus broadcasting is only used the very first time a server is contacted. After that, the kernel tables provide the necessary information.

To summarize, locating a put-port requires two mappings:

1. From the put-port to the FLIP address (done by the RPC layer).
2. From the FLIP address to the network address (done by the FLIP layer).

The reason for this two-stage process is twofold. First, FLIP has been designed as a general-purpose protocol for use in distributed systems, including non-Amoeba systems. Since these systems generally do not use Amoeba-style ports, the mapping of put-ports to FLIP addresses has not been built into the FLIP layer. Other users of FLIP may just use FLIP addresses directly.

Second, a put-port really identifies a *service* rather than a *server*. A service may be provided by multiple servers to enhance performance and reliability. Although all the servers listen to the same put-port, each one has its own private FLIP address. When a client's RPC layer issues a broadcast to find the FLIP address corresponding to a put-port, any or all of the servers may respond. Since each server has a different FLIP address, each response creates a different entry in the put-port table of Figure 5.

The advantage of this scheme over having just a single (port, network address) cache is that it permits servers to migrate to new machines or have their machines be wheeled over to new networks and plugged in without requiring any manual reconfiguration, as say, TCP/IP does. There is a strong analogy here with a person moving and being assigned the same telephone number at the new residence as he had at the old one. (For the record, Amoeba does not currently support process migration, but it could be added later.)

The advantage over having clients and servers use FLIP addresses directly is that FLIP addresses are temporary, whereas ports may be valid for a long time. If a server crashes, it will pick a new FLIP address when it reboots. Attempts to use the old FLIP address will time out, allowing the RPC layer to indicate failure to the client. This mechanism is how at-most-once semantics are guaranteed. The client, however, can just try again with the same put-port if it wishes, since that is not necessarily invalidated by server crashes.

5.3.5 FLIP over wide-area networks

FLIP also works transparently over wide-area networks. In Figure 14 we have three local-area networks connected by a wide-area network. Suppose the client A wants to do an RPC with the server E. A's RPC layer first tries to locate the put-port using a maximum hop count of 1.

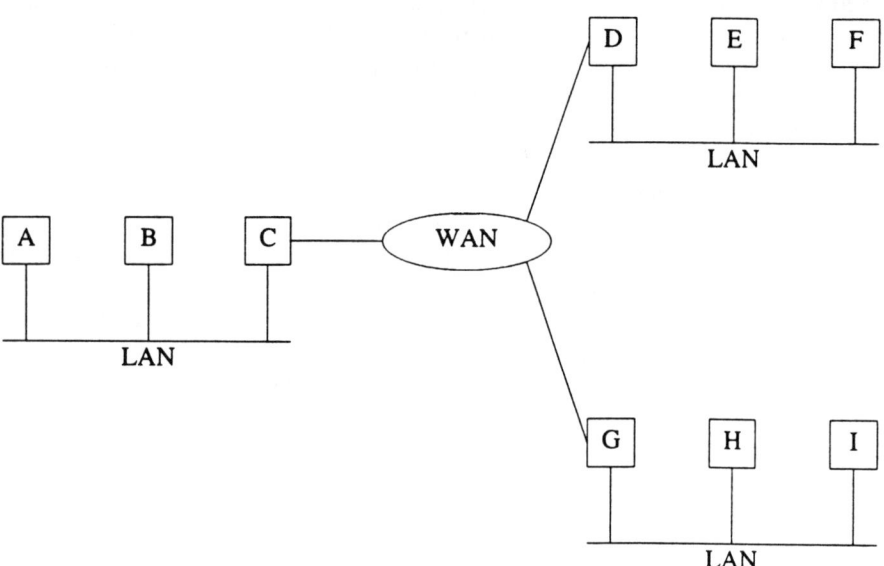

Figure 14. Three LANs connected by a WAN.

When that fails, it tries again with a maximum hop count of 2. This time, C forwards the broadcast packet to all the routers that are connected to the wide-area network, namely, D and G. Effectively, C simulates broadcast over the wide-area network by sending individual messages to all the other routers. When this broadcast fails to turn up the server, a third broadcast is sent, this time with a maximum hop count of 3. This one succeeds. The reply contains E's network address and FLIP address, which are then entered into A's routing table. From this point on, communication between A and E happens using normal point-to-point communication. No more broadcasts are needed.

Communication over the wide-area network is encapsulated in whatever protocol the wide-area network requires. For example, on a TCP/IP network, C might have open connections to D and G all the time. Alternatively, the implementation might decide to close any connection not used for a certain length of time.

Although this method does not scale to large networks, we expect that for modest numbers it may be usable, based on our initial experiments with an internetwork of five networks on two continents. In practice, few servers move between sites, so that once a server has been located by broadcasting, subsequent requests will use the cached entries. Using this method, a modest number of machines all over the world can work together in a totally transparent way. An RPC to a thread in the caller's address space and an RPC to a thread halfway around the world are done in exactly the same way.

Group communication also uses FLIP. When a message is sent to multiple destinations, FLIP uses the hardware multicast or broadcast on those networks where it is available. On those that do not have it, broadcast is simulated by sending individual messages, just as we saw on the wide-area network. The choice of mechanism is done by the FLIP layer, with the same user semantics in all cases.

6 Summary

The Amoeba microkernel manages process and memory, and handles communication. At the lowest level, processes are started by generating a process descriptor and doing an RPC with the kernel thread responsible for starting new processes on the target machine. Higher level services help with locating a suitable machine to run on.

Memory is based on the concept of segments, which can be mapped into and out of processes address spaces at arbitrary addresses.

Communication comes in two forms: RPC and group communication. The former is for sending point-to-point messages, and the latter is for sending many-to-one messages reliable, in the face of various errors. Both use the FLIP protocol for actual data transport.

Amoeba has been operational for several years. It is now available for use. Interested parties should contact the first author by electronic mail.

7 Acknowledgments

We would like to thank Greg Sharp and Mark Wood for their comments on the manuscript.

8 References

1. Birman, K.P. and Joseph, T.: "Reliable Communication in the Presence of Failures," *ACM Trans. on Computer Systems*, Vol. 5, pp. 47-76, Feb. 1987.

2. Birrell, A.D., and Nelson, B.J.: "Implementing Remote Procedure Calls," *ACM Trans. on Computer Systems,* Vol. 2, pp. 39-59, Feb. 1984.

3. Chang, J. and Maxemchuk, N.F.: "Reliable Broadcast Protocols," *ACM Trans. on Computer Systems*, Vol. 2, pp. 251-273, Aug. 1984.

4. Evans, A., Kantrowitz, W., and Weiss, E. A.: "User Authentication Scheme Not Requiring Secrecy in the Computer," *Commun. ACM,* Vol. 17, pp. 437-442, Aug. 1974.

5. Garcia-Molina, H.: "Elections in a Distributed Computing System," *IEEE Trans. on Computers*, Vol. 31, pp. 48-59, Jan. 1982.

6. Kaashoek, M.F., Renesse, R. van, Staveren, H. van, and Tanenbaum, A.S.: "FLIP: an Internetwork Protocol for Supporting Distributed Systems," Report IR-251, Dept. of Math. and Computer Science, Vrije Univ., 1991.

7. Mullender, S.J., Rossum, G. van, Tanenbaum, A.S., Renesse, R. van, and Staveren, H. van: "Amoeba — A Distributed Operating System for the 1990s," *IEEE Computer Magazine*, Vol. 23, pp. 44-53, May 1990.

8. Tanenbaum, A.S., Mullender, S.J., and Renesse, R. van: "Using Sparse Capabilities in a Distributed Operating System," *Proc. Sixth International Conf. on Distr. Computer Systems*, IEEE, pp. 558-663, 1986.

9. Tanenbaum, A.S., Renesse, R. van, Staveren, H. van., Sharp, G.J., Mullender, S.J., Jansen, J., and Rossum, G. van: "Experiences with the Amoeba Distributed Operating System," *Commun. ACM,* Vol. 33, pp. 46-63, Dec. 1990.

10. Tanenbaum, A.S., Mullender, S.J., and Renesse, R. van: "Using Sparse Capabilities in a Distributed Operating System," *Proc. Sixth International Conf. on Distr. Computer Systems*, IEEE, 1986.

11. Tseung, L.N.: "Guaranteed, Reliable, Secure Broadcast Networks," *IEEE Network Magazine*, Vol. 3, pp. 33-37. Nov. 1989.

A New Look at Microkernel-Based UNIX Operating Systems: Lessons in Performance and Compatibility

Allan Bricker
Michel Gien
Marc Guillemont,

Jim Lipkis
Doug Orr
Marc Rozier

Chorus systèmes
6, avenue Gustave Eiffel
F-78182 Saint Quentin-en-Yvelines Cedex
France

Abstract

An important trend in operating system development is the restructuring of the traditional monolithic operating system kernel into independent servers running on top of a minimal nucleus or "microkernel." This approach arises out of the need for modularity and flexibility in managing the ever-growing complexity caused by the introduction of new functions and new architectures. In particular, it provides a solid architectural basis for distribution, fault tolerance, and security. Microkernel-based operating systems have been a focus of research for a number of years, and are now beginning to play a role in commercial UNIX systems.

The ultimate feasibility of this attractive approach is not yet widely recognised, however. A primary concern is efficiency: can a microkernel-based modular operating system provide performance comparable to that of a monolithic kernel when running on comparable architectures? The elegance and flexibility of the client-server model may exact a cost in message-handling and context-switching overhead. If this penalty is too great, commercial acceptance will be limited. Another pragmatic concern is compatibility: in an industry relying increasingly on portability and standardisation, compatible interfaces are needed not only at the level of application programs, but also for device drivers, streams modules, and other components. In many cases, binary as well as source compatibility is required. These concerns affect the structure and organisation of the operating system.

The Chorus team has spent the past six years studying and experimenting with UNIX "kernelisation" as an aspect of its work in modular distributed and real-time systems. In this paper we examine aspects of the current CHORUS* system in terms of its evolution from the previous version. Our focus is on pragmatic issues such as performance and compatibility, as well as considerations of modularity and software engineering.

---

* CHORUS is a registered trademark of Chorus systèmes.

1 Microkernel architectures

A recent trend in operating system development consists of structuring the operating system as a modular set of system servers which sit on top of a minimal microkernel, rather than using the traditional monolithic structure. This new approach promises to help meet system and platform builders' needs for a sophisticated operating system development environment that can cope with growing complexity, new architectures, and changing market conditions. In this operating system architecture, the microkernel provides system servers with generic services, such as processor scheduling and memory management, independent of a specific operating system. The microkernel also provides a simple Inter-Process Communication (IPC) facility that allows system servers to call each other and exchange data independent of where they are executed, in a multiprocessor, multicomputer, or network configuration.

This combination of primitive services forms a standard base which in turn supports the implementation of functions that are specific to a particular operating system or environment. These system-specific functions can then be configured, as appropriate, into system servers managing the other physical and logical resources of a computer system, such as files, devices and high-level communication services. We refer to such a set of system servers as a *subsystem*. Real-time systems tend to be built along similar lines, with a very simple generic executive supporting application-specific real-time tasks.

1.1 UNIX and microkernels

UNIX introduced the concept of a standard, hardware-independent operating system, whose portability allowed platform builders to reduce their time to market by obviating the need to develop proprietary operating systems for each new platform.

However, as more function and flexibility is continually demanded, it is unavoidable that today's versions become increasingly more complex. For example, UNIX is being extended with facilities for real-time applications and on-line transaction processing. Even more fundamental is the move toward distributed systems. It is desirable in today's computing environments that new hardware and software resources, such as specialised servers and applications, be integrated into a single system, distributed over a network. The range of communication media commonly encountered includes shared memory, buses, high-speed networks, local-area networks, and wide-area networks. This trend to integrate new hardware and software components will become fundamental as collective computing environments emerge.

To support the addition of function to UNIX and its migration to distributed environments, it is desirable to map UNIX onto a microkernel architecture, where machine dependencies may be isolated from unrelated abstractions and facilities for distribution may be incorporated at a very low level.

The attempt to reorganise UNIX to work within a microkernel framework poses problems, however, if the resultant system is to behave exactly as a traditional UNIX implementation. A primary concern is efficiency: a microkernel-based modular operating system must provide performance comparable to that of a monolithic kernel. The elegance and flexibility of the client-server model may exact a cost in message-handling and context-switching overhead. If this penalty is too great, commercial acceptance will be limited. Another pragmatic concern is compatibility: in an industry relying increasingly upon portability and standardisation, compatible interfaces are needed not only at the level of application programs, but also for device drivers, streams modules, and other components. In many cases binary as well as source compatibility is required. These concerns affect the structure and organisation of the operating system.

There is work in progress on a number of fronts to emulate UNIX on top of a microkernel architecture, including the Mach [Gol90], V [Che90], and Amoeba [Tan90] projects. Plan 9 from

Bell Labs [Pik91] is a distributed UNIX-like system based on the "minimalist" approach. CHORUS versions V2 and V3 represent the work we have done to solve the problems of compatibility and efficiency.

1.2 The CHORUS microkernel technology

The Chorus team has spent the past six years studying and experimenting with UNIX "kernelisation" as an aspect of its work in modular, distributed and real-time systems. The first implementation of a UNIX-compatible microkernel-based system was developed during 1984 through 1986 as a research project at INRIA. Among the goals of this project were to explore the feasibility of shifting as much function as possible out of the kernel and to demonstrate that UNIX could be implemented as a set of modules that did not share memory. In late 1986, an effort to create a new version, based on an entirely rewritten CHORUS nucleus, was launched at Chorus systèmes. The current version maintains many of the goals of its predecessor and adds some new ones, including real-time support and — not incidentally — commercial viability. A UNIX subsystem compatible with System V Release 3.2 is currently available, with System V Release 4.0 and 4.4BSD systems under development. The System V Release 3.2 implementation performs comparably with well established monolithic-kernel systems on the same hardware, and better in some respects. As a testament to its commercial viability, the system has been adopted for use in commercial products ranging from X terminals and telecommunication systems to mainframe UNIX machines.

In this paper we examine aspects of the current CHORUS system in terms of its evolution from the previous version. Our focus is on pragmatic issues such as performance and compatibility, as well as considerations of modularity and software engineering.

In section 2, we review the previous CHORUS version. Section 3 evaluates the previous version and discusses how the lessons learned from its implementation led to the main design decisions for the current version. The subsequent sections focus on specific aspects of the current design.

2 CHORUS V2 overview

The CHORUS project, while at INRIA, began researching distributed operating systems with CHORUS V0 and V1. These versions proved the viability of a modular, message-based distributed operating system, examined its potential performance, and explored its impact on distributed applications programming.

Based on this experience, CHORUS V2 [Arm86, Roz87] was developed. It represented the first intrusion of UNIX into the peaceful CHORUS landscape. The goals of this third implementation of CHORUS were:

1. To add UNIX emulation to the distributed system technology of CHORUS V1;
2. To explore the outer limits of "kernelisation"; demonstrate the feasibility of a UNIX implementation with a minimal kernel and semi-autonomous servers;
3. To explore the distribution of UNIX services;
4. And to integrate support for a distributed environment into the UNIX interface.

Since its birth, the CHORUS architecture has always consisted of a modular set of servers running on top of a microkernel (the nucleus) which included all of the necessary support for distribution.

The basic execution entities supported by the V2 nucleus were monothreaded *actors* running in user mode and isolated in protected address spaces. Execution of actors consisted of a sequence of "processing-steps" which mimicked atomic transactions: ports represented operations to be performed; messages would trigger their invocation and provide arguments. The execution of remote operations were synchronised at explicit "commit" points. An ever-present concern in the design of CHORUS was that fault-tolerance and distribution are tightly coupled; hardware redundancy both increases the probability of faults and gives a better chance to recover from these faults.

Communication in CHORUS V2 was, as in many current systems, based upon the exchange of messages through *ports*. Ports were attached to actors, and had the ability to migrate from one actor to another. Furthermore, ports could be gathered into *port groups*, which allowed message broadcasting as well as functional addressing. For example, a message could be directed to all members of a port group or to a single member port which resided on a specified site. The port group mechanism provided a flexible set of client-server mapping semantics including dynamic reconfiguration of servers.

Ports, port groups, and actors were given global unique names, constructed in a distributed fashion by each nucleus for use only by the nucleus and system servers. Private, context-dependent names were exported to user actors. These *port descriptors* were inherited in the same fashion as UNIX file descriptors.

2.1 UNIX

On top of this architecture, a full UNIX System V was built.

In V2, the whole of UNIX was split into three servers: a Process Manager, dedicated to process management, a File Manager for block device and file system management, and a Device Manager for character device management. In addition, the nucleus was complemented with two servers, one which managed ports and port groups, and another which managed remote communications (see Figure 1). UNIX network facilities (sockets) were not implemented at this time.

A UNIX process was implemented as a CHORUS actor. All interactions of the process with its environment, i.e. all system calls, were performed as exchanges of messages between the process and system servers. Signals were also implemented as messages.

This "modularisation" impacted UNIX in the following ways:

1. UNIX data structures were split between the nucleus and several servers. Splitting the data structures, rather than replicating them, was done to avoid consistency problems. Messages between these servers contained the information managed by one server and required by another in order to provide its service. Careful thought was given to how UNIX data structures were split between servers to minimise communication costs.
2. Most UNIX objects, files in particular, were designated by network-wide capabilities which could be exchanged freely between subsystem servers and sites. The context of a process contained a set of capabilities representing the objects accessed by the process.

As many of the UNIX system calls as possible were implemented by a process-level library. The process context was stored in process-specific library data at a fixed, read-only location within the process address space. The library invoked the servers, when necessary, using an RPC facility. For example, the Process Manager was invoked to handle a `fork(2)` system call and the File Manager for a `read(2)` system call on a file.

This library offered only source-level compatibility with UNIX, but was acceptable because binary compatibility was not a project goal. The library resided at a predefined user virtual address in a write-protected area. Library data holding the process context information was not

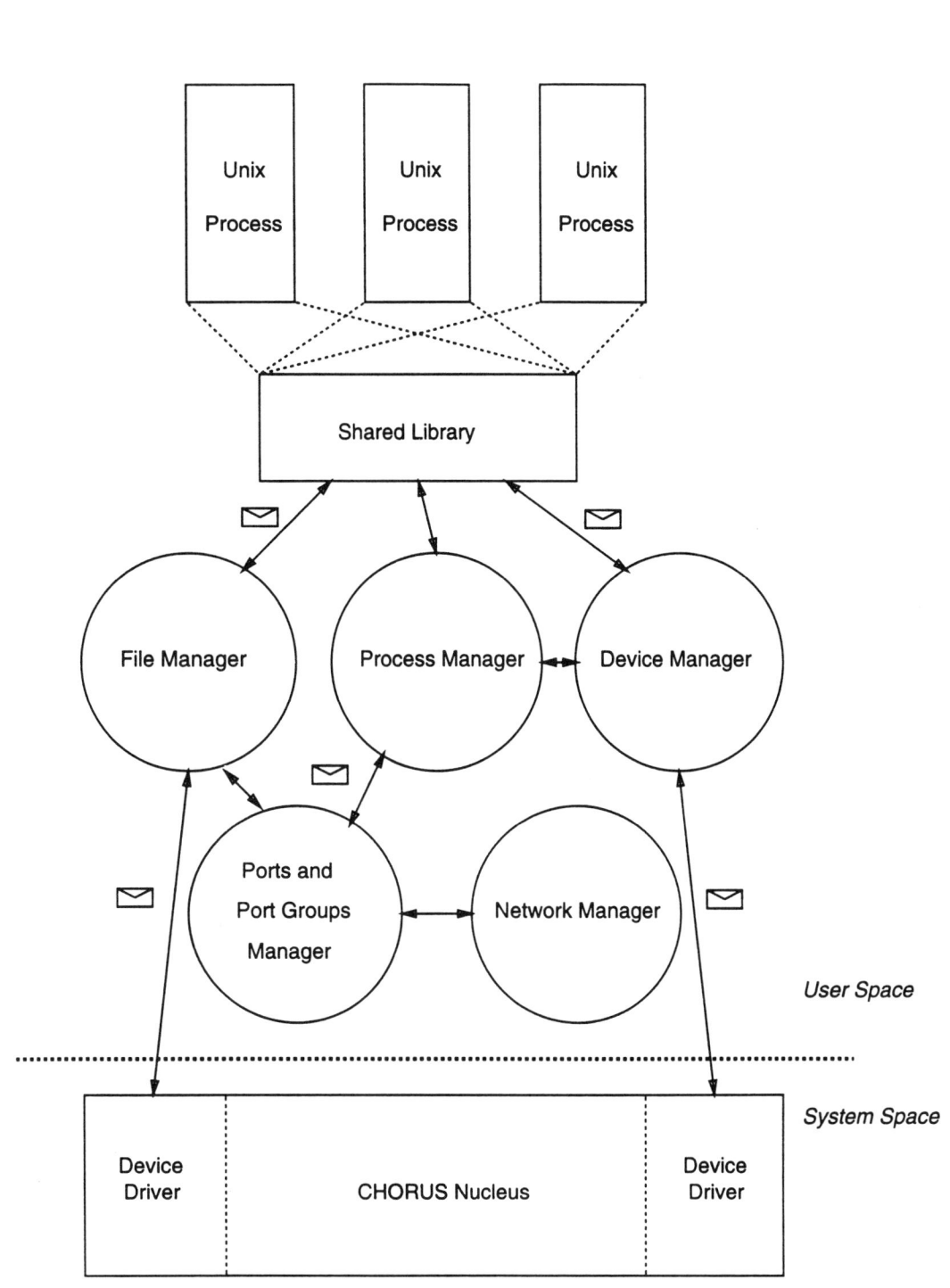

Figure 1. CHORUS-V2 architecture.

completely secure from malicious or unintentional modification by the user. Thus, errant programs could experience new, unexpected error behaviour. In addition, programs that depended upon the standard UNIX address space layout could cease to function because of the additional address space contents.

2.2 Extended UNIX services

CHORUS V2 extended UNIX services in two ways:

- by allowing their distribution while retaining their original interface (e.g. remote process creation and remote file access).
- by providing access to new services without breaking existing UNIX semantics (e.g. CHORUS IPC).

2.2.1 Distribution of UNIX Services

Access to files and processes extended naturally to the remote case due to the modularity of CHORUS's UNIX and its inherent protocols. Files and processes, whether local or remote, were manipulated using CHORUS IPC through the use of location-transparent capabilities.

In addition, CHORUS V2 extended UNIX file semantics with *port nodes*. A port node was an entry in the file system which had a CHORUS port associated with it. When a port node was encountered during path-name analysis, a message containing the remainder of the path to be analysed was sent to the associated port. Port nodes were used to automatically interconnect file trees.

For processes, new protocols between Process Managers were developed in order to distribute `fork` and `exec` operations. Remote `fork` and `exec` were facilitated because:

- the management of a process context was not distributed; each process context was managed entirely by only one system server (the Process Manager),
- a process context contained only global references to resources (capabilities).

Therefore, creating a remote process could be done almost entirely by transferring the process context from one Process Manager to another.

Since signals were implemented as messages, their distribution was trivial due to the location transparency of CHORUS IPC.

2.2.2 Introduction of new services

CHORUS IPC was introduced at user-level. Its UNIX interface was designed in the standard UNIX style:

1. Ports and port groups were known, from within processes, by local identifiers. Access to a port was controlled in a fashion analogous to the access to a file.
2. Ports and port groups were protected in a similar fashion to files (with *uids* and *gids*).
3. Port and port group access rights were inherited on `fork` and `exec` exactly as are file descriptors.

3 Analysis of CHORUS V2

Experience developing and using CHORUS V2 gave us valuable insight into the basic operating system services that a microkernel must provide to implement a rich operating system environment such as UNIX. CHORUS V2 was our third reimplementation of the CHORUS nucleus, but represented our first attempt at integrating an existing, complex operating system interface with microkernel technology. This research exercise was not without faults. However, it demonstrated that we did a number of things correctly. The CHORUS V2 basic IPC abstractions — location transparency, untyped messages, asynchronous and RPC protocols, ports, and port groups — have proven to be very well suited to the implementation of distributed operating systems and applications. These abstractions have been entirely retained for CHORUS V3; only their interface has been enriched to make their use more efficient.

The basic modular architecture of the UNIX subsystem has also been retained in the implementation of CHORUS V3 UNIX subsystems. Some new servers, such as a BSD Socket Manager, have been added to provide new function that was not included in CHORUS V2.

Version 3 of the CHORUS nucleus has been completely redesigned and reimplemented around a new set of project goals. These goals were put in place as a direct result of our experience implementing our first distributed UNIX system.

In the following subsections we briefly state our new goals and then explain how these new goals affected the design of CHORUS V3.

3.1 CHORUS V3 goals

The design of CHORUS V3 system [Arm89, Arm90, Her88, Roz88] has been strongly influenced by a new major goal: to design a microkernel technology suitable for the implementation of commercial operating systems. CHORUS V2 was a UNIX-compatible distributed operating system. The CHORUS V3 microkernel is able to support operating system standards while meeting the new needs of commercial systems builders.

These new goals determined new guidelines for the design of the CHORUS V3 technology:

- **Portability:** the CHORUS V3 microkernel must be highly portable to many machine architectures. In particular, this guideline motivated the design of an architecture-independent memory management system [Abr89], taking the place of the hardware-specific CHORUS V2 memory management.
- **Generality:** the CHORUS V3 microkernel must provide a set of functions that are sufficiently generic to allow the implementation of many different sets of operating system semantics; some UNIX-related features had to be removed from the CHORUS V2 nucleus. The nucleus must maintain its simplicity and efficiency for users or subsystems which do not require high level services.
- **Compatibility:** UNIX source compatibility in CHORUS V2 had to be extended to binary compatibility in V3, both for user applications and device drivers. In particular, the CHORUS V3 nucleus had to provide tools to allow subsystems to build binary compatible interfaces.
- **Real-time:** process control and telecommunication systems comprise important targets for distributed systems. In this area, the responsiveness of the system is of prime importance. The CHORUS V3 nucleus is, first and foremost, a distributed real-time executive. The real-time features may be used by any subsystem, allowing for example, a UNIX subsystem to be naturally extended to be suitable for real-time applications needs.
- **Performance:** for commercial viability, good performance is essential in an operating system. While offering the base for building modular, well-structured operating systems, the nucleus interface must allow these operating systems to reach at least the same performance as conventional, monolithic, implementations.

These new goals forced us to reconsider CHORUS V2 design choices. In most cases, the architectural elements were retained in CHORUS V3; only their interface evolved. Whenever possible, the V3 interface reflects our desire to leave it to the subsystem designer to negotiate the tradeoffs between simplicity and efficiency, on the one hand, and more sophisticated function, on the other.

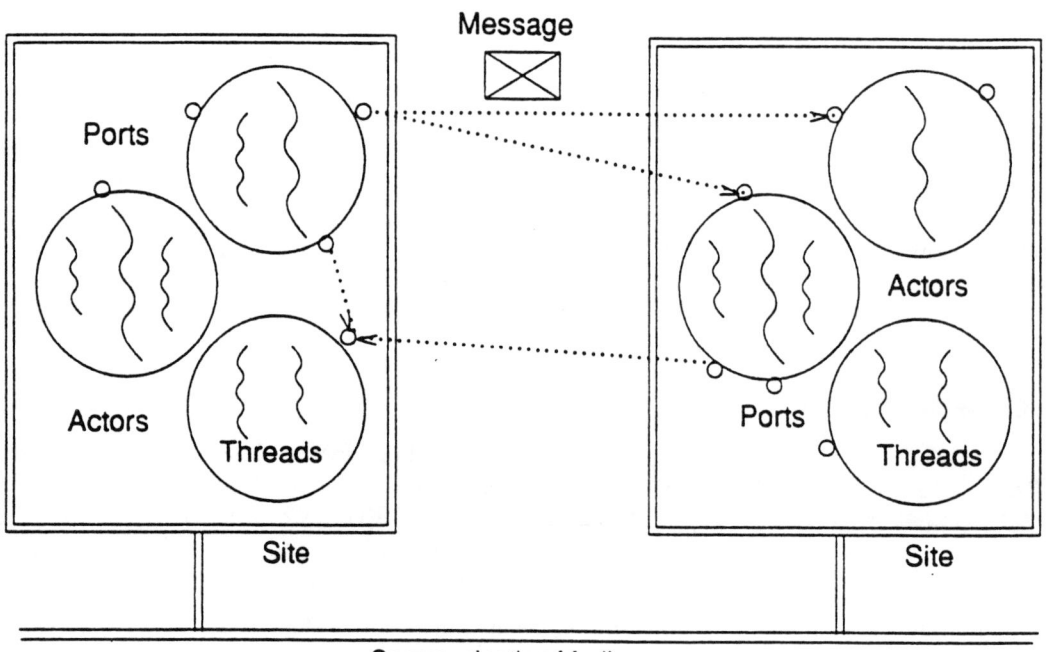

Figure 2. CHORUS V3 nucleus abstractions.

3.2 CHORUS processing model

Problems arose with the CHORUS V2 processing model when UNIX signals were first implemented. To treat asynchronous signals in V2 monothreaded actors, it was necessary to introduce the concept of priorities within messages to expedite the invocation of a signaling operation. Even so, the priorities went into effect only at fixed synchronisation points, making it impossible to perfectly emulate UNIX signal behaviour. Further work has shown that signals are one of the major stumbling blocks for building fault tolerant UNIX systems.

> **Lesson:** *We found the processing-step model of computation to be a poor fit with the asynchronous signal model of exception handling. In order to provide full UNIX emulation, a more general computational model was necessary for CHORUS V3.*

The solution to this problem gave rise to the V3 multi-threaded processing model. A CHORUS V3 actor is merely a resource container, offering, in particular, an address space in which multiple threads may execute. Threads are scheduled as independent entities, allowing real parallelism on a multiprocessor architecture. In addition, multiple threads allow the simplification of the control structure of server-based applications. New nucleus services, such as thread execution control and synchronisation have been introduced.

3.3 CHORUS inter-process communication

As a consequence of the change to the basic processing model, the inter-process communication model also evolved. In the V2 processing-step model, IPC and execution were tightly bound, yielding a mechanism that resembled atomic transactions.

This tight binding of communication to execution did not necessarily make sense in a multi-threaded CHORUS V3 system. Thus, the atomic transactions of V2 have been replaced, in V3, by the remote procedure call (RPC) paradigm and has since evolved into a very efficient lightweight RPC protocol.

One aspect of the IPC mechanism that has not changed in CHORUS V3 is that messages remain untyped. The CHORUS IPC mechanism is simple and efficient when communicating among homogeneous sites. When communicating between heterogeneous sites, higher-level protocols are used, as needed. A guideline in the design of CHORUS V2, retained in V3, was to allow the construction of simple and efficient applications without forcing them to pay a penalty for sophisticated mechanisms which were required only by specific classes of programs.

3.4 CHORUS ports

A number of enhancements concerning CHORUS ports have been made to provide more generality and efficiency in the most common cases.

3.4.1 Port naming

Recall that in V2 context-dependent port names were exported to the user-level while global port names were used by the nucleus and system servers. The user-level context-dependent port names of V2 were intended to provide security and ease of use. It was difficult, however, for applications to exchange port names, since it required intervention by the nucleus and posed bootstrapping problems. As a result, context-dependent names were inconvenient for distributed applications, such as name servers. In addition, many applications had no need of the added security the context-dependent names provided.

> **Lesson:** *CHORUS V3 makes global names of ports and port groups (Unique Identifiers) visible to the user, discarding the UNIX-like CHORUS V2 contextual naming scheme. Contextual identifiers turned out not to be an effective paradigm.*

The first consequence of using Unique Identifiers is simplicity: port and port group names may be freely exchanged by nucleus users, avoiding the need for the nucleus to maintain complex actor context. The second consequence is a lower level of protection: the CHORUS V3 philosophy is to provide subsystems with the means for implementing their own level and style of protection rather than enforcing protection directly in the microkernel. For example, if the security of V2 context-dependent names is desired, a subsystem can easily and efficiently export a protected name-space server. V3 Unique Identifiers have proven to be key to providing distributed UNIX services in an efficient manner.

3.4.2 Port implementation

A goal of the V2 project was to determine what were the minimal set of functions that a microkernel should have in order to support a robust base of computing. To that end, the management of ports and port groups was put into a server external to the nucleus. Providing the ability to replace a portion of the IPC did not prove to be useful, however, since IPC was a fundamental and critical element of all nucleus operations. Maintaining it in a separate server rendered it more expensive to use.

> **Lesson:** *We found that actors, ports, and port groups are basic nucleus abstractions. Splitting their management did not provide significant benefit, but did impact system performance. Actor, port, and port group management has been moved back into the nucleus for V3.*

3.4.3 UNIX port extensions

When extending the UNIX interface to give access to CHORUS IPC, we maintained normal UNIX-style semantics. Employing the same form as the UNIX file descriptor for port descriptors was intended to provide uniformity of model. The semantics of ports were sufficiently different from the semantics of files to negate this advantage. In operations such as `fork`, for example, it did not make sense to share port descriptors in the same fashion as file descriptors. Attempting to force ports into the UNIX model resulted in confusion.

> **Lesson:** *A user-level IPC interface was important, but giving it UNIX semantics was cumbersome and unnecessary. This lesson is an example of a larger principle; the nucleus abstractions should be primitive and generally applicable — they should not be coerced into the framework of a specific operating system.*

V3 avoids this issue by, as previously mentioned, exporting global names. Since the V3 nucleus no longer manages the sharing of global port and port group names, it is up to the individual subsystem servers to do so. In particular, if counting the number of references to a given port is important to a subsystem, it is the subsystem itself that must maintain the reference count. On the other hand, a subsystem that has no need for reference counting is not penalised by the nucleus.

Using V2 port nodes to interconnect file systems was a simple, but extremely powerful, extension to UNIX. Since all access to files was via CHORUS messages, port nodes provided network transparent access to regular files as well as to device nodes. They also, however, introduced a new file type into the file system. This caused many system utilities, such as `ls` and `find`, to not function properly. Thus, all such utilities had to be modified to take the new file type into account.

Port nodes have been maintained in CHORUS V3 (however, they are now called *"symbolic ports"*). In future CHORUS UNIX systems, the file type "symbolic port" may be eliminated by inserting the port into the file system hierarchy using the `mount` system call. These *"port mount points"* would carry the same semantics as a normal mounted file system.

3.5 Virtual memory

The virtual memory subsystem has undergone significant change. The machine dependent virtual memory system of CHORUS V2 has been replaced, in V3, by highly portable VM system. The VM abstractions presented by the V3 nucleus include "segments" and "regions." Segments encapsulate data within a CHORUS system and typically represent some form of backing store, such as a swap area on a disk. A region is a contiguous range of virtual addresses within an actor that map a portion of a segment into its address space. Requests to read or to modify data within a region are converted by the virtual memory system into read or modify requests within the segment. "External Mappers" interact with the virtual memory system using a nucleus-to-Mapper protocol to manage data represented by segments. Mappers also provide the needed synchronisation to implement distributed shared memory. For more details on the CHORUS V3 virtual memory system, see [Abr89].

3.6 Actor context

CHORUS V2 was built around a "pure" message-passing model, in which strict protection was incorporated at the lowest level; all servers were implemented in protected user address spaces. This distinct separation enforced a clean, modular design of a subsystem. However, it also led to several problems:

- A UNIX subsystem based on CHORUS V2 required the use of user-level system call stubs and altered the memory layout of a process and, therefore, could never provide 100% binary compatibility;
- All device drivers were required to reside within the nucleus;
- Context switching expense was prohibitively high.

The most fundamental enhancement made between CHORUS V2 and V3 was the introduction of the *Supervisor Actor*. Supervisor actors share the supervisor address space and whose threads execute in a privileged machine state. Although they reside within the supervisor address space, supervisor actors are truly separate entities; they are compiled, link edited, and loaded independently of the nucleus and of each other.

The introduction of supervisor actors creates several opportunities for system enhancement in the areas of compatibility and performance. Section 4 discusses the ramifications of supervisor actors in-depth.

3.7 UNIX subsystem

As a consequence of these nucleus evolutions, the UNIX subsystem implementation has also evolved. In particular, full UNIX binary compatibility has been achieved. Internally, the UNIX subsystem makes use of new nucleus services, such as multi-threading and supervisor actors. The CHORUS V2 user-level UNIX system-call library has been moved inside the Process Manager and is now invoked directly by system-call traps.

Experience with the decomposition of UNIX System V for V2 showed, not surprisingly, that performing this modularisation is difficult. Care must be taken to decompose the data structures and function along meaningful boundaries. Performing this decomposition is an iterative process. The system is first decomposed along broad functional lines. The data structures are then split accordingly, possibly impacting the functional decomposition.

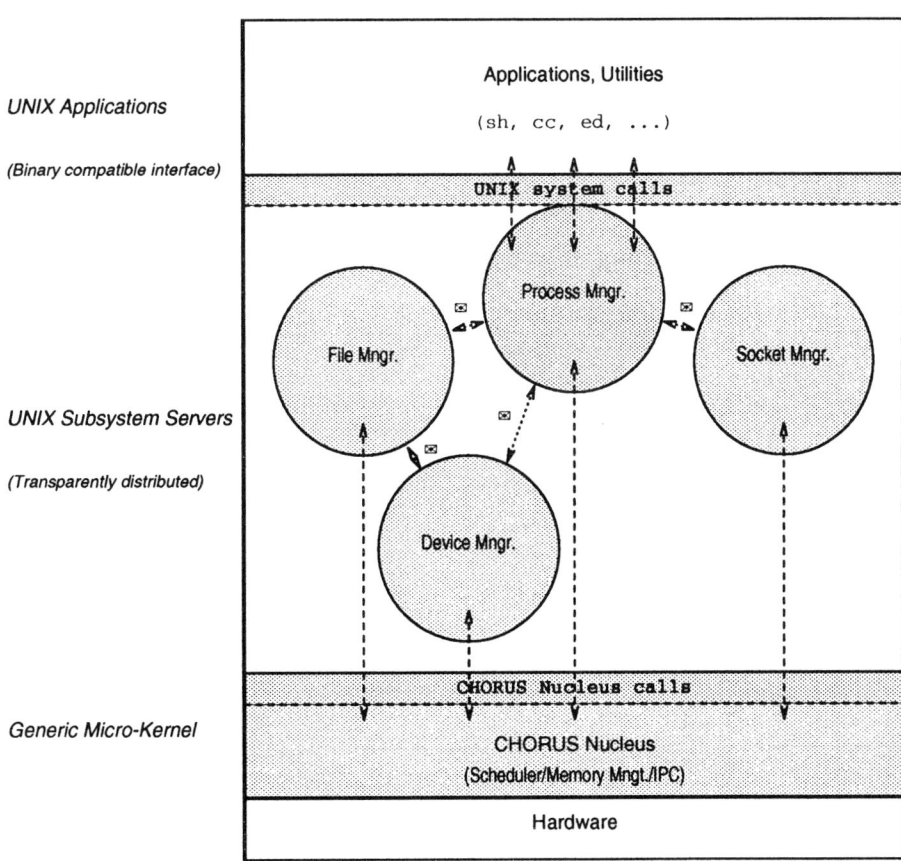

Figure 3. CHORUS/MiX-V3 architecture.

4 Evolution in nucleus support for subsystems: supervisor actors

Supervisor actors, as mentioned above, share the supervisor address space and whose threads execute in a privileged machine state, usually implying, among other things, the ability to execute privileged instructions. Otherwise, supervisor actors are fundamentally very similar to regular user actors. They may create multiple ports and threads, and their threads access the same nucleus interface. Any user program can be run as a supervisor actor, and any supervisor actor which does not make use of privileged instructions or *connected handlers* (see below) can be run as a user actor. In both cases a recompilation of the program is not needed (a relink is required, however). Although they share the supervisor address space, supervisor actors are paged just as user actors and may be dynamically loaded and deleted.

Supervisor actors alone are granted direct access to the hardware event facilities. Using a standard nucleus interface, any supervisor actor may dynamically establish a handler for any particular hardware interrupt, system call trap, or program exception. A connected handler executes as an ordinary subroutine, called directly from the corresponding low-level handler in the nucleus. Several arguments are passed, including the interrupt/trap/exception number and the processor context of the executing thread. The handler routine may take various actions, such as processing an event and/or awakening a regular thread in the actor. The handler routine then returns to the nucleus.

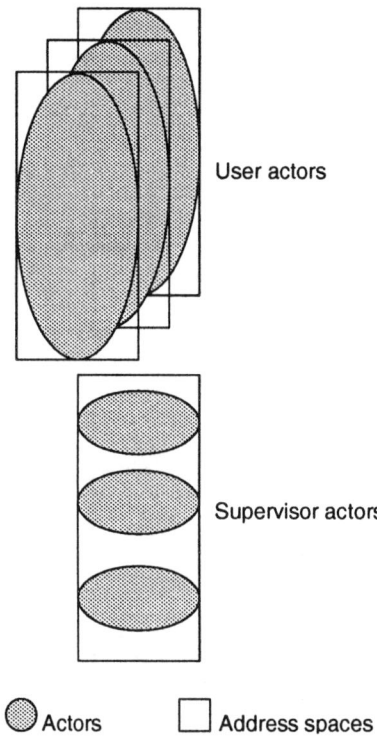

Figure 4. Supervisor actors.

4.1 External device drivers

It is important to note that no subsystem in CHORUS V3 is ever required to use connected handlers or supervisor actors. For example, a subsystem designer may choose to export a programming interface based entirely upon messages rather than upon traps. The CHORUS nucleus can handle program exceptions either by sending an RPC message to a designated exception port or by calling a connected exception handler. Only actors that process device interrupts are required to be implemented as supervisor actors. Even so, device drivers may be split into two parts, if desired; a "stub" supervisor actor to translate interrupts into messages and a user-mode actor that processes these interrupt messages. Connected handlers, however, provide significant advantages in both performance and binary compatibility:

- The nucleus need not be modified each time that a new device type is to be supported on a given machine;
- Interrupt processing time is greatly reduced, allowing real-time applications to be implemented outside of the nucleus.

Connected interrupt handlers allow device drivers to exist entirely outside of the nucleus, and to be dynamically loaded and deleted, with no loss in interrupt response or overall performance. For example, to demonstrate the power and flexibility of the CHORUS V3 nucleus, we have constructed a user-mode File Manager that communicates using CHORUS IPC with a supervisor actor which manages a physical disk. Both the supervisor actor and the user-mode File Manager can be dynamically loaded from a remote site. Additionally, the user-mode File Manager can be debugged using standard debuggers.

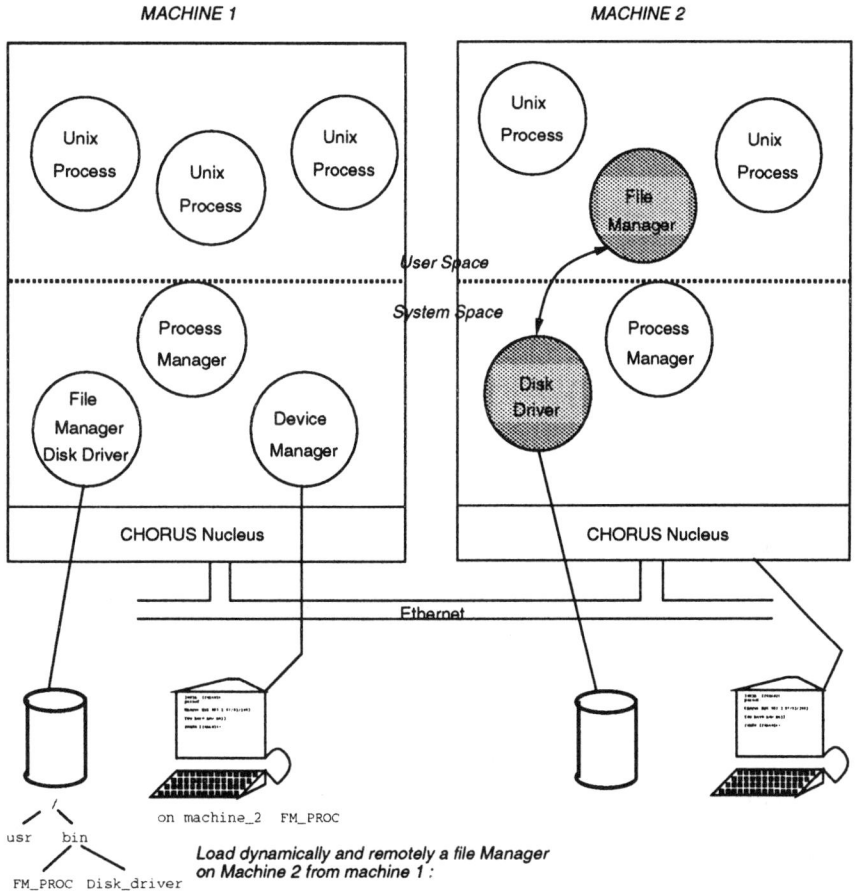

Figure 5. CHORUS/MiX File Manager as a UNIX process in user space.

Interrupt handlers may be stacked, since multiple device types often share a single interrupt level. In this case the sequence of handlers is executed in priority order until one of them returns a code indicating that no further handlers should be called. Connected interrupt handlers have been designed to allow subsystems to incorporate proprietary, object-only device drivers that conform to one of the relevant binary standards that are emerging in this area. Without this mechanism, object compatibility would require incorporating entire device drivers within the nucleus.

4.2 Compatibility

System call trap handlers are essential for both performance and, as it has been pointed out in [Tan90], binary compatibility. Any subsystem may dynamically connect either a general trap-handling routine or a table of specific system call handlers, the latter providing an optimised path for UNIX-style interfaces. An alternative mechanism, the system-wide user-level shared library used in CHORUS V2, would seem to provide equivalent system call performance. However, we found that it is difficult to protect subsystem data that share the address space of the user program, especially if processes are multi-threaded. As we have seen, malicious or innocent but erroneous programs can change the behaviour of system calls. If functions must be moved from the shared library into separate servers for protection, increased IPC traffic results. Finally, the presence of the library code and data in the user context can interfere with binary programs that use a large portion of the address space or manage the address space in some particular fashion. Traps to supervisor actors, by contrast, provide a low overhead, self-authenticating transfer to a protected server, while maintaining full transparency for the user program.

Lesson: *Use of shared libraries produces compatibility and error-detection problems. For 100% UNIX binary compatibility, it is necessary to maintain the standard UNIX trap interface and address space layout.*

4.3 Performance benefits

Performance benefits of supervisor actors come in several areas. Memory and processor context switches are minimised through use of connected handlers rather than messages, and in general through address-space sharing of actors of a common subsystem which happen to be running on a single site. Trap expense can be avoided for nucleus system calls executed by supervisor actors. Finally, supervisor actors allow a new level of RPC efficiency. The "lightweight RPC" mechanism of [Ber90] optimises pure RPC for the case where client and server reside on the same site. We further optimise for the case where no protection barrier need be crossed between client and server. This "featherweight" RPC is substantially lower in overhead, while still mediated by the nucleus and still using an interface similar to that of pure RPC.

Lesson: *Implementing part of an operating system in user-level servers, while elegant, imposes prohibitive message passing and context switching overheads not present in a monolithic implementation of the system. To allow microkernel technology to compete in the marketplace, it was necessary to provide a solution to these problems. Supervisor actors provide the advantages of a modular system while minimally sacrificing performance.*

4.4 Construction of subsystems

Subsystems may be constructed using combinations of supervisor or user actors. Any server may itself belong to a subsystem, such as UNIX, as long as it does not produce any infinite recursions, and may be either local or remote. Servers that need to issue privileged instructions or that are responsible for handling traps or interrupts must be supervisor actors.

4.5 Protection issues

Computer systems often give rise to tradeoffs between security and performance, and we must consider the nature of the sacrifice being made when multiple servers and the microkernel share the supervisor address space. Protection barriers are weakened, but only among mutually trusted system servers. The ramifications of the weakening of protection barriers can be minimised by systematically adhering to the following design rule: individual servers must never pass data through shared memory.

Allowing a server to explicitly access other servers' data would completely break system modularity. This rule being enforced, the only genuine sacrifice for using supervisor actors is a degree of bug isolation among the components of a running system. This is somewhat mitigated by the fact that subsystem servers may be debugged in user mode. In fact, this forms our day-to-day development activity: servers are developed and debugged in user mode. When validated, they are loaded as supervisor actors for better performance, if desired. However, the overall CHORUS philosophy is to allow the subsystem designer or even a system manager to choose between protection and performance on a case-by-case basis, and to alter those choices easily.

5 Evolution in CHORUS IPC

CHORUS V3 IPC is based on the accumulated experience gained since CHORUS V0. Here again, the main characteristics of the IPC facilities are their simplicity and performance.

5.1 Naming

The first aspect which has evolved since V2 is naming: for many reasons, distributed applications need to transfer names among their individual components. This is most efficiently achieved with a single space of global names that are usable in any context, from nucleus to application level. The main difficulty with this style of naming is protection.

In CHORUS V3, ports and port groups are named using Unique Identifiers which are visible at every level. Basic protection for these names is threefold:

1. All messages are stamped by the nucleus with the sending port's Unique Identifier as well as its *Protection Identifier*. Protection Identifiers allow the source of a message to be reliably identified as they may be modified only by trusted actors. Using these facilities provided by the nucleus, subsystems have the choice to implement their own more stringent user authentication mechanisms if needed.
2. Global names are randomly generated in a large, sparse name space; knowing a valid global name does not help much in finding other valid names.
3. Objects within CHORUS may be named using capabilities which consist of a <name, key> tuple. Capabilities are constructed using whatever techniques are deemed appropriate by the server that provides them, and may incorporate protection schemes.

Port groups, as implemented by the nucleus, have keys related to the group name by means of a non-invertible function. Knowledge of the group name conveys the right to send messages to the group, but knowledge of the key is required to insert or delete members from the group.

Higher degrees of port and/or message security can be implemented by individual subsystems, as required. Subsystems may act as intermediaries in message communications to provide protection, or may choose to completely exclude CHORUS IPC from the set of abstractions they export to user tasks.

5.2 Message structure

A second area of evolution in the CHORUS V3 IPC is message structure.

The memory management units of most modern machines allow moving data from the address space of one actor to the address space of another actor by remapping. This facility is exploited in CHORUS V3 IPC, which allows transmission of message bodies between actors within a single site by means of address remapping. In situations where data is to be copied and not moved between address spaces, CHORUS V3 has copy-on-write facilities that allow the data to be efficiently transferred only as needed. The typical communication that makes use of this facility involves the exchange of a large amount of data (e.g. I/O operations).

It is often the case that messages contain a large data area, accompanied by some auxiliary information such as a header or some parameters, such as a path-name, a size, or the result of an I/O operation. Frequently, the auxiliary information is physically disjoint from the primary data. In CHORUS V2, assembling these two discontiguous fragments into a single message required that extra copying be done by the user.

CHORUS V3 splits message data into two parts:

- a message body, which has a variable size and may be copied or moved; it typically contains the raw data;
- the message annex, which has a fixed size and is always copied; it typically contains the associated parameters or headers.

This division also allows one software layer to provide data, while another provides header or parameter information. For example, the V3 implementation of the `write` system call receives the address of a data buffer from the caller and appends a header describing the data area and sends both to the device responsible for performing the operation.

5.3 Processing vs. communication

A third issue is the relationship between the processing model and communication model. The CHORUS V2 execution model was event or communication-driven. In CHORUS V3, the processing model has been inverted actors are multi-threaded and the basic mechanism for inter-process synchronisation is RPC. Thus, the CHORUS V3 model is much closer to the traditional procedural model of computation. Multi-threading allows the multiplexing of servers, simplifying their control structure while potentially increasing concurrency and parallelism. RPC is well understood and straightforward to program.

In addition, for applications that require basic, low-level communication, asynchronous IPC is provided. This IPC has very simple semantics — it provides unidirectional communication incorporating location transparency, with no error detection or flow control. Higher-level protocol layers provided by the user or subsystem can be built on top of this minimal nucleus function.

6 Conclusion

With CHORUS V2, we experimented with a first-generation microkernel-based UNIX system. UNIX emulation was built as an application of a pure message-based microkernel. Our microkernel approach proved its applicability to building UNIX operating systems for distributed architecture in a research environment.

The challenge in designing CHORUS V3 was to make this technology suitable for commercial systems requirements; to provide performance comparable to similar monolithic systems and to provide full compatibility with these systems. Our second-generation microkernel design was driven by these requirements and we were forced to reconsider the role of the microkernel. Instead of strictly enforcing a single, rigid, system architecture, the microkernel is now comprised of a set of basic, flexible, and versatile tools. Our experience with CHORUS V2 taught us that some functions, such as IPC management, belong within the microkernel. Device drivers and support for heterogeneity, on the other hand, are best handled by separate servers and protocols. Supervisor actors are crucial to both performance and binary compatibility with existing systems. A global name space is necessary to simplify the interactions between system servers and the nucleus. Using CHORUS V3, subsystem designers have the freedom to define their operating system architecture and to select the most appropriate tools. Decisions, such as the choice between high security and high performance, are not enforced a priori by the microkernel.

The CHORUS V3 microkernel has met its requirements: the CHORUS/MiX microkernel-based UNIX system provides the level of performance of real-time executives, is compatible with UNIX at the binary level, and is truly modular and fully distributed. It has been adopted by a number of manufacturers for real-time and distributed commercial UNIX systems.

Further work will concentrate on exploiting this technology to provide advanced operating system features, such as a distributed UNIX with a single system image and fault tolerance.

References

[Abr89] V. Abrossimov, M. Rozier, and M. Shapiro, "Generic Virtual Memory Management for Operating System Kernels," in *Proceedings of the 12th ACM Symposium on Operating Systems Principles*, Litchfield Park, AZ (USA), (December 1989).

[Arm86] François Armand, Michel Gien, Marc Guillemont, and Pierre Léonard, "Towards a Distributed UNIX System — The CHORUS Approach," in *Proceedings of the EUUG Autumn '86 Conference*, Manchester, England, (Autumn 1986).

[Arm89] François Armand, Michel Gien, Frédéric Herrmann, and Marc Rozier, "Revolution 89 or 'Distributing UNIX Brings it Back to its Original Virtues'," in *Workshop on Experiences with Building Distributed and Multiprocessor Systems*, Ft. Lauderdale, FL (USA), (October 1989).

[Arm90] François Armand, Frédéric Herrmann, Jim Lipkis, and Marc Rozier, "Multi-threaded Processes in CHORUS/MiX," in *Proceedings of the EUUG Spring '90 Conference*, Munich, Germany, (April 1990), pp. 1-13.

[Ber90] Brian N. Bershad, Thomas E. Anderson, Edward D. Lazowska, and Henry M. Levy, "Lightweight Remote Procedure Call," *ACM Transactions on Computer Systems*, vol. 8, no. 1, (February 1990), pp. 37-55.

[Che90] David R. Cheriton, Gregory R. Whitehead, and Edward W. Sznyter, "Binary Emulation of UNIX using the V Kernel," in *Proceedings of the Summer 1990 USENIX Conference*, Anaheim, CA (USA), (June 1990), pp. 73-86.

[Gol90] Davic Golub, Randall Dean, Alessandro Forin, and Richard Rashid, "UNIX as an Application Program," in *Proceedings of the Summer 1990 USENIX Conference*, Anaheim, CA (USA), (June 1990), pp. 87-96.

[Her88] Frédéric Herrmann, François Armand, Marc Rozier, Vadim Abrossimov, Ivan Boule, Michel Gien, Marc Guillemont, Pierre Léonard, Sylvain Langlois, and Will Neuhauser, "CHORUS, a New Technology for Building UNIX Systems," in *Proceedings of the EUUG Autumn '88 Conference*, Cascais, Portugal, (October 1988), pp. 1-18.

[Pik91] Rob Pike, Dave Presotto, Ken Thompson, and Howard Trickey, "Designing Plan 9," *Dr. Dobb's Journal*, vol. 16, no. 1, (January 1991), pp. 49-60.

[Roz87] Marc Rozier and José Legatheaux-Martins, "The CHORUS Distributed Operating System: Some Design Issues," in *Distributed Operating Systems, Theory and Practice*, Springer-Verlag, Berlin, BRD, (1987), pp. 261-286.

[Roz88] Marc Rozier, Vadim Abrossimov, François Armand, Ivan Boule, Michel Gien, Marc Guillemont, Frédéric Herrmann, Claude Kaiser, Sylvain Langlois, Pierre Léonard, and Will Neuhauser, "CHORUS Distributed Operating Systems," *Computing Systems Journal*, vol. 1, no. 4, The Usenix Association, (December 1988), pp. 305-370.

[Tan90] Andrew Tanenbaum, Robbert van Renesse, Hans van Staveren, Gregory J. Sharp, Sape J. Mullender, Jack Jansen, and Guido van Rossum, "Experiences with the Amoeba Distributed Operating System," *Communications of the ACM*, vol. 33, no. 12, (December 1990), pp. 46-63.

Plan 9: A Distributed System

Dave Presotto Ken Thompson Howard Trickey
Rob Pike   Phil Winterbottom

AT&T Bell Laboratories
Murray Hill, New Jersey 07974

Abstract

Plan 9 is a computing environment physically distributed across many machines. The distribution itself is transparent to most programs giving both users and administrators wide latitude in configuring the topology of the environment. Two properties make this possible: a virtual name space and uniform access to all resources by representing them as files.

1 Introduction

Plan 9 is a general-purpose, multi-user, portable distributed system implemented on a variety of computers and networks. Because commands, libraries, and system calls are similar to those of the UNIX operating system, it is possible to port many UNIX programs to Plan 9 with little or no changes. A casual user would find little difference between the two systems.

What distinguishes Plan 9 is its organization. The goals of this organization were to reduce administration and to promote resource sharing. Our programming style was minimalism. We believe that a small number of well-chosen abstractions can, with much less code, provide most of the function of a larger system. This is the approach that made the UNIX operating system so much smaller than its contemporaries such as Multics. In building Plan 9, we generalized proven ideas from the UNIX operating system rather than add new untried concepts.

Plan 9 is divided along lines of service function. Diskless CPU servers concentrate computing power into large multiprocessors; file servers provide repositories for storage; and terminals give each user of the system a dedicated computer with bitmap screen and mouse on which to run a window system. The sharing of computing and file storage services provides a sense of community for a group of programmers, amortizes costs, and centralizes and hence simplifies management and administration.

Since both CPU servers and terminals use the same kernel, users may choose whether to run programs locally on their terminals or remotely on CPU servers. Plan 9 provides this flexibility without constraining the choice. Therefore, both users and administrators can configure their environment to be as distributed or centralized as they wish. At work, users tend to use their terminals more like workstations running all interactive programs locally and reserving the CPU servers for data or compute intensive jobs such as compiling and computing chess end games. At home, connected via a dedicated 9600 baud line to work, users choose what they run locally and remotely to reduce communication cost. Some applications, such as the editor [Pik87], are split into multiple programs to make this choice even more flexible.

An earlier version of this paper was published in *Proceedings of EurOpen Spring '91 Conference*, 1991, Tromsø, Norway.

Figure 1 in any Plan 9 paper shows how we have configured our environment. Multiprocessor CPU and file servers are clustered in a few computer rooms and connected via 7 megabyte/sec point-to-point links [Pre88]. This permits the CPU servers to be used as high performance compute engines without becoming starved for data. Terminals are connected to the servers via lower speed, lower cost distribution networks such as the 10 megabit Ethernet [Met80] and 2 megabit Incon [Kal, Res]. By emphasizing the shared service clusters we can quickly and cheaply incorporate new technologies as they arise. At the same time, users wishing more autonomy can incorporate as much computing power as they wish in their own offices without losing the advantage of transparently sharing other resources.

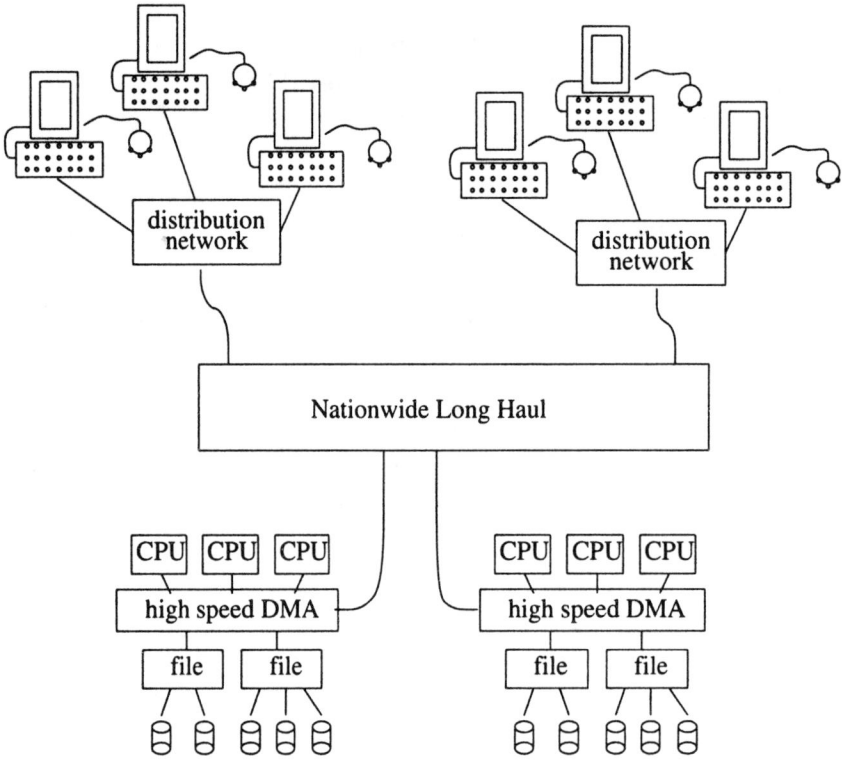

Figure 1. Plan 9 topology

The rest of this paper describes the features of Plan 9 that make possible such a flexible topology. For more information on hardware and use of the system, see our previous paper [Pik90]. For details of the file server, see [Qui].

2 Minimalism

All resources that a process can access, aside from program memory, reside in one name space and are accessed uniformly. Simply stated, all resources are implemented to look like file systems and, henceforth, we shall call them file systems. A file system is a strict tree with no links. File systems can be the traditional type representing persistent storage on a disk as implemented by the shared file servers. They can also represent physical devices such as terminals or complex abstractions such as processes. The file systems can be implemented by kernel resident drivers, by user level processes, or by remote servers.

A file system representing a physical device normally contains one or two files. For example, an RS232 line is represented as a directory containing a `data` and a `ctl` file. The `data` file is the stream of bytes transmitted/received on the line. The `ctl` file is a control channel used to change device parameters such as baud rate.*

Some file systems represent software concepts. Environment variables (as in UNIX) are implemented as files in a kernel resident file system. Even processes themselves are represented as directories with separate files representing different aspects of the process such as memory, text file, and control. Many things that require a system call in other operating systems are represented by I/O operations on files in Plan 9; reading the id of a process, the user id associated with a process, the time, etc.

A kernel data structure, called a *channel*, is used as a pointer to a file. A user level file descriptor is just a handle for a kernel channel. All I/O system calls eventually translate into nine primitive operations on channels. They are:

- attach   point a channel to the root of a file system. The file system is told which user is attaching.
- clone   make a copy of a channel. The new channel points to the same file as the old one.
- walk   do a one level directory lookup on the channel and point it to the new file (or directory).
- stat   get the attributes of the file pointed to.
- wstat   change the attributes of the file pointed to.
- open   check permissions prior to I/O on the channel.
- read   read from the opened file.
- write   write to the opened file.
- close   close the opened file.

Each kernel resident file system is implemented by a *device driver* containing a procedure for each primitive operation. The device drivers are accessed indirectly via a kernel array, `devtab`, which contains 9 pointers per driver, one to each primitive procedure. Each channel contains an offset into `devtab` indicating the driver to be used in accessing the file it points to.

Accessing file systems not resident in the kernel is via a special device driver, the *mount driver*. All channels pointing to this driver contain a pointer to a communication channel. The mount driver turns operations on such channels into request messages written to the communication channel. The mount driver is written as a multiplexer allowing multiple outstanding messages. Because the messages on the communication channel are transmitted using `reads` and `writes`, any type of channel can be used: a pipe to a process, a network connection, even an RS232 line. The `mount` system call, described below, is used to create a new mount device channel and supply a communication channel for it.

All Plan 9 components are connected using this file system protocol. The code used to encapsulate the primitives into request and reply messages is 580 lines long. The mount driver is 899 lines long. Compared to the equivalent NFS code implementing vnodes and XDR this is tiny.

Including all device drivers, protocols, and architecture specific code for 7 architectures, the Plan 9 kernel consists of 49159 lines of code. Of that, 11058 lines perform the basic functions of memory management, process management, and system calls. Each architecture requires approximately 2000 lines of C code and from 300 to 800 lines of assembler. The remaining code consists of 55 file systems implementing devices, networks, process control, etc. Since most of the

---

* We neither need nor have a system call.

file systems are completely self contained, the complexity of the kernel code is much lower than its 49000 lines would imply. A working, albeit not very useful, kernel can be configured containing only the file systems implementing pipes, a local root, and a console. For the SGI Power Series architecture this totals 14377 lines of commented C code (counted using `wc *.[ch]`) plus 760 lines of assembler. As a comparison, Mach's microkernel without device drivers has 25530 lines of C code (calculated, we are told, by counting semicolons). By the same metric our smallest runable kernel is only 6766 lines long, about 1/4 the size. In fact, our largest configurable kernel is still smaller than the Mach microkernel.

One might note the similarities between `devtab` and parts of the UNIX operating system; the block device switch, character device switch, file system switch and vnodes. One advantage of Plan 9 is that we have recognized that these are all essentially the same mechanism and have implemented them as such.

3 Virtual name space

When a user boots a terminal or connects to a cpu server, a new name space is created for her processes. This initial name space contains at minimum a root (`/`), some binaries for the processor the processes are running on (`/bin/*`), and some local devices (`/dev/*`). The processes can then either add to or rearrange their name space using two systems calls, mount and bind. The mount call is used to attach a new (not kernel resident) file system to a point in the name space. Its syntax is

```
mount(int fd, char *old, int flags, ...)
```

where *fd* is a file descriptor for a communication stream such as a pipe or a network connection and *old* is the name of an existing file in the current name space where the file system will be attached. The attachment creates a new mount device channel whose communication channel is that referred to by *fd*. Subsequent accesses to *old* and any files below it in the hierarchy become request messages written to the communication stream.

The bind call is used to attach a kernel resident file system to the name space and also to rearrange pieces of the name space. Its syntax is

```
bind(char *new, char *old, int flags)
```

where *new* is a name in the current name space[++] and *old* is the same as in mount.

How the attachment works depends on the *flags* specified in the call. One possibility is that the old file is replaced by the new one. However, when both files are directories, Plan 9 allows another possibility. The result can be the union of the two directories. The effect is that of putting one directory behind the other. In the case of name conflicts for files contained in the directories, the one in front wins. *Flags* specifies whether the new directory replaces, goes in front of, or goes behind the old one. This concept is essentially the same as the search paths used in the UNIX libraries and the various shells. In fact, Plan 9 has no search paths and uses these *union directories* in their place. When a command is executed, Plan 9 uses the directory `/bin` the same way UNIX uses an execution path.

[++] Local kernel resources are referred to by a syntactic escape (hack) in the name space. Any name starting with a "#" refers to a local resource. The first character following the "#" specifies the type of resource and the remaining characters are a parameter specifying the instance of the resource. Thus, to bind the local console to a standard place in the name space, one would use `bind("#c","/dev", FRONT)`.

The ability to specify the complete name space for a process that contains all resources the process can access forms the basis for a true virtual machine. Any aspect of a process' world can be rearranged. Remote objects can be substituted for local ones. Processes can implement part or all of the name space of other processes. This capability is the basis for a number of important services, three of which we present here.

3.1 The cpu command

We consider the shared CPU servers as accelerators for our terminals, someplace where commands can run while maintaining the same environment. It is important that as little as possible change when running on the CPU server. The virtual name space provides us with a means to make the CPU servers actually feel this way to our users. A command, cpu, calls a CPU server across a network. A daemon process on the server answers the call, sets up a name space, and starts a shell process. The name space set up is an analogue of the name space of the calling process on the terminal. In particular, local resources on the terminal, such as the screen and the mouse, become visible to the server processes at the same place in the name space as on the terminal. The standard input, standard output, standard error, and current directory of the cpu command become those of the remote shell. The directories mounted on /bin are changed to be those that contain executables for the CPU server's processor type (the terminal may be a 68020 while a CPU server could be a MIPS). In general, a user typing the cpu command just notices that things such as compilations speed up while graphics operations slow down.

After the initial handshake to pass information describing the caller's environment, the cpu command becomes a file server answering file system requests from the network connection. The server daemon mounts the network connection to the terminal in a standard place, /mnt/term, and then binds the resources it decides to keep into the same places in the new name space. For example, it binds

```
/mnt/term/dev/mouse onto /dev/mouse,
/mnt/term/dev/bitblt onto /dev/bitblt, etc.
```

Subsequent accesses to those files are converted by the mount driver in the CPU server into file system messages sent to the terminal.

3.2 The window system

The user interface is made up of three files:

```
/dev/bitblt — writes represent bitblt operations to the screen
/dev/mouse — reads return mouse events, i.e., button clicks and movement
/dev/cons — reads return keyboard input, writes put characters to the screen.
```

Between them, these devices represent all I/O to the user. The window system, 8.5 [Pik91], offers processes a multiplexed view to these devices. When a window is opened, the window system starts a new name space for a command (usually a shell) that will run in that window. The name space is a copy of that of window system. In that name space, the window system then mounts a pipe to itself in front of /dev. Subsequent references by the new process group to /dev/bitblt, /dev/mouse, or /dev/cons are sent as file system messages to the window server. 8.5 interprets those requests as accesses of the window instead of the whole screen. Similarly, 8.5 multiplexes the mouse and the keyboard so that mouse and keyboard input is available to processes only when their window is selected.

The result is that any program written to use the kernel resident user interface will also work inside a window. Because this is also true of the window system itself, new versions of the window system can be run and debugged in windows of the current window system.

3.3 Network gateways

One, sometimes insurmountable, problem is accessing a network to which a system is not physically attached. For example, a system may be connected to our Datakit [Fra80] network but not to the DoD Internet. Many gateways exist that try to solve this problem by performing protocol to protocol translation. Unfortunately, few transport protocols have completely equivalent concepts. In order to perform the best translation, it is be necessary to know the semantics requested by the program. For example, TP4 has message delimiters but TCP does not. A protocol translator going from TCP to TP4 would not know which bytes correspond to a single write by the sender.

In Plan 9, every network interface is a file system. A gateway is a file server that serves its own network interfaces to other machines. A process that wants to get at a remote network connects to the gateway and mounts the gateway's interface to the remote network into its name space. Whenever the process accesses the interface, the mount driver will send the request to the gateway. Thus, the gateway sees exactly what the process does.

4 File caching

In building our environment, we have been reluctant to add local disk file systems to any of our terminals or CPU servers. There are essentially two reasons for this choice. The first is administration. Anyone with a local disk must administer it. Any disk that has unique long term state requires both knowledge and time to administer. In fact, the Bell Labs computer center at Murray Hill is doing a lucrative business maintaining other peoples' disked Sun workstations because the owners have neither the time nor the experience necessary to do it themselves.

The second reason is sharing. Although most workstations can export access to their local file systems, when left up to individual users, this rarely happens. Terminals become personified and users become tied to a particular room to do their work.

Plan 9 survives without local disk file systems thanks partially to hardware and partially to caching. The CPU servers do so because their links to the file servers transfer at a substantial percentage of memory speed. The file servers maintain large main memory caches for their disk file systems. These servers are configured with 128 megabytes or more of main memory to ensure that there is plenty of room for cache. Getting a file from a file server is generally faster than it would be to get it from a local disk.

Office terminals are connected to the file servers by shared 1 or 10 megabit/sec links. Home terminals use 9600 or 19200 baud links. In both cases, the link is much slower than access to a local disk would be. To avoid the obvious performance hit, we use caching. To keep the caches coherent, we use file identifiers supplied by the file server. The identifiers are unique 64 bit quantities. 32 bits identify the file, the other 32 bits identify the version of the file. The version number is incremented each time the file is modified. Each time a file is opened the file server returns the identifier with the reply. Therefore, it is possible to guarantee coherency at each opening of a file.

Office terminals only cache pages of executable files. Whenever a program terminates, its unmodified text and data pages are not immediately freed. Instead they are retained until the space is required by other programs. When a program is rerun its executable file is reopened and the current version number returned. If the version number has not changed and pages remain from the last run, they are reused. If the version number has changed, any remaining pages of the stale version are discarded. Since most data intensive work is done on the CPU servers, this simple cache saves most of the traffic between office terminals and the file servers. Other caching could be helpful but would require much more complexity.

This cache might also have sufficed for home terminals if it were persistent, but it is not. Therefore, we have added disks to our home terminals to be used as write through caches of the file server files. As a write through cache, it contains no state that is not duplicated on the file servers. Therefore, it needs little maintenance compared to a local file system. If the code discovers a disk problem, it reformats the disk discarding the current contents. If the user should suspect that the cache is contaminated, she can request that it be reformatted at the next boot. The system slows down until subsequent use refills the cache but no information is lost. The user need not consciously update the disk because the cache uses file identifiers to maintain coherency with the file servers. Each time a file is opened, the cache discards any stale data it might have for that file. The user does not have to copy what she needs to the disk because it is done as a consequence of her using the data.

The disk based cache is implemented by a process that resides between the kernel and the file server connection. For every read request, the process satisfies as much as it can with data cached on the disk. It gets the rest from the file server. Any new data that passes through it is saved on the disk. When the cache fills up the least recently used file is discarded. The amount of data cached for any one file is limited to 1.75 megabytes to prevent one file from displacing all others.

Because the disk based cache only checks for coherency when a file is opened, it provides slightly different semantics than that seen on office terminals which do not cache data files. This looser coherency constraint forces programs that communicate via files to ensure an open between each transaction. Thus far we have not had to change any programs because of it.

5 Conclusion

We have presented a distributed system that is simple in structure and flexible in its use. Both the flexibility and simplicity are the result of two properties, a per process group name space and a single resource interface. Coupled with some minimal caching we provide a simple system that is as usable at home as at work.

6 Availability

Plan 9 has been ported to a number of commercial architectures; SGI Power Series, 68040 Nextstation, MIPS Magnum, SUN SLC, and IBM compatible 386/486 PCs. Two universities have an experimental release. Send electronic mail to research!rob or rob@research.att.com for further information.

7 Acknowledgments

Many people helped build the system. We would like especially to thank Bart Locanthi, who built our terminal, the Gnot, and encouraged us to program it; Tom Duff, who wrote the command interpreter `rc`; Tom Killian, who built and programmed the Gnot's SCSI interface; Ted Kowalski, who cheerfully endured early versions of the software; and Dennis Ritchie, who frequently provided us with much-needed wisdom.

References

Fra80. A.G. Fraser, "Datakit — A Modular Network for Synchronous and Asynchronous Traffic," in *Proc. Int'l Conf. on Commun.*, Boston, MA (June 1980).

Kal. C.R. Kalmanek, "INCON: Network Maintenance and Privacy," Internal Memorandum 220106-0450, AT&T Bell Laboratories.

Met80. R. Metcalfe, D. Boggs, C. Crane, E. Taft, J. Shoch, and J. Hupp, "The Ethernet Local Network: Three Reports," CSL-80-2, XEROX Palo Alto Research Centers (February, 1980).

Pik91. R. Pike, "8.5, The Plan 9 Window System," *1991 USENIX Summer Conference Proceedings*, (1991).

Pik87. R. Pike, "The Text Editor sam," *Software — Practice and Experience*, Vol. 17(11), pp. 813-845 (November 1987).

Pik90. R. Pike, D. Presotto, K. Thompson, and H. Trickey, "Plan 9 from Bell Labs," in *UKUUG Proceedings of the Summer 1990 Conference*, London, England (July, 1990).

Pre88. D. Presotto, "Plan 9 from Bell Labs — The Network," in *EUUG Proceedings of the Spring 1988 Conference*, London, England (April, 1988).

Qui. S. Quinlan, "A Cached WORM File System," *Software — Practice and Experience*, (To appear).

Res. R.C. Restrick, "INCON Wire Interface Integrated Circuit Design," Internal Memorandum 52413-860314-01TM, AT&T Bell Laboratories.

A Distributed Computing Environment Framework: An OSF Perspective

Brad Curtis Johnson*

Abstract

This paper articulates an architectural framework, and the fundamental mechanisms that are required to support that framework, for a distributed computing environment. The emphasis of this framework is on open distributed systems. That is, it serves as a model that supports many of the requirements of a distributed system, such as the need for interoperability, the need to support the client/server distributed application model, and the need to account for the characteristics and challenges that are unique to a distributed environment.

This paper will describe a number of commonalities and differences between the stand-alone environment and the distributed environment. In doing so, it will raise a number of distributed system issues that must be resolved in order to satisfy the needs of an open distributed system.

Finally, this paper will also articulate the need and process for building an open distributed system so that it behaves like a system rather than a set of disparate components.

1 Introduction

The most significant characteristic of computing in the 90s will be the evolution of distributed computing environments. This sentiment is echoed by people involved in development, research,[1] and management. This gradual change is predicated on the ability of the industry (that is, both research and development organizations) to develop at least one architecture that can satisfy several key needs: increasing demand for interoperability among systems, support for the client/server distributed application development model, and the ability to account for the characteristics and challenges that are inherent in a distributed computing environment.

Such an architecture would be considered appropriate if it were applicable to a wide variety of physical topologies (that is, a variety of hardware platforms), to a wide variety of management topologies (such as centralized or decentralized), and to a wide variety of software topologies (such as operating systems and development languages). The architecture would be considered appropriate if it were able to adapt to changing requirements, such as the ones just mentioned, over time. And finally, the architecture would be considered appropriate if its components behaved predictably and coherently, that is, if they behaved like a system rather than a set of disparate pieces. Now let us take a closer look at some of the needs that must be accounted for in this architecture.

1.1 Interoperability

Interoperability is usually a concern only in an environment that contains dissimilar fundamental hardware or software services (that is, a heterogeneous environment). This, in a

---

* Brad Johnson is currently Methodology Manager at OpenVision.

"A Distributed Computing Environment Framework: An OSF Perspective," B.C. Johnson, previously published in *Proceedings of EurOpen Spring '91 Conference*, 1991, Tromsø, Norway, and as an Open Software Foundation technical report. Copyright ©1991, Open Software Foundation, Inc. Reprinted with permission.

nutshell, is the difference between a distributed operating (homogeneous) system and a distributed networking (heterogeneous) system. A distributed operating system is not preoccupied with interoperability because homogeneity is a fundamental characteristic of its environment. Each system that is cooperating in the distributed operating environment runs the same set of underlying operating system services. Although there is occasionally a need for homogeneity in some environments, this is not typical.

The need for a distributed networking system, on the other hand, is typically based on the need for some degree of heterogeneity. For example, in many organizations computing resources are acquired by satisfying the needs of the local department. This typically is done with little or no attention to the prospect of integrating these resources with other departments. This results in a diverse set of hardware and software services. And even in the case where this integration is anticipated, it is reasonable to assume that the specific requirements of each department will lead to the accumulation of dissimilar hardware and software services. However, specialization too can drive the need for interoperability. That is, the demand for a special device or service (for example, a high-capacity disk drive, a high-performance graphics workstation, or a multiprocessor operating system) is what drives a variety of organizations to solve that need. For example, the demand for a low-priced multiuser workstation has led to many different implementations. Inherently, these implementations are not interoperable unless additional services are introduced.

Put another way, the need for interoperability is great because there are only a few situations that demand a homogeneous rather than a heterogeneous environment. A distributed computing environment architecture needs to support the requirement of interoperability because it is assumed that most environments have varying degrees of dissimilar fundamental hardware or software services.

1.2 Client/server model

One of the most widely used models in the development of distributed applications is the client/server model (see Figure 1). This model is based on the premise an application, referred to as the client, makes a request of a particular service, referred to as the server. Although this is the canonical definition of the client/server model, it needs to be extended.

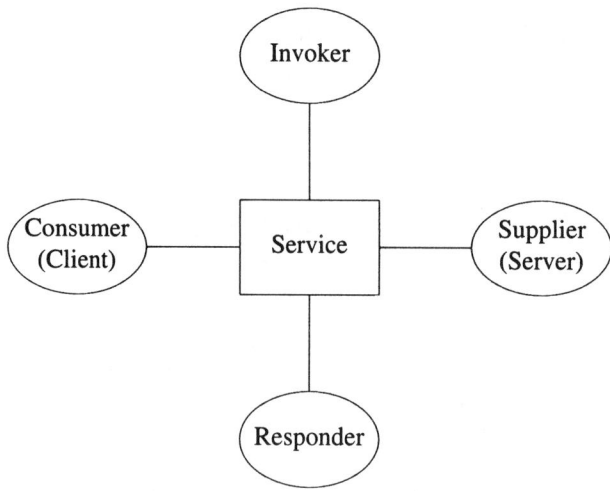

Figure 1. Extended client/server model

The new definition is based on the premise that the client receives the benefit of the service. Therefore, the model is defined by the application that receives a service rather than the application that initiated it. Each service has a consumer and a supplier as well as an invoker and a responder. The current definition can be thought of as a pull-down approach to services. The invoker is associated with the consumer (the client) and the responder is associated with the supplier (the server). This would typically be the case for a distributed file server, a remote procedure call, or a distributed name service request. However, for other applications that fit into the client/server model, the invoker is associated with the supplier and the responder is associated with the consumer. This is the case for many distributed system management applications.[2] For example, imagine an application which performs backups of systems on the network. This task, in many cases, would be initiated centrally by a system administrator and be executed remotely on all of the managed systems. In this case, the client is the consumer of the service, although the request was initiated at the supplier — a push-down approach.

1.3 Defining a distributed environment

Logically, people understand that the difference between a distributed computing environment and an environment which is not distributed (either a stand-alone system or a collection of stand-alone systems) is that related code can be executing on more than one system in the network. If the code is not related, then two systems executing completely unrelated code on two different systems would not constitute a distributed environment. Additionally, it is not a requirement that related code execute on more than one system, but it needs to be possible. That is, an extensible architecture is defined by assuming that the components of a distributed environment will be distributed. The degenerate case occurs when all of the components are on the same system. The reverse is true of services developed for a stand-alone system, which assumes that all of the components are local.

Ideally, this functionality should have a desired amount of transparency. This is somewhat different from the need for total transparency in that the users of the system should have the ability to require (manage) non-transparency if it is appropriate. For example, in a distributed environment which supports load balancing (the ability to maximize the usage of idle CPUs, or conversely, the ability to avoid overwhelming any particular CPU), it is desirable to have the ability to specify which systems are and which are not participating in the load-balancing algorithm. Without this capability, the load-balancing software would transparently (indiscriminately) choose from any of the systems on the network.

Architecturally, the approach to defining a distributed computing environment is to consider the characteristics which distinguish a distributed environment from a stand-alone environment and then engineer a solution which is responsive to those characteristics. This solution must take into account any challenges that are associated with a distributed environment.

1.3.1 Characteristics

Following is a list which articulates some of the characteristics which help distinguish a distributed environment from a stand-alone environment.

- Physical separation

    Through the use of both local area network (LAN) and wide area network (WAN) hardware capabilities, the computing environment can be physically dispersed and potentially extended over a large geographical area.

- Scalability

  The number of software components such as a file server, a name server, or a time server and the number of hardware processing entities such as a multiuser time sharing system, a printer, or a disk server can range from small to quite large. Realistically, a large distributed environment might have tens of thousands of components and processing entities.

- Administrative autonomy

  Especially as the distributed environment grows, as defined by both physical separation and scale, there is likely to be an increasing need to support a variety of administrative policies. Each administrative domain needs to be able to dictate administrative policies (for example, based on national language, organizational requirements, or geographical restrictions) independent of other domains.

- Heterogeneity

  Again, especially as the distributed environment grows, there is likely to be an increasing variety of both hardware and software capabilities. This variety can be realized in two ways: one, the preservation of the current installation base, and two, the anticipation of solutions which are delivered by different organizations. The need to support or coexist with the current installation base (for example, hardware and operating systems) is not just a marketing requirement but an acknowledgment of how new technologies are typically integrated: by evolution. In addition, it is only reasonable to expect that there will be more than one supplier of either hardware or software for any particular service. All of these issues help to drive the distributed environment to be increasingly heterogeneous.

1.3.2 Challenges

Following is a list which articulates some of the challenges which help distinguish a distributed environment from a stand-alone environment.

- Naming

  As in a stand-alone system, the ability to retrieve information associated with a name (object) is a primary function of the distributed system. The name could be associated with, for example, a file, a device, or an application. In a distributed environment, however, this information needs to be available from anyplace in the network. Additionally, a name should reveal the same information regardless of where the name is referenced.

- Security

  Again, similar to a stand-alone environment, the need to control access to resources is a primary function of the system. However, a distributed environment introduces new vulnerabilities in managing access to a resource. For example, information typically flows across a physical medium (like an

Ethernet) which cannot be assumed to be trustworthy. That is, a user can maliciously or unintentionally read or change data as it propagates around the network. Additionally, in many cases a resource (such as a file, a printer, or a disk) is not physically close to the people who would like to manage it; therefore, security can not be assumed because of physical proximity.

- Manageability

  As related to the characteristic of administrative autonomy, portions, or domains, of the network will be managed in different ways. The distributed computing environment architecture needs to support a variety of management policies without imposing undue restrictions or constraints on these management implementations. Additionally, in order to work effectively in a distributed environment, the management functions must have the same qualities as the fundamental distributed system technologies. For example, they must execute in a heterogeneous environment and scale to large networks.

- Indeterminacy

  Although the ability to have true parallelism is a trademark of an effective distributed environment, it is also the root of one of the most significant challenges, that of indeterminacy. Indeterminacy can be manifested by inconsistency of multiple copies of data, by asynchrony (for example, related functions running in parallel on separate systems), by latency (that is, functions that may succeed, temporarily fail, or completely fail at varying and unpredictable rates), and by event-ordering (that is, the ability to accurately determine the order of events as they occur on separate systems).

2 Motivation for distributed computing

One explanation for the necessity of distributed computing can be expressed by answering two questions. Why do we need to think in terms of being distributed? And what are the benefits of being distributed?

2.1 Why do we need to think in terms of being distributed?

The main reason we need to think in terms of being distributed is because we exist in a distributed world that is becoming increasingly distributed.[3] That is, by definition a network is a collection of connected systems (such as, multiuser workstations, personal computers, and mainframes). Except for the case in which there is one and only one storage mechanism, data is stored on many different systems in many different ways, and the users of the systems either want to or are required to share this information.

Two factors increase the likelihood of distribution.

- The user community prefers to support open systems (that is, standard interfaces and protocols) as a means of increasing the opportunity to share information and services.
- The overall decrease in costs of hardware components and the increase in price-performance ratios allows more people to become investors in low-cost personal computers and mid-range computing systems.

It should be noted that people have been thinking in terms of being distributed for quite some time. Until recently, however, the state of technology, or lack thereof, prevented distributed environments from becoming more prevalent.

2.2 What are the benefits of being distributed?

In the previous section a distributed computing environment was defined in terms of a set of characteristics and challenges. If these characteristics and challenges can be addressed in a distributed systems architecture, potential advantages can be realized in the resulting distributed computing environment. They include

- Resource sharing

  Resource providers reach a wider consumer audience in a distributed computing environment than in a stand-alone environment, and conversely, resource consumers can choose from a wider selection of providers.

- Performance

  Similar to a multiprocessor system, a distributed environment can execute a number of operations simultaneously. The key benefit to performing tasks in parallel is increased throughput — through the advantage of decreased latency in processing separable functions.

- Availability

  By taking advantage of the parallel nature of a distributed environment, the availability of services can be increased because there is potentially no single-point of failure. That is, one instance of a service can continue to run in the event that another instance of the same service cannot due to, for example, heavy loading, temporary network failure, or complete failure of the system it is running on.

3 Developing the distributed computing architectural framework

The question of how to define such an architectural framework remains. One way is to resolve two general issues, first, to define the paradigms that are essential to support the development environment, and second, to define a process which will produce instantiations of these paradigms. Let us take a look at each of these issues.

3.1 Necessary distributed computing paradigms

Although many differences have been articulated between the stand-alone and distributed environment, there is some set of issues common to both. That is, in all programming environments, some set of paradigms must exist to support the development of applications. Historically, this has been done in the stand-alone environment by many different organizations in many different ways. However, at the root of these development environments is the support for a set of fundamental programming paradigms. Following is a description of how these paradigms have been actualized in stand-alone systems and an indication of how they would be applied to a distributed system.

Execution space

>On almost all operating systems, the execution space is defined as the process. For multiprocess operating systems, the local execution space is a process and the global space is the collection of all processes. The focal point of administration for the system is determined by the current state of a process or set of processes.
>
>In the distributed environment, the local execution space can be thought of as a host (system) and the global space as the collection of all systems. Components of a distributed application usually are instantiated as a process, or set of processes, on some particular system. Therefore, the focal point of administration in the distributed environment is determined by the current state of a system or set of systems.

Physical data exchange and interexecution space communication

>In the stand-alone environment, the standard means for execution spaces to exchange data is through main memory. This can be achieved in many ways. For example, a single process might use a local procedure call which would take advantage of a common address space, and multiple processes might use an interprocess communication (IPC) mechanism which would take advantage of some memory-management technique such as shared memory.
>
>In the distributed environment, the standard data-exchange mechanism is the network (for example, the Ethernet). Given that the execution is defined across multiple systems, the data-exchange mechanism needs to support inter-procedure communication paths that will probably occur over the network. Therefore, it logically should behave similarly to the local procedure call except that the sending and receiving functions may be on different systems.

Primary stable data storage

>A key mechanism for any type of non-transient system is the ability to store information that persists longer than the duration of a process. This is commonly referred to as stable storage. The type of device used to satisfy this need (whether it be a floppy, a tape, a hard disk, or a write once optical disk) is unimportant. In the stand-alone environment, the stable storage mechanism is typically a local file system.
>
>In the distributed environment, a similar type of technology is needed for the same reasons. In this case, a file system which allows a consistent view of files from anywhere on the network is needed. For the distributed environment, the concepts of the local file system need to be extended to support the same operations, and provide similar benefits and guarantees, across many systems in the network.

Concurrent programming

>The idea of a component in the computing system working on more than one thing at a time is very appealing. The hope is that such a scheme would allow

more tasks to be completed. This idea is referred to as concurrent programming and it has been accomplished in a number of ways. Multitasking uniprocessor systems achieve concurrency by swapping out processes that are waiting for another event to complete (or because the process has used up some (pre)determined time-slice) and swapping in another process that can execute. Multiprocessor systems achieve concurrent programming by actually running code on more than one processor at the same time. Another alternative is time-slicing activities within a given process. By allowing a single process to have multiple execution code segments, the segment ready to execute can continue. Therefore, other segments which are potentially waiting for the completion of some event (such as input or output) can be suspended.

A network is inherently a concurrent programming environment because autonomous computing systems can be independently running a process on their own dedicated processor(s). Although this concept is applicable to a stand-alone environment, concurrent programming becomes a necessary component in the distributed system. Typically, a server is required to service more than one client request at a time. Without this mechanism, all requests to the server would be handled sequentially and would not satisfy certain requirements of the distributed environment — such as the need to scale to support large numbers of systems.

Event ordering

In the stand-alone environment there are at least two types of event ordering. One type occurs when a process is pending on a system resource to become available. For example, a process has made some synchronous request and waits in a pending state until that request has been satisfied; the process could be waiting for some I/O to complete, for a semaphore to clear, or for some other locked resource to become available. Another type occurs when a process needs to make an ordering decision based on the time-stamp of some well known event. It typically does so by checking a time-stamp associated with a file or an object in a file (such as a database). In the stand-alone environment, a decision based on a time-stamp is trustworthy because there is only one provider of the time within the environment — the local operating system.

In a distributed environment each system has its own representation of time; therefore any decision based on the time-stamp associated with events (such as file modification) from different systems is suspect. Hence, a mechanism is needed to ensure that applications can continue to make decisions based on the order of events within the distributed environment.

Stable data storage for execution space

A process normally makes reference to data in two storage areas, temporary and permanent. Temporary data can be thought of as anything stored in memory (physical, virtual, or shared) and permanent data as anything stored in stable storage. In any event, things stored in stable storage are data constructs that need to persist longer than the duration of the process;[1] such as, administrative, transaction, configuration, or log information.

In a distributed environment, there is also a need to access data that persists longer than the duration of any particular process or system. Such data also needs to be consistently available to any process on any system in the network.

Secure access to objects

In the stand-alone execution space, there are usually two types of objects that need an access control (security) mechanism: process objects and file objects. The local operating system is usually responsible for process objects (such as shared memory or IPC channels) and the local file system is responsible for file objects[2]. The goal is to control access to a particular resource.

In the distributed environment, there is a similar need to control access to objects. However, in this environment the objects may be dispersed or even migrate among many systems. Additionally, there are new security issues that do not exist in the local environment. For example, the location of a resource may not be known until it is referenced or a resource will be accessible by users who are not defined in the local system.

These paradigms are available for most application development environments. Their implementation can take many forms, but their existence is a necessity. The distributed computing environment is just another example of an application development environment which needs to provide solutions for these paradigms. However, there are characteristics and challenges specific to the distributed environment.

3.2 A process for defining a distributed computing environment

Most people would agree that the prospect of developing a distributed computing environment architecture is a formidable task. The effort required to meet such a diverse set of needs, requirements, and challenges makes it difficult to understand the entire problem. However, the issue of diversity also leads to an appropriate method for addressing these issues. That is, given that the problem area is diverse, it makes sense to formulate a potential solution by reviewing and incorporating a diverse set of perspectives.

This is exactly what the Open Software Foundation (OSF) did: it used an open process to design the architectural framework as part of its distributed computing environment request for technology effort. The evaluation team reviewed many distributed system architectures[3] and

---

[1] This does not rule out the possibility of storing temporary data in stable storage.

[2] It should be noted that in some operating systems, another object that requires access control, and is not explicitly either a process or a file object, is a device — such as a disk drive, a floppy drive, or a network controller. In this case, the device is usually accessed through a special file but is handled by the operating system.

[3] For example, A Distributed Systems Architecture for the 1990s,[4] Network Computing Architecture,[5] Advanced Networked Systems Architecture,[6] Open Distributed Processing,[7] and The Digital Distributed System Security Architecture.[8]

solicited the opinions of leading developers, researchers,[4] and users in an effort to push forward the state of open distributed systems. The key aspect of this process was to use these opinions in influencing the design. In this respect, the design is in fact a conglomeration of a diverse set of viewpoints and requirements.

4 Putting it all together

There are three requirements for an appropriate distributed computing environment architecture. First, there must be mechanisms to support the needs of the fundamental application development paradigms. Second, these fundamental technologies must account for the characteristics and challenges which are unique to a distributed environment. And third, these technologies must be incorporated in such a way that they have the qualities of a well formed system.

4.1 Fundamental technologies

As stated above, a set of fundamental programming paradigms must exist to support the development of applications, in this case distributed applications. Following are the necessary technologies which can support these paradigms in the distributed environment and a brief description of their capabilities.

Physical data exchange and interexecution space communication

Remote procedure call

The remote procedure call (RPC) provides programmers a familiar programming model by extending the local procedure call to a distributed environment. RPC maintains the useful aspects of the local programming model while handling purely distributed issues such as operation semantics (for example, at-most-once), server selection (binding), and communication or server failures. RPC also provides a convenient and consistent mechanism for specifying the interactions between components of a distributed system.[5]

In addition to basic RPC features, such as supporting a variety of data types and transport independence, the remote procedure call needs to support extended features such as

- context handles, allowing a server to reclaim resources when either the communications or client fails

---

[4] Dr. Andrew Birrell at the Digital Equipment Corporation Systems Research Center, Professor David Cheriton at the Stanford University Computer Science Department, Dr. Paul Mockapetris at the University of Southern California Information Sciences Institute, Dr. Sape Mullender at the Centrum voor Wiskunde en Informatica, Dr. Roger Needham at the University of Cambridge Computer Laboratory, Dr. Michael D. Schroeder at the Digital Equipment Corporation Systems Research Center, and Dr. Peter J. Weinberger at AT&T Bell Laboratories.

[5] It should be noted that there is some debate about the difference between procedure- and message-oriented systems. I believe, as Lauer and Needham[9] stated, that these categories are duals of each other. My extension to their theory is that it applies not just to local operating systems but to distributed systems as well.

- mutable pointers, allowing pointer-handling capabilities that mimic local pointer semantics
- multiple language bindings, allowing applications to be implemented in different programming languages
- orderly quit, allowing the application to cancel outstanding requests
- national language support, allowing data types from multibyte character sets to be supported

Primary stable data storage

Distributed file system

Distributed file system technology provides the ability to access and store data at remote locations. It extends the local file system model to a distributed environment.

To do this, it needs to

- provide transparent access to both local and remote files
- support local functionality, such as file locking and sharing, when accessing remote files
- allow users to address files with the same pathname from anywhere in the system, regardless of the computer that is being used
- provide high availability to all accessible data resources
- serve a very large number of concurrent requests with good performance
- work in a wide area network configuration
- provide secure access to local and remote files and directories
- ensure that the logical view of a file is independent of its physical location

Concurrent programming

Threads

Threads provide a useful model for structuring applications to allow them to exploit parallelism. To a large degree, this is accomplished by taking advantage of multiple processors in a multiprocessor system. In a single processor system this is accomplished by allowing the application to overlap operations. That is, when one thread is blocked (for example, because it is waiting for an I/O call to complete) another thread in the same process can be executed.

This technique is useful in client applications and is most important in servers, which must handle requests from multiple clients concurrently. For example, in a typical client/server scenario, a server program can be processing the data from a read request while it is waiting (that is, blocking on the next read request) for another chunk of data to be received. Threads use re-entrant programming techniques that allow simpler designs than other parallelism alternatives such as multiprocess implementations using shared memory, or explicit asynchronous operations.

To do this, threads must support features such as:

- mutexes: a way to synchronize threads access to shared data
- condition variables: used to develop race-free multithreaded applications (that is, coordinate threads within an application)
- alerts: used to provide graceful and reliable thread termination

Event ordering

Distributed time service

The purpose of a time service is to synchronize the clock of a local computer with Universal Coordinated Time (UTC), as well as clocks of other computers on the network. Distributed services that compare dates generated at different computers require some mechanism for determining the appropriate order of events as they occur across different systems within the network. Distributed file systems and authentication are two examples of such services.

The network consists of local system clocks that are divided into clients and servers. Clients take the time from servers, whereas servers synchronize with each other. Because any single server can fail or be inaccurate, a requester, either client or server, needs to ask the time from a number of servers. Additionally, the time service needs to handle error situations like faulty servers and a temporary breakdown of the network as well as avoiding instabilities that arise from loops (that is, the same two servers asking time from each other) and topology changes (for example, the addition of new servers).

Stable data storage for execution space

Directory or name service

The purpose of a naming or directory service in a distributed computing environment is to map user-oriented names to computer-oriented entries in a special-purpose distributed database that describes the objects of interest. Objects contain information for such things as organizations, persons, groups, organizational roles, computers, printers, files, processes, and application services and their interfaces. The clients of the directory service span a wide range from other services comprising the distributed environment, such as remote procedure call and management programs, to applications, such as print spoolers and mail services. The basic added-value of a directory service is its ability to provide location- and routing-independence. It allows objects to be addressed by human readable names, regardless of the locations of the directory client and of the named object, or of the communications path between the two.

The directory service needs to support features such as:

- white pages: the ability to perform straightforward name-to-entry lookups
- yellow pages: the ability to perform lookups based on object attributes

- link or alias service: the ability to perform name-to-different-name mappings
- group service: the ability to map a single name into a set of names

Secure access to objects

Security services

Security consists of authentication of entities (or principals) in an open system, authorization of principals for using resources, and guarantees of integrity and privacy of messages sent over the network. Authentication in an open network context is the verification of a given principal's identity (such as a user or service). In a network system, authenticated communication is necessary because messages are subject to forgery and therefore cannot necessarily be trusted. Authorization is concerned with granting privileges with respect to resources, such as access to files.

Because messages on an open network can be read and forged, a way of determining whether a message from a given principal arrived intact and unaltered is needed. This assurance provides message integrity based on the identity of the invoking principal. While guarantees of message integrity are an absolute minimum requirement, some applications require that the confidentiality of the data be guaranteed as well. This is done by encrypting the message contents, which provides message privacy. It should be noted that although authentication and authorization are essential in a distributed computing environment, the use of security mechanisms is expensive (in terms of overhead applied to each request); therefore different levels of security may be appropriate for different applications.

4.2 Fundamental technology design mechanisms

As pointed out earlier, one of the keys to understanding the makeup of open distributed systems is to understand the characteristics, challenges, and benefits that distinguish a distributed environment from a stand-alone environment. In addition a number of fundamental paradigms are necessary to support the development of applications in both a stand-alone and a distributed environment. The task, then, is to design services that support these paradigms in a way that accounts for the issues that are unique to the distributed environment.

Following is a list of design goals that should be considered in the development of the fundamental technologies, and for that matter, in the development of distributed applications in general. Listed with each goal are some of the common mechanisms that should be used to achieve that goal.

- Autonomy

    The principle behind autonomy within a distributed environment is that each site has its own set of execution and management policies. Therefore, it is difficult, if not impossible, to predict which policies will be acceptable for a given site. In fact, each site may have a number of administrative domains that have varying degrees of policy conformity. Moreover, those policies typically change over time.

Therefore, with respect to autonomy, the technology developer must strive to meet the following design objectives:

- minimize the number of predetermined execution and management parameters
- maximize the number of system parameters that can be reconfigured

- Availability

A resource accessible via only one mechanism would become unavailable if the mechanism failed. Therefore, the key to increasing the availability of any resource in a system is to increase the probability that no single point of failure would prohibit access to that resource.

Hence, with respect to availability, the technology developer must consider the following design objective: there must be alternate mechanisms to access valuable resources. This typically is done by using either replication or duplication techniques. The key distinction between these mechanisms is that replication algorithms attempt to coordinate copies of the information automatically, and duplication algorithms do not. For example, a directory service attempts to ensure that all references to any particular piece of data reveal the same result independent of where that data is referenced.

- Hardware and operating system independence

Hardware and operating system independence is important in the distributed system because applications need to be ported to, execute in, and interoperate in a heterogeneous environment. The key to providing both hardware and operating system independence is to not rely on any features, side effects, or traits that are specific to any particular system.

This would include

- services that only exist in certain environments. For example, the availability of a broadcast mechanism is endemic to a local area network. Therefore, reliance on its availability might prohibit a service from working in a wide area network.
- local services that parallel distributed fundamental services. Often, services within the local operating system parallel services in the distributed system. An example is the use of an interprocess communication mechanism versus a remote procedure call. In general, a service should be developed by assuming that all resources are remote. Otherwise, reliance on a local mechanism might impede the ability for this service to execute remotely or execute on a dissimilar system.

- Indeterminacy

A distributed environment includes a certain set of execution characteristics that are not typically provided in the stand-alone environment. For example, if there are problems accessing main memory in the stand-alone environment, the system probably needs to be rebooted to correct the problem. In the distributed environment, however, there are a variety of problems that could temporarily affect access to the network.

Therefore, with respect to indeterminacy, it is necessary for the technology developer to make the following assumptions:

- all access to the network may result in failure and a subsequent access may succeed; this is typically handled by using retry mechanisms.
- any access to the network may not relinquish control to the calling program; this is typically handled by using threads, polling, or time-out mechanisms.

- Scalability

  One of the most important objectives of a distributed service is to ensure acceptable operation as the number of users increase. This growth typically occurs because more systems are added to the current environment. In general, the issues associated with scalability tend to dictate what mechanisms are appropriate for a distributed application. That is, if the target audience for a given application is known to be small, there are a variety of approaches that can be used to solve a particular problem. When the target audience is known to be large, usually only a few methodologies will be appropriate. This is analogous to determining an appropriate search algorithm. When the sample is small, there is practically no difference in using a binary or a linear search. However, as the sample size increases, the appropriateness of a linear search decreases. Therefore, it is incumbent upon the technology developer to assume that the demand on the application will always be large. In general, mechanisms that work when the sample size is large will work when it is small. The reverse, however, usually is not true.

4.3 Requirements of the distributed system

Now the issue is how to put all of this information together in a way that will lead us to the appropriate architectural framework and the appropriate set of mechanisms to support this framework. There are two key goals in making this happen: define a minimal set of mechanisms and integrate them into a system.

The core of the distributed system needs to be defined as a minimal set of fundamental mechanisms. A mechanism is fundamental if it is required for the development of other distributed applications (such as distributed system management or distributed development tools). The core is expected to be that set of mechanisms which support the previously described application development paradigms. Figure 2 depicts the framework which defines this minimal set of fundamental mechanisms.[10]

Several issues should be considered when reviewing the information in Figure 2.

- It is not an interface definition. For example, it is explicitly expected that distributed applications will make direct calls to the remote procedure call or threads interface(s).

Distributed Open Systems

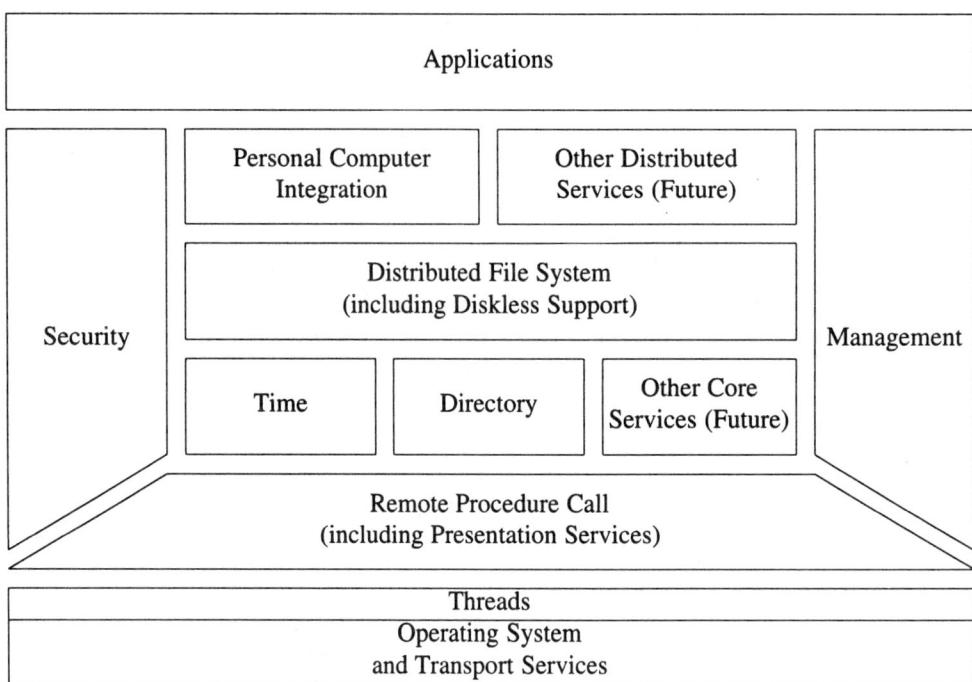

Figure 2. OSF distributed computing environment architectural framework.

- Threads is shown close to the operating system because it is an essential distributed system service but may be implemented in the local operating system.
- The Other Core Services area is intended to be a repository only for other fundamental technologies, that is, those necessary for the development of other applications. An example is event notification.

The fundamental services such as file, time, directory, remote procedure call, management, and threads provide a layer between the application and the operating system and network. These services are necessary for the development of applications in the distributed environment. The security, remote procedure call, and management services form the architectural infrastructure. The remote procedure call is the application development communication mechanism, and the security and management services are a part of all of the fundamental services. The directory service is central to the whole architecture because it provides the mechanism in which all objects are referenced and located.

The need to put this distributed environment together to create a distributed system, rather than a disparate set of technologies was articulated by Lampson, Schroeder, and Birrell.[4] Basically, there needs to be one set of interfaces to the fundamental technologies. For example, there is only one set of exposed interfaces to the remote procedure call, to threads, or to the naming/directory service. Additionally, the fundamental technologies themselves need to use these same interfaces. For example, all of the fundamental technologies should use the threads technology to achieve concurrent programming benefits. Furthermore, all of the fundamental technologies should use the remote procedure call technology to achieve interprocess communication across systems. The information in Figure 3 indicates the level of integration that

	Threads	Time	Security	RPC	Directory
Threads	–	n.a.	n.a.	n.a.	n.a.
Time	x	–	x	x	x
Security	x	x	–	x	x
RPC	x	x	x	–	x
Directory	x	x	x	x	–
File	x	x	x	x	x

Legend:

x denotes an explicit integration point; for example, the Security, RPC, Directory, and the File services are integrated with the Threads service.

n.a. denotes a non-applicable integration point; the threads technology does not integrate with the other services because it executes only within a process on the local operating system (and therefore does not require the functionality provided by the other distributed services).

– denotes an intersection of a technology with itself.

Figure 3. Fundamental technology integration matrix.

needs to exist in the fundamental technologies to support the distributed computing environment architecture. Note that the technologies listed vertically use the technologies listed horizontally.

4.4 The makings of a system

Without this level of integration, the distributed environment becomes less predictable and more complex. This is true from both a statistical and an intuitive sense. Statistically the complexity of the environment increases with the number of interfaces because there are more potential outcomes during the execution of a process. For example, if each fundamental service had its own interface(s) (represented by n) to support threads, time, security, remote procedure call, and directory services, the total number of interface invocations would (more likely) be on the order of $n*n$ rather than just n. Intuitively, the environment would be more complex because there are more potential failure points, debugging paths, and administrative issues. Additionally, it would be more likely that this collection of components would grow apart in time because each would be following its own evolutionary path rather than evolving as a system.

With this level of integration, the fundamental technologies have the qualitative characteristics and benefits of a system. This is analogous to the local operating system. That is, the local operating environment is viewed as a system which provides a common set of fundamental services, such as memory management, interprocess communication, and interprocess synchronization. Without these common services, the application developer is burdened with the task of providing some level of support for these mechanisms. Therefore, by designing an integrated system, the application developer is relieved of many programming complexities. For example, the RPC service will automatically use the security service to ensure both message integrity and privacy. It also will automatically use threads to ensure maximum throughput for multiple requests from a single process. Without an integrated system, the application developer needs to explicitly call all of these services to obtain the benefits that they provide. This additional programming makes it difficult to write distributed applications.

It should be noted that the comprehensive integration of the distributed technologies, and the adherence to a standard set of interfaces to them, is what distinguishes this type of system (that is, this architecture and the technologies that support it) from other distributed networking systems.[6] These are the attributes that make the system coherent and allow the system to account for the characteristics and challenges that distinguish a distributed environment.

5 Future directions for the OSF DCE

Before describing enhancements and new capabilities that may be added to future versions of the OSF DCE, there are two characteristics to keep in mind with respect to an OSF technology release. The first is that OSF delivers technology in the form of source code. In general, organizations acquire DCE and modify it to run in their environments. These modifications can include, for example, operating system-specific changes (such as, porting it to run on MVS), value-added extensions (such as, a graphical user interface to the administrative programs), and porting their distributed applications to use DCE functionality (APIs).

Because end-users do not typically get DCE directly from OSF, development is centered on portable, core functions. That is, OSF does not concentrate on vendor- or ISV-specific issues such as a particular hardware platform, operating system, or compiler. Therefore, there is a class of implementation changes that OSF does not address.

The second characteristic is that OSF makes decisions on what to add or change by considering input from a variety of sources. These include in-house technical experts, standards organizations, OSF member organizations, and OSF special-interest groups (SIGs, which are working groups comprised of individual contributors from OSF member organizations).

OSF released the original version of DCE in January 1992 and began working on the first update release. With respect to future directions, we have defined three general areas to address in the next one to three years; they are performance, functional enhancements, and additional technologies.

5.1 Performance

As with almost all software, the first demand from users after the basic functionality has been supplied is for better performance. Although the OSF release model assumes that the source will be modified to suit vendor- and ISV-specific needs, there are a number of performance changes that can be considered that are beneficial to almost all target environments. These types of changes include, but are not limited to:

Threads and RPC: given the fundamental nature of Threads and RPC (all other DCE components rely on them) any performance enhancements to these components will benefit the entire DCE system. Examples include fine tuning the Threads syncronization (mutex) code path or making RPC packet-size optimizations for both connection-oriented or connectionless (datagram) transport protocols.

Directory Services: like Threads and RPC, all of the other DCE components use Directory Services. Any performance improvements to these services therefore benefit the system — especially object look-up (normally, the most used functionality). These changes might include optimizing current look-up code paths, as well as adding code to provide caching of key information such as often referenced objects, RPC binding handles, and security principals.

---

[6] Distributed operating systems have this level of integration among the fundamental services; however, this type of system is usually only applicable to a homogeneous distributed environment.

5.2 Functional enhancements

Another area for change is adding extensions to the existing source base. This work falls into two general categories. One area includes delegation of security principals, hierarchical cells, C2 security auditing, and support for the OSF Distributed Management Environment technologies. The other area includes well understood changes such as general code clean-up, high-profile code-path optimizations, and internationalization. For the latter, areas such as locale handling, use of XPG messaging, character (multibyte) manipulation, and handling a variety of code and encoding sets (for example, ISO 8859 or EUC or Shift-JIS varieties) must be addressed.

5.3 Additional technologies

The third general area for future work is to consider adding core-level technologies. Our efforts are concentrated in an area that was defined as part of the original DCE architecture (see Figure 2), that is, event-notification. In principle, we would like to integrate an event notification service in the same way we integrated the other DCE technologies (see Figure 3). The two basic characteristics we would expect of such a service are error notification (that is, common error function calls, standardized error message format, message suppression and destination selection) and tracing (that is, common trace function calls, standardized trace data format, and active trace hooks).

6. What we learned

OSF learned many lessons through the complex project of selecting and integrating the technologies for the OSF DCE. They fall into two areas: technical issues (concerning the architecture, design, and implementation) and software engineering issues (concerning project management).

6.1 Technical

In software development there is an on-going dichotomy of creating things (for example, functions) that are completely general and things that are optimized for a specific environment — sometimes referred to as the power/generality tradeoff. The former, if done correctly, tends to be more extensible and widely applicable and the latter tends to be more efficient and specifically applicable. Within DCE we strive to provide limited generality. That is, for often used and fundamental mechanisms we use a common API which offers several distinct options. For example, there is a common interface (XDS) to the directory services; the application can use either (or both) the global directory service (GDS — which is based on the ISO X.500 standard) or the local, or cell, directory service (CDS). There is also a common RPC interface that allows the application to use either the connectionless (datagram) or the connection-oriented transport protocol. We are currently considering extending the security service to embrace the same philosophy by offering a common API to request either public key or private key authentication.

6.2 Software engineering

The DCE project is a unique, on-going software engineering project. It involves the cooperation of six companies, several which are normally competing with each other on several hardware and software fronts. Its goal is to create a base for distributed applications which will, to varying degrees, replace or dramatically change the original technology that each company submitted. For example, the distributed file system has been modified to integrate with completely new Threads, RPC, security, and directory services. As a result, this project requires that many of these companies ensure that their technologies execute correctly on a hardware architecture and operating system that they would not normally have or use. And most of all, it requires engineers to make design (including architecture) and implementation changes at the request of other development organizations and companies.

Yet, in most ways this project is just like other software development efforts except that the operating conditions are exaggerated. They are exaggerated by geography, by company and country cultures, and by the requirement to abide by decisions through indirect management (that is, outside of their own company hierarchy).

Of the many things we learned from working in this kind of environment, there are a few which warrant mention.

First, and foremost, is to always state the obvious. Because of the opportunity for confusion caused by these operating conditions, it is important to ensure that communications are based on common understandings. We have found that statements such as "it is done," and "it is tested," and "I will call you soon," were interpreted quite differently by different participants. In addition, expectations for common project documents such as the project plan, testing plan, or a functional specification varied widely. It is therefore imperative to question and clarify almost every statement.

We also learned that it is important to have frequent and well documented communication forums. These include conference calls, email, and regular face-to-face meetings. These are necessary to help ensure a common understanding of fundamental issues so that the separate parallel activities do not diverge (too much) from each other. This level of communication requires an on-gong effort by everyone to explicitly state assumptions so that they can be challenged and clarified.

And finally, we learned that although tracking standards (that is, implementing code that represents a standard specification) is a beneficial and necessary process, it is not easy to do. Tracking a well-known standard like ISO X.500 is frustrating because of the latency between requesting a change and that change actually appearing in the specification. Tracking emerging standards like POSIX Threads is difficult because the standard is still in draft form and there can be inconsistencies and lack of closure between draft versions. And tracking unstable standards like ISO RPC is virtually impossible because of potential dramatic architectural changes from one meeting to the next.

7 Conclusion

We are compelled to think about and solve problems associated with distributed computing because we live in a distributed world and a distributed computing environment offers many potential benefits. In order to effectively deal with the complexity of a distributed environment, we need to define an architecture which accounts for a certain set of distributed environment issues. For example, it needs to support useful distributed application development models (such as the client/server model) and account for interoperability issues (such as heterogeneous software and hardware platforms). The architecture needs to be designed by considering and solving for key characteristics and challenges that are endemic to a distributed computing environment. Additionally, there is historical evidence which suggests that there are a certain set of necessary application development paradigms that apply to both the stand-alone environment as well as the distributed environment.

While it is certainly true that no one architecture will satisfy all of the needs of all of the people, the architecture developed by the Open Software Foundation is an example that satisfies the needs of many diverse organizations and many of the architectural demands of a distributed environment. To realize the potential of a distributed computing environment will require supporting such an architecture as well as providing implementations which satisfy two key requirements. One, the mechanisms that support the fundamental application development paradigms must account for the characteristics and challenges that are unique to a distributed environment. And two, these mechanisms need to be integrated with each other so that they behave like a system rather than a collection of disparate technologies.

Acknowledgments

I would like to especially thank Dr. Walter Tuvell for his keen insights into shaping the direction of this paper and Ann Hewitt for her valuable editing comments. Their input has significantly improved the quality and clarity of the paper. I would also like to thank Doug Hartman, David Lounsbury, and Jon Gossels for their reviewing comments. And finally, I would like to pay special tribute to the rest of the Open Software Foundation distributed computing environment evaluation team: Richard Mackey, Norbert Leser, Dietmar Fauth, Chi Shue, and Todd Smith. The efforts of this team made this paper possible.

This paper was originally presented at the 1991 EurOpen Conference in Tromsø, Norway and updated for this book (specifically, sections *Future Directions* and *What We Learned*)

References

1. Sape J. Mullender, "Introduction," *An Advanced Course on Distributed Computing*, pp. 3-17, ACM Press, Fingerlakes, New York, 1989.

2. Brad C. Johnson and David M. Griffin, "Remote System Management in Network Environments," *Digital Technical Journal*, No. 9, pp. 29-35, Maynard, Massachusetts, June 1989.

3. B.W. Lampson, M. Paul, and H.J. Siegert, ed. "Motivations, Objectives and Characterization of Distributed Systems," *Distributed Systems: Architecture and Implementation*, pp. 1-19, Springer-Verlag, New York, 1981.

4. Butler W. Lampson, Michael D. Schroeder and Andrew D. Birrell, *A Distributed Systems Architecture for the 1990s*, Digital Systems Research Center, Palo Alto, California, 1989.

5. Apollo Computing Inc., *Network Computing Architecture*, Prentice Hall, Englewood Cliffs, New Jersey, 1989.

6. Architecture Projects Management Limited, *Advanced Networked Systems Architecture*, Cambridge, United Kingdom, 1989.

7. International Standards Organization (ISO), *Basic Reference Model of Open Distributed Processing*, ISO/IEC JTC1/SC21/WG7, The Netherlands, 1990.

8. Morrie Gasser, Andy Goldstein, Charlie Kaufman, and Butler Lampson, *The Digital Distributed System Security Architecture*, Boxborough, Massachusetts, 1989.

9. H.C. Lauer, and R.M. Needham, "On the Duality of Operating System Structures," *Proceedings of the Second International Symposium on Operating Systems, IRIA*, October 1978, reprinted in *Operating Systems Review*, 12,2, April 1979, pp. 3-19.

10. Open Software Foundation, *Distributed Computing Environment Request for Technology: DCE Framework — Preliminary Position Paper*, Cambridge, Massachusetts, 1990.

OSF is a trademark of the Open Software Foundation, Inc.
MVS is a trademark of the International Business Machines Corporation

The Evolution of the Kerberos Authentication Service*

John T. Kohl
Digital Equipment Corporation

B. Clifford Neuman
Information Sciences Institute
University of Southern California

Theodore Y. Ts'o
Massachusetts Institute of Technology

Abstract

The Kerberos Authentication Service, developed at MIT, has been widely adopted by other organizations to identify clients of network services across an insecure network and to protect the privacy and integrity of communication with those services. While Version 4 was a step up from traditional security in networked systems, extensions were needed to allow its wider application in environments with different characteristics than that at MIT. This paper discusses some of the limitations of Version 4 of Kerberos and presents the solutions provided by Version 5.

1 Introduction

The Kerberos Authentication Service was developed by the Massachusetts Institute of Technology (MIT) to protect the emerging network services provided by Project Athena. Versions 1 through 3 were used internally. Although designed primarily for use by Project Athena, Version 4 of the protocol has achieved widespread use beyond MIT. Models for administration and use of computer services differ from site to site and some environments require support that is not present in Version 4. Version 5 of the Kerberos protocol incorporates new features suggested by experience with Version 4, making it useful in more situations. Version 5 was based in part upon input from many contributors familiar with Version 4.

This paper begins by describing the Kerberos model and basic protocol exchanges. Section 3 discusses the limitations of Version 4 of Kerberos. The fourth section reviews new features found in Version 5. Section 5 describes the implementation of Version 5 and support for converting existing applications from Version 4. The paper concludes with status and plans for future work.

1.1 Terminology and conventions

A *principal* is the basic entity that participates in authentication. In most cases a principal represents a user or an instantiation of a network service on a particular host. Each principal is uniquely named by its *principal identifier*.

---

* The work described here was done while Kohl was at MIT, and in part while Neuman was at the University of Washington.

An earlier version of this paper was published in *Proceedings of EurOpen Spring '91 Conference*, 1991, Tromsø, Norway.

Encryption is the process of transforming data into a form that cannot be understood without applying a second transformation. The transformation is affected by an *encryption key* in such a manner that the second transformation can only be applied by someone in possession of the corresponding *decryption key*.

A *secret-key cryptosystem* such as that defined by the Data Encryption Standard (DES) [Sta77a] uses a single key for both encryption and decryption. Such an encryption key is called a *secret* key.

A *public-key cryptosystem* such as RSA [Riv78a] uses different keys for encryption and decryption. One of the keys in the pair can be publicly known while the other must be kept private. These keys are referred to as *public* and *private* keys respectively.

Plaintext is a message in its unencrypted form, either before the encryption transformation has been applied, or after the corresponding decryption transformation is complete. *Ciphertext* is the encrypted form of a message, the output of the encryption transformation.

In figures, encryption is denoted by showing the plaintext surrounded by curly braces ({ }) followed by a key (K) whose subscript denotes the principals who possess or have access to that key. Thus, "abc" encrypted under c's key is represented as $\{abc\} K_c$.

2 The *Kerberos* Model

Kerberos was developed to enable network applications to securely identify their peers. To achieve this, the client (initiating party) conducts a three-party message exchange to prove its identity to the server (the contacted party). The client proves its identity by presenting to the server a *ticket* (shown in figures as $T_{c,s}$) which identifies a principal and establishes a temporary encryption key that may be used to communicate with that principal, and an *authenticator* (shown in figures as $A_{c,s}$) which proves that the client is in possession of the temporary encryption key that was assigned to the principal identified by the ticket. The authenticator prevents an intruder from replaying the same ticket to the server in a future session.

Tickets are issued by a trusted third party *Key Distribution Center* (KDC). The KDC, proposed by Needham and Schroeder [Nee78a], is trusted to hold in confidence secret keys known by each client and server on the network (the secret keys are established out-of-band or through an encrypted channel). The key shared with the KDC forms the basis upon which a client or server believes the authenticity of the tickets it receives. A Kerberos ticket is valid for a finite interval called its *lifetime*. When the interval ends, the ticket expires; any later authentication exchanges require a new ticket from the KDC.

Each installation comprises an autonomously administered *realm* and establishes its own KDC. Most currently-operating sites have chosen realm names that parallel their names under the Internet domain name system (e.g. Project Athena's realm is ATHENA.MIT.EDU). Clients in separate realms can authenticate to each other if the administrators of those realms have previously arranged a shared secret.

2.1 The initial ticket exchange

Figure 1 shows the messages[*] required for a client to prove its identity to a server. The basic messages are the same for Versions 4 and 5 of Kerberos though the details of the encoding differ. A typical application uses this exchange when it first establishes a connection to a server. Subsequent connections to the same server require only the final message in the exchange (client caching eliminates the need for the first two messages until the ticket expires).

---

[*] For clarity, the figures show a simplified version of the messages. Other message fields present in the actual messages are less relevant to the present discussion.

In the first message the client contacts the KDC, identifies itself, presents a nonce (a timestamp or other non-repeating identifier for the request), and requests credentials for use with a particular server.

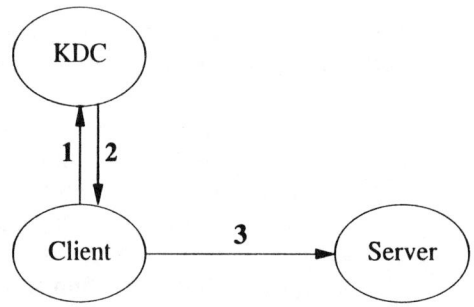

1. Client → KDC: c, s, n
2. KDC → Client: $\{K_{c,s}, n\}K_c, \{T_{c,s}\}K_s$
3. Client → Server: $\{A_c\}K_{c,s}, \{T_{c,s}\}K_s$

(In version 4, message 2 is $\{K_{c,s}, n, \{T_{c,s}\}K_s\}K_c$)

Figure 1. Getting and using an initial ticket.

Upon receipt of the message the KDC selects a random encryption key $K_{c,s}$, called the *session key*, and generates the requested ticket. The ticket identifies the client, specifies the session key $K_{c,s}$, lists the start and expiration times, and is encrypted in the key K_s shared by the KDC and the server. Because the ticket is encrypted in a key known only by the KDC and the server, nobody else can read it or change the identity of the client specified within it. The KDC next assembles a response, the second message, which it sends to the client. The response includes the session key, the nonce, and the ticket. The session key and nonce are encrypted with the client's secret key K_c (in Version 4 all fields are encrypted in K_c).

Upon receiving the response the client decrypts it using its secret key (usually derived from a password). After checking the nonce, the client caches the ticket and associated session key for future use.

In the third message the client presents the ticket and a freshly-generated authenticator to the server. The authenticator contains a timestamp and is encrypted in the session key $K_{c,s}$. Upon receipt the server decrypts the ticket using the key it shares with the KDC (this key is kept in secure storage on the server's host) and extracts the identity of the client and the session key $K_{c,s}$. To verify the identity of the client, the sever decrypts the authenticator (using the session key $K_{c,s}$ from the ticket) and verifies that the timestamp is current.

Successful verification of the authenticator proves that the client possesses the session key $K_{c,s}$, which it only could have obtained if it were able to decrypt the response from the KDC. Since the response from the KDC was encrypted in K_c, the key of the user named in the ticket, the server may reasonably be assured that identity of the client is in fact the principal named in the ticket.

If the client requests mutual authentication from the server, the server responds with a fresh message encrypted using the session key. This proves to the client that the server possesses the session key, which it could only have obtained if it was able to decrypt the ticket. Since the ticket is encrypted in a key known only by the KDC and the server, the response proves the identity of the server.

For greater detail on the messages in Version 4 of Kerberos the reader is referred to [Ste88a] and [Mil87a]. Details about Version 5 can be found in [Koh92a].

2.2 The additional ticket exchange

To reduce the risk of exposure of the client's secret key K_c and to make the use of Kerberos more transparent to the user, the exchange above is used primarily to obtain a ticket for a special *ticket-granting server* (TGS). The client erases its copy of the client's secret key once this ticket-granting ticket (TGT) has been obtained.

The TGS is logically distinct from the KDC which provides the initial ticket service, but the TGS runs on the same host and has access to the same database of clients and keys used by the KDC (see Figure 2). A client presents its TGT (along with other request data) to the TGS as it would present it to any other server (in an application request); the TGS verifies the ticket, authenticator, and accompanying request, and replies with a ticket for a new server. The protected part of the reply is encrypted with the session key from the TGT, so the client need not retain the original secret key K_c to decrypt and use this reply. The client then uses these new credentials as before to authenticate itself to the server, and perhaps to verify the identity of the server.

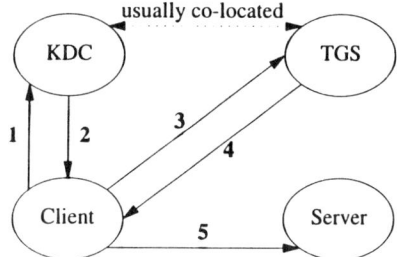

1. Client $\to$ KDC: c, tgs, n
2. KDC $\to$ Client: $\{K_{c,tgs}, n\}K_c, \{T_{c,tgs}\}K_{tgs}$
3. Client $\to$ TGS: $\{A_c\}K_{c,tgs}, \{T_{c,tgs}\}K_{tgs}$, s, n
4. TGS $\to$ Client: $\{K_{c,s}, n\}K_{c,tgs}, \{T_{c,s}\}K_s$
5. Client $\to$ Server: $\{A_c\}K_{c,s}, \{T_{c,s}\}K_s$

(In version 4, message **2** is $\{K_{c,tgs}, n, \{T_{c,tgs}\}K_{tgs}\}K_c$, and message **4** is $\{K_{c,s}, n, \{T_{c,s}\}K_s\}K_{c,tgs}$)

Figure 2. Getting a service ticket.

Once the authentication is established, the client and server share a common session key $K_{c,s}$, which has never been transmitted over the network without being encrypted. They may use this key to protect subsequent messages from disclosure or modification. Kerberos provides message formats which an application may generate as needed to assure the integrity or both the integrity and privacy of a message.

3 Limitations of Version 4

Version 4 of Kerberos is in widespread use, but some sites require functionality that it does not provide, while others have a computing environment or administrative procedures that differ from that at MIT. As a result, work on Kerberos Version 5 commenced in 1989, fueled by discussions with Version 4 users and administrators about their experiences with the protocol and MIT's implementation.

3.1 Environmental shortcomings

Kerberos Version 4 was targeted primarily for Project Athena [Cha90a], and as such in some areas it makes assumptions and takes approaches that are not appropriate universally:

Encryption system dependence: The Version 4 protocol uses only the Data Encryption Standard (DES) to encrypt messages. The export of DES from the USA is restricted by the U.S. Government, making truly widespread use of Version 4 difficult.

Internet protocol dependence: Version 4 requires the use of Internet Protocol (IP) addresses, which makes it unsuitable for some environments.

Message byte ordering: Version 4 uses a "receiver makes right" philosophy for encoding multi-byte values in network messages, where the sending host encodes the value in its own natural byte order and the receiver must convert this byte order to its own native order. While this makes communication between two hosts with the same byte order simple, it does not follow established conventions and will preclude interoperability of a machine with an unusual byte order not understood by the receiver.

Ticket lifetimes: The valid life of a ticket in Version 4 is encoded by a UNIX timestamp issue date and an 8-bit lifetime quantity in units of five minutes, resulting in a maximum lifetime of 21 ¼ hours. Some environments require longer lifetimes for proper operation (e.g. a long-running simulation which requires valid Kerberos credentials during its entire execution).

Authentication forwarding: Version 4 has no provision for allowing credentials issued to a client on one host to be forwarded to some other host and used by another client. Support for this might be useful if an intermediate server needs to access some resource with the rights of the client (e.g. a print server needs access to the file server to retrieve a client's file for printing), or if a user logs into another host on the network and wishes to pursue activities there with the privileges and authentication available on the originating host.

Principal naming: In Version 4, principals are named with three components: name, instance, and realm, each of which may be up to 39 characters long. These sizes are too short for some applications and installation environments. In addition, due to implementation-imposed conventions the normal character set allowed for the name portion excludes the period (.), which is used in account names on some systems. These same conventions dictate that the account name match the name portion of the principal identifier, which is unacceptable in situations where Kerberos is being installed in an existing network with non-unique account names.

Inter-realm authentication: Version 4 provides cooperation between authentication realms by allowing each pair of cooperating realms to exchange an encryption key to be used as a secondary key for the ticket-granting service. A client can obtain tickets for services from a foreign realm's KDC by first obtaining a ticket-granting ticket for the foreign realm from its local KDC and then using that TGT to obtain tickets for the foreign application server (see Figure 3). This pair-wise key exchange makes inter-realm ticket requests and verification easy to implement, but requires $O(n^2)$ key exchanges to interconnect n realms (see Figure 4). Even with only a few cooperating realms, the assignment and management of the inter-realm keys is an expansive task.

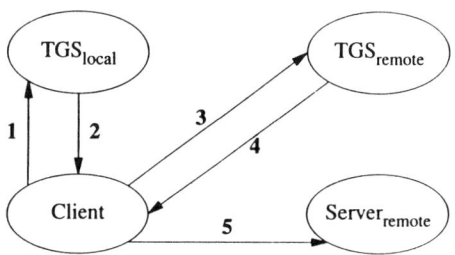

1. Client → TGS_{local}: $\{A_c\}K_{c,tgs}, \{T_{c,tgs}\}K_{tgs}, tgs_{rem}$
2. TGS_{local} → Client: $\{K_{c,tgs_{rem}}\}K_{c,tgs}, \{T_{c,tgs_{rem}}\}K_{tgs_{rem}}$
3. Client → TGS_{remote}: $\{A_c\}K_{c,tgs_{rem}}, \{T_{c,tgs_{rem}}\}K_{tgs_{rem}}, s_{rem}$
4. TGS_{remote} → Client: $\{K_{c,s_{rem}}\}K_{c,tgs_{rem}}, \{T_{c,s_{rem}}\}K_{s_{rem}}$
5. Client → $Server_{remote}$: $\{A_c\}K_{c,s_{rem}}, \{T_{c,s_{rem}}\}K_{s_{rem}}$

(In version 4, message 2 is $\{K_{c,tgs_{rem}}, \{T_{c,tgs_{rem}}\}K_{tgs_{rem}}\}K_{c,tgs}$, and message 4 is $\{K_{c,s_{rem}}, \{T_{c,s_{rem}}\}K_{s_{rem}}\}K_{c,tgs_{rem}}$)

Figure 3. Getting a foreign realm service ticket.

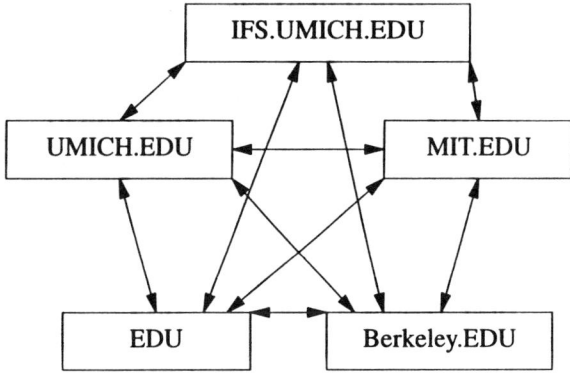

Figure 4. Version 4 realm interconnections.

3.2 Technical deficiencies

In addition to the environmental problems, there are some technical deficiencies in Version 4 and its implementation. Bellovin and Merritt [Bel90a] provide detailed analyses of some of these issues.

Double Encryption: As shown in Figure 1, the ticket issued by the Kerberos server in Version 4 is encrypted twice when transmitted to the client, and only once when sent to the application server. There is no need to encrypt it in the message from the KDC to the client, and doing so can be wasteful of processing time if encryption is computationally intensive (as will be the case for most software-based encryption implementations; see [Mer90a] for discussion of fast software-based encryption methods).

PCBC encryption: Kerberos Version 4 uses a non-standard mode of DES to encrypt its messages. FIPS 81 [Sta80a] describes the normal cipher-block-chaining (CBC) mode of DES. Version 4 uses a modified Version called plain- and cipher-block-chaining mode (PCBC). This mode was an attempt to provide data encryption and integrity protection in one operation. Unfortunately, it allows an intruder to modify a message with a special block-exchange attack which may not be detected by the recipient [Koh89a].

Authenticators and replay detection: Kerberos Version 4 uses an encrypted timestamp to verify the freshness of messages and prevent an intruder from staging a successful replay attack. If an authenticator (which contains the timestamp) is out of date or is being replayed, the application server rejects the authentication. However, maintaining a list of unexpired authenticators which have already been presented to a service can be hard to implement properly (and indeed is not implemented in the Version 4 implementation distributed by MIT).

Password attacks: The initial exchange with the Kerberos server encrypts the response with a client's secret key, which in the case of a user is algorithmically derived from a password. An intruder is able to record an exchange of this sort and, without alerting any system administrators, attempt to discover the user's password by decrypting the response with each password guess. Since the response from the Kerberos server includes verifiable plaintext [Lom89a], the intruder can try as many passwords as are available and will know when the proper password has been found (the decrypted response will make sense).

Session keys: Each ticket issued by the KDC contains a key specific to that ticket, called a session key, which may be used by the client and server to protect their communications once authentication has been established. However, since many clients use a ticket multiple times during a user's session, it may be possible for an intruder to replay messages from a previous connection to clients or servers which do not properly protect themselves (again, MIT's Version 4 implementation does not fully implement this protection for the KRB_SAFE and KRB_PRIV messages). Additionally, there are situations in which a client wishes to share a session key with several servers. This requires special non-standard application negotiations in Version 4.

Cryptographic checksum: The cryptographic checksum (sometimes called a message authentication code or hash or digest function) used in Version 4 is based on the quadratic algorithm described in [Jue85a]. The MIT implementation does not perform this function as described; the suitability of the modified version as a cryptographic checksum function is unknown.

4 Changes for Version 5

Version 5 of the protocol has evolved over the past two years based on implementation experience and discussions within the community of Kerberos users. Its final specification has reached closure, and a description of the protocol is available [Koh92a]. Version 5 addresses the concerns described above and provides additional functionality.

4.1 Changes between Versions 4 and 5

4.1.1 Use of Encryption

To improve modularity and ease export-regulation considerations for Version 5, the use of encryption has been separated into distinct software modules which can be replaced or removed by the programmer as needed. When encryption is used in a protocol message, the ciphertext is tagged with a type identifier so that the recipient can identify the appropriate decryption algorithm necessary to interpret the message.

Encryption keys are also tagged with a type and length when they appear in messages. Since it is conceivable to use the same key type in multiple encryption systems (e.g. different variations on DES encryption), the key type may not map one-to-one to the encryption type.

Each encryption algorithm is responsible for providing sufficient integrity protection for the plaintext so that the receiver can verify that the ciphertext was not altered in transit. If the algorithm does not have such properties, it can be augmented by including a checksum in the plaintext before encryption. By doing this, we can discard the PCBC DES mode, and use the standard CBC mode with an embedded checksum over the plaintext. It is important to consider the effects of chosen plaintext attacks when analyzing the message integrity properties of candidate encryption algorithms. Some potential weaknesses were found with encryption and checksum methods in initial drafts of the Version 5 protocol [Stu92a]. These weaknesses were corrected in subsequent revisions.

4.1.2 Network addresses

When network addresses appear in protocol messages, they are similarly tagged with a type and length field so the recipient can interpret them properly. If a host supports multiple network protocols or has multiple addresses of a single type, all types and all addresses can be provided in a ticket.

4.1.3 Message encoding

Network messages in Version 5 are described using the Abstract Syntax Notation One (ASN.1) syntax [Sta87b] and encoded according to the basic encoding rules [Sta87a]. This avoids the problem of independently specifying the encoding for multi-byte quantities as was done in Version 4. It makes the protocol description look quite different from Version 4, but it is primarily the presentation of the message fields that changes; the essence of the Kerberos Version 4 protocol remains.

4.1.4 Ticket changes

The Kerberos Version 5 ticket has an expanded format to accommodate the required changes from the Version 4 ticket. It is split into two parts, one encrypted and the other plaintext. The server's name in the ticket is plaintext since a server with multiple identities, e.g. an inter-realm TGS, may need the name to select a key with which to decrypt the remainder of the ticket (the name of the server is bookkeeping information only and its protection is not necessary for secure authentication). Everything else remains encrypted. The ticket lifetime is encoded as a starting time and an expiration time (rather than a specific lifetime field), affording nearly limitless ticket lifetimes. The new ticket also contains a new flags field and other new fields used to enable the new features described later.

4.1.5 Naming principles

Principal identifiers are multi-component names in Kerberos Version 5. The identifier is encoded in two parts, the realm and the remainder of the name. The realm is separate to facilitate easy implementation of realm-traversal routines and realm-sensitive access checks. The remainder of the name is a sequence of however many components are needed to name the principal. The realm and each component of the remainder are encoded as separate ASN.1 `GeneralStrings`, so there are few practical restrictions on the characters available for principal names.

4.1.6 Inter-realm support

In Version 5, Kerberos realms cooperate through a hierarchy based on the name of the realm (see Figure 5). A source realm is interoperable with a destination realm if it shares an inter-realm key directly with the destination realm, or if it shares a key with an intermediate realm that is itself interoperable with the destination realm. Each realm exchanges a different pair of inter-realm keys with its parent node and each child. These keys are used in a common encryption system to obtain tickets for each successive realm along the path. This arrangement reduces the number of key exchanges to $O(\log(n))$.

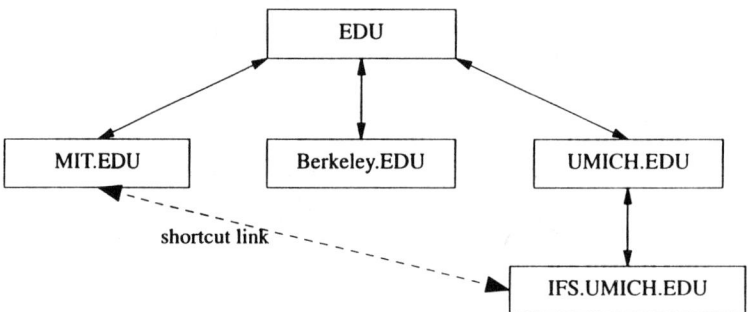

Figure 5. A Version 5 hierarchy of realms.

When an application needs to contact a server in a foreign realm, it "walks" up and down the tree toward the destination realm, contacting each realm's KDC in turn, asking for a ticket-granting ticket to the foreign realm. In most cases, the KDC will issue a ticket for the next node in the proper direction on the tree. If a realm has established a "shortcut" spanning link with some realm further in the path, it issues a ticket-granting ticket for that realm instead. This way every realm can interoperate, and heavily-traveled paths can be optimized with a direct link.

When a ticket for the end service is finally issued, it will contain an enumeration of all the realms consulted in the process of requesting the ticket. An application server which applies strict authorization rules is permitted to reject authentication which passes through certain untrusted realms.

4.2 New protocol features in Version 5

In addition to the changes discussed above, several new features are supported in Version 5.

4.2.1 Tickets

Version 5 tickets contain several additional timestamps and a flags field. These changes allow greater flexibility in the use of tickets than was available in Version 4.

Each ticket issued by the KDC using the initial ticket exchange is flagged as such. This allows servers such as a password changing server to require that a client present a ticket obtained by direct use of the client's secret key K_c instead of one obtained using a TGT. Such a requirement prevents an attacker from walking up to an unattended but logged in workstation and changing another user's password.

Tickets may be issued as renewable tickets with two expiration times, one for a time in the near future, and one later. The ticket expires as usual at the earlier time, but if it is presented to the KDC in a renewal request before this earlier expiration time, a replacement ticket is returned which is valid for an additional period of time. The KDC will not renew a ticket beyond the second expiration indicated in the ticket. This mechanism has the advantage that although the credentials can be used for long periods of time, the KDC may refuse to renew tickets which are reported as stolen and thereby thwart their continued use.

A similar mechanism is available to assist authentication during batch processing. A ticket issued as postdated and invalid will not be valid until its post-dated starting time passes and it is replaced with a validated ticket. The client validates the ticket by presenting it to the KDC as described above for renewable tickets.

Authentication forwarding can be implemented by contacting the KDC with the additional ticket exchange and requesting a ticket valid for a different set of addresses than the TGT used in the request. The KDC will not issue such tickets unless the presented TGT has a flag set indicating that this is a permissible use of the ticket. When the entity on the remote host is granted only limited rights to use the authentication, the forwarded credentials are referred to as a *proxy* (after the proxy used in legal and financial affairs). Proxies are handled similarly to forwarded tickets, except that new proxy tickets will not be issued for a ticket-granting service; they will only be issued for application server tickets.

In certain situations, an application server (such as an X Window System server) will not have reliable, protected access to an encryption key necessary for normal participation as a server in the authentication exchanges. In such cases, if the server has access to a user's ticket-granting ticket and associated session key (which in the case of single-user workstations may well be the case), it can send this ticket-granting ticket to the client, who presents it and the user's own ticket-granting ticket to the KDC. The KDC then issues a ticket encrypted in the session key from the server's ticket-granting ticket; the application server has the proper key to decrypt and process this ticket. The details of such an exchange are presented in [Dav90a].

4.2.2 Authorization data

Kerberos is concerned primarily with authentication; it is not directly concerned with the related security functions of authorization and accounting. To support the implementation of these related functions by other services, Version 5 of Kerberos provides a mechanism for the tamper-proof transmission of authorization and accounting information as part of a ticket. This information takes the form of restrictions on the use of a ticket. The encoding of each restriction is not a concern of the Kerberos protocol, but is instead defined by the authorization or accounting mechanism in use. Restrictions are carried in the *authorization data* field of the ticket.

When a ticket is requested, restrictions are sent to the KDC where they are inserted into the ticket, encrypted, and thus protected from tampering. In the protocol's most general form, a client may request that the KDC include or add such data to a new ticket. The KDC does not remove any authorization data from a ticket; the TGS always copies it from the TGT into the new ticket, and then adds any requested additional authorization data. Upon decryption of a ticket, the authorization data is available to the application server. While Kerberos makes no interpretation of the data, the application server is expected to use the authorization data to appropriately restrict the client's access to its resources.

Among other uses, the *authorization data* field can be used in a proxy ticket to create a capability. The client requesting the proxy from the KDC specifies any authorization restrictions in the authorization data, then securely transmits the proxy and session key to another party, which uses the ticket to obtain limited service from an application server. Neuman [Neu91a] discusses possible uses of the *authorization data* field in detail.

The Open Software Foundation's Distributed Computing Environment uses the *authorization data* field for the generation of privilege attribute certificates (PACs). Privilege information is maintained by a privilege server. When a PAC is requested by a client the privilege server requests a Kerberos ticket identifying the privilege server itself, but restricting the groups to which the client belongs and specifying a DCE specific user ID. The ticket is then returned to the client which uses it to assert its DCE user ID and prove membership in the listed groups. In essence, the privilege server grants the client a proxy authorizing the client to act as the privilege server to assert the listed DCE user ID and membership in the listed groups. If the ticket did not include restrictions, it would indicate that the client was the privilege server, allowing the client to assert any user ID and membership in any group.

4.2.3 Pre-authentication data

In an effort to complicate the theft of passwords, the Kerberos Version 5 protocol provides fields in the initial- and additional-ticket exchanges to support password alternatives such as hand-held authenticators (devices which have internal circuitry used to generate a continually changing password). In the initial ticket exchange, these fields can be used to alter the key K_c in which the reply is encrypted. This makes a stolen password useless since fresh information from a physical device is needed to decrypt a response. The field can also be used to prove the client's identity to the KDC before any ticket is issued. Doing this makes it a little more difficult for an attacker to obtain a message that can be used to verify password guesses.

This pre-authentication data field is used by the client in the additional ticket exchange to pass the ticket-granting ticket to the KDC; since it is a variable-length array, other values may be sent in the additional-ticket exchange.

4.2.4 Subsession key negotiation

Tickets are cached by clients for later use. To avoid problems caused by the reuse of a ticket's session key across multiple connections, a server and client can cooperate to choose a new *subsession key* which is used to protect a single connection. This subsession key is discarded once the connection is closed.

Negotiation of subsession keys allows an application to protect the privacy of messages broadcast to several recipients. The application can individually negotiate with each recipient to use a common subsession key before beginning the broadcasts.

4.2.5 Sequence numbers

Kerberos provides two message formats for applications to protect their communications. The KRB_SAFE message uses a cryptographic checksum to insure data integrity. The KRB_PRIV message uses encryption to insure integrity and privacy. In Version 4 these messages included as control information a timestamp and the sender's network address. With Version 5, an application may elect to use a timestamp (as before) or a sequence number. If the timestamp is used, the receiver must record the known timestamps to avoid replay attacks; if a sequence number is used the receiver must verify that the messages arrive in the proper order without gaps. There are situations where one choice makes applications simpler (or even possible) to implement; see the discussions in [Koh92a].

5 Implementation features

5.1 The base implementation

The MIT implementation of the Version 5 protocols is composed of several run-time libraries with which a program may link. The core library functions will probably be used by all applications; other libraries or subsystems may be replaced or omitted as needed by an application programmer. All code is currently written in "C."

The base functions: The core Kerberos library contains the routines which assemble, disassemble and interpret the network messages. This includes ASN.1 encoding and decoding functions which convert from a machine's native format to the network encoding (currently based on the ISODE package, but another ASN.1 support package may be substituted), routines which verify that requests are answered as expected, and routines to determine which messages are necessary. This core set of routines calls out to the remaining portions of the library as required. A programmer may replace those portions at certain specified interfaces.

Encryption routines: Since multiple encryption types may be in use simultaneously, the core functions call encryption routines through a function table which has entries provided by each encryption system implementation. The core library provides a default cryptosystem table, initialized to list the known encryption types. A programmer may load his own cryptosystem table to replace the default table and avoid linking with the default encryption libraries.

In an attempt to alleviate some possible export restrictions, MIT's implementation distributes its encryption systems separately from the remainder of the system. Only DES is currently available from MIT.

Checksum routines: In a similar fashion to the encryption routines, the core routines call any needed checksum functions through a function table, and compute any necessary sizes based on the information in the table. Certain applications of checksum technology require that the checksum have certain properties. The table entry indicates whether the checksum is keyed (its algorithm is perturbed by an encryption key which cannot be discovered with knowledge only of the algorithm and the checksummed text) and whether the checksum is collision proof (it is computationally infeasible to discover a different checksum text which has the same checksum). The core library provides a replaceable default checksum table.

Four checksums are currently available from MIT: the CRC-32, which is neither keyed nor collision proof (but it is useful for integrity checks within encryption systems); the DES message authentication code (MAC), which is both keyed and collision proof, and MD4 [Riv92a] and MD5 [Riv92b], both of which are collision proof but not keyed.

Credentials cache and key table routines: When clients store tickets and credentials in a cache, the core routines call out through a credentials cache table entry to a separate library module which implements the storing and searching routines for credentials caches. An environment variable can be used to specify the default type and location of a credentials cache, so a user can switch between different types and locations of caches as needed (perhaps to keep the credentials for two roles separate). MIT's implementation provides two credentials cache implementations, one built on C "`stdio`" routines and the other built on UNIX file-descriptor semantics. Other implementations could provide shared-memory or kernel-resident caches.

Servers likewise store their secret keys K_s in key tables accessed by the core routines through a function table. MIT's implementation provides a key table library built on C "`stdio`" routines.

KDC database support: All accesses to the KDC's principal database by the KDC and administrative programs are mediated by a database library which can be replaced if needed. MIT's implementation uses the UNIX *dbm* database system. Since *dbm* does not provide any record or database locking, its use is augmented with separate locking code to mediate between writers and readers. Administrative requests (e.g. adding entries, changing keys or passwords) can be handled on-line.

Operating system support: Although it is targeted for UNIX systems, the MIT implementation is careful to access operating system features only from a few well-contained modules. An operating system support library performs all the accesses required by the rest of the code, such as transmitting and receiving network messages, examining configuration files, checking the system's time-of-day, translating from account names to Kerberos names (and vice versa), and performing rudimentary account access checks.

5.2 User interaction

If all parts of Kerberos are working properly, users will not normally be aware that Kerberos authentication is in use by their applications. The normal login process obtains and caches an initial ticket-granting ticket, and applications automatically obtain and cache service tickets as required. Only when authentication fails will users become aware of the underlying use of Kerberos.

If users need to refresh tickets (e.g., if they expire), then they can use the *kinit* program, which will get a new ticket-granting ticket after reading a password from the keyboard. Users examine the cached tickets with *klist* and destroy the cache with *kdestroy*.

When principal names need to be displayed to human users, by convention[*] they are represented as the sequence of name components separated by slashes (/), followed by an at-sign (@), and the realm name. Thus, a principal with two name components `userX` and `role2` in the realm `ATHENA.MIT.EDU` would be represented as `userX/role2@ATHENA.MIT.EDU`.

5.2.1 Password to key conversion

Since users are not good at remembering binary encryption keys, Kerberos provides routines which convert passwords into keys. The algorithm used to convert a password into an encryption key performs a non-invertible transformation, so that an attacker cannot discover a user's password knowing only K_c. In Version 5, the conversion can be seeded with an additional

---

[*] Please note that this is only a *convention*, and other implementations may display the principal names differently.

string (often the realm name) which perturbs the output key, so that a user who is registered in multiple realms and uses the same password in two of those realms will have a different K_c in each realm. Without this perturbation, an attacker discovering the user's key in one realm could impersonate that user in the other realm, without needing to know the user's password. When no additional perturbation string is supplied, the resulting key is the same as the key produced by the Version 4 algorithm.

5.3 Compatibility support for Version 4

There is a small but growing base of Kerberos Version 4 applications, and a number of sites running a Kerberos Version 4 authentication server. MIT's implementation of Version 5 provides several compatibility features which can help sites and programmers convert to Version 5.

Interface compatibility: MIT's implementation of Version 5 includes a "glue library" which presents a Kerberos Version 4 application programming interface (API) but which uses Version 5 protocol messages and routines. This library converts data structures as much as possible between the differing Version 4 and Version 5 data structures. In many cases (especially those that use only a common subset of the Version 4 library functions), an application originally written for Kerberos Version 4 need only be re-linked with this library and the remainder of the Version 5 code to use Version 5 protocols. However, such applications will no longer be compatible with older peer processes, which would still expect the Version 4 messages, and continued maintenance may be made more difficult.

A generic authentication interface: The Generic Security Services API (GSSAPI) [Lin91a] is an authentication-system independent programming interface which is currently being developed by the Common Authentication Technology Working Group within the Internet Engineering Task Force. The GSSAPI provides a convenient abstraction boundary for applications writers who wish to take advantage of multiple authentication systems (even ones not yet invented), without needing to be aware of any of the details of those systems. Since the GSSAPI only provides access to those basic authentication services which form a common denominator across different authentication systems, applications which need access to specialized features provided by a particular authentication system will still need to code to that system's native interface. However, the basic functionality to which the GSSAPI provides access should be sufficient for the majority of applications. MIT provides a binding of this interface to the Kerberos Version 5 implementation.

Protocol compatibility: For those sites which wish to convert the Kerberos server to provide the features of Version 5, a compatibility mode may be enabled on the KDC which causes it to accept Version 4 format KDC requests and respond with Version 4 format tickets and messages, as well as accepting Version 5 format requests. This allows an administrator to convert a Version 4 installation to Version 5 slowly, by supporting the old users with the compatibility code. After some grace period, the Version 4 compatibility would be turned off. If a user wishes to use both Version 4 and Version 5 programs simultaneously, the user's key must be encoded using the Version 4 style string-to-key algorithm; the Version 5 response will include information in the pre-authentication data of the ticket response to indicate which string-to-key algorithm should be used by the Version 5 client.

Interface coexistence: The MIT Version 5 libraries were purposely designed to allow an application to simultaneously support both Versions 4 and 5, and this is the suggested compatibility mode. The telnet [Pos83a] program distributed with the MIT code can automatically choose an authentication system to use when it connects to a remote system, based on what credentials the user holds and what Versions of authentication the remote telnet server will accept. It implements the current draft specifications of the authentication [Bor92a] and encryption [Bor91a] options for both Kerberos Version 5 [Bor92b] and Kerberos Version 4 [Bor92c] authentication systems.

Program compatibility: Another possible compatibility mode can be fabricated by maintaining separate copies of network applications which use Version 4 and Version 5 protocol messages. The user would use a generic name for the application, and the application would try each authentication system in turn, by executing a separate copy of the program for each system (see Figure 6). When authentication is successfully completed, the application would proceed as normal. On both the client and server sides of the application, this approach requires two copies of the same program, each linked with a different authentication system. The different versions of the server would each accept requests at different network ports, and the different clients would only send a request to the server which supports its authentication type.

This approach could be mixed with the glue library and/or single-server approaches, by creating the separate clients using the glue library and/or using a single server program which understands both protocols.

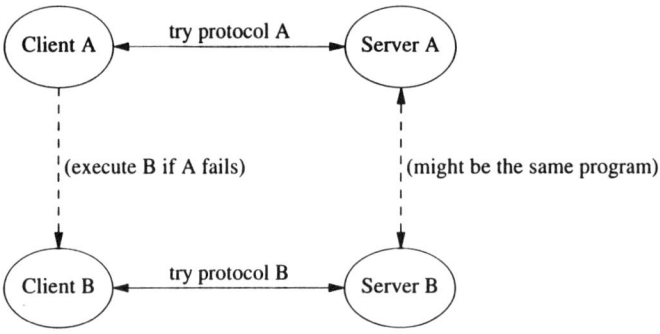

FIGURE 6. Implementing protocol compatibility by executing separate programs.

6 Future work

Version 5 of Kerberos is a step toward the design of an authentication system that is widely applicable. We believe the framework is flexible enough to accommodate future requirements. Some items we expect to add to Kerberos in the near future include:

Public-key cryptosystems: The encryption specifications in Kerberos Version 5 are designed primarily for secret-key cryptosystems, but we are considering support for public-key cryptosystems. One advantage of such support will be the ability to interoperate with the evolving certificate infrastructure for Privacy Enhanced Mail. There is also work proceeding on the development of a hybrid Internet Authentication System (IAS) that will provide interoperability between Kerberos and public key based systems such as Digital Equipment Corporation's DASS [Tar91a].

"Smartcards": Several companies manufacture hand-held devices which can be used to augment normal password security methods, and there is strong interest within the industry to integrate one or more of these systems with Kerberos. Work is underway to use the pre-authentication data field to pass the additional information needed to use such devices.

In the more distant future it might also be possible to program a smartcard to directly take part in the Kerberos protocol. To do so would require special hardware to support communication between the smartcard and the workstation (so that the smartcard could communicate with the KDC). The advantage of such an approach is that the initial Kerberos exchange could take place without making the user's password available to a potentially untrusted workstation.

Remote administration: The current protocol specifications do not specify an administrative interface to the KDC database. MIT's implementation provides a sample remote administration program which allows administrators to add and modify entries and users to change their keys. We would like to standardize such a protocol. Some features we would like to add include remote extraction of server key tables, password "quality checks," and a provision for servers to change their secret keys automatically every so often.

Database propagation: The current implementation provides reliable KDC service by a periodic bulk-copy of the KDC database to slave KDC machines. It might be more convenient and/or efficient to build the KDC on distributed database technologies. However, to insure that an attacker cannot illegitimately obtain any database entry, the technology must provide for private secure transmission of the database elements to each server,

Validation suites: The current implementation does not include a complete validation suite to verify that the protocol is properly implemented. Such a suite could prevent future security problems in the case of a faulty implementation, and would help facilitate interoperation of diverse implementations.

Applications: There are many network applications that would benefit from the addition of authentication. Among the highly visible examples are electronic mail, popular bulletin-board systems (such as Usenet), and distributed file systems. It is hoped that application designers will consider authentication and related security services when designing their protocols. The generic application programming interface should go a long way toward making it possible to do so.

Acknowledgments

The work described here has been the result of many MIT Project Athena and MIT Network Services staff members' visions, ideas, and hard work.

The authors would especially like to thank Steve Bellovin, Jennifer Steiner, and Ralph Swick for their comments on early drafts of this paper.

References

[Bel90a] S.M. Bellovin and M. Merritt, "Limitations of the Kerberos Authentication System," *Computer Communications Review*, **20**, 5, pp. 119-132 (October 1990).

[Bor91a] D. Borman, Editor, "Telnet Encryption Option," Internet-Draft, Internet Engineering Task Force, Telnet Working Group (July 1991).

[Bor92a] D. Borman, Editor, "Telnet Authentication Option," Internet-Draft, Internet Engineering Task Force, Telnet Working Group (February 1992).

[Bor92b] D. Borman, Editor, "Telnet Authentication: Kerberos Version 5," Internet-Draft, Internet Engineering Task Force, Telnet Working Group (February 1992).

[Bor92c] D. Borman, Editor, "Telnet Authentication: Kerberos Version 4," Internet-Draft, Internet Engineering Task Force, Telnet Working Group (February 1992).

[Cha90a] George A. Champine, Daniel E. Geer, and William N. Ruh, "Project Athena as a Distributed Computer System," *IEEE Computer*, **23**, 9, pp. 40-50 (September 1990).

[Dav90a] Don Davis and Ralph Swick, "Workstation Services and Kerberos Authentication at Project Athena," Technical Memorandum TM-424, MIT Laboratory for Computer Science (February 1990).

[Jue85a] R.R. Jueneman, S.M. Matyas, and C.H. Meyer, "Message Authentication," *IEEE Communications*, **23**, 9, pp. 29-40 (September 1985).

[Koh89a] John T. Kohl, "The Use of Encryption in Kerberos for Network Authentication," in *Crypto '89 Conference Proceedings,* International Association for Cryptologic Research, Santa Barbara, CA (August 1989).

[Koh92a] John T. Kohl and B. Clifford Neuman, "The Kerberos Network Authentication Service," Version 5 Revision 5, Project Athena, Massachusetts Institute of Technology (April 1992).

[Lin91a] John Linn, "Generic Security Service Application Program Interface," Internet-Draft, Internet Engineering Task Force, Common Authentication Technology Working Group (June 1991).

[Lom89a] T. Mark A. Lomas, Li Gong, Jerome H. Saltzer, and Roger M. Needham, "Reducing Risks from Poorly Chosen Keys," *Operating Systems Review,* **23**, 5, pp. 14-18 (December 1989).

[Mer90a] Ralph C. Merkle, "Fast Software Encryption Functions," in *Crypto '90 Conference Proceedings*, International Association for Cryptologic Research, Santa Barbara, CA (August 1990).

[Mil87a] S.P. Miller, B.C. Neuman, J.I. Schiller, and J.H. Saltzer, "Section E.2.1: Kerberos Authentication and Authorization System," Project Athena Technical Plan, M.I.T. Project Athena, Cambridge, Massachusetts (December 21, 1987).

[Nee78a] Roger M. Needham and Michael D. Schroeder, "Using Encryption for Authentication in Large Networks of Computers," *Communications of the ACM*, **21**, 12, pp. 993-999 (December, 1978).

[Neu91a] B. Clifford Neuman, "Proxy-Based Authorization and Accounting for Distributed Systems," Technical Report 91-02-01, Department of Computer Science and Engineering, University of Washington (March 1991).

[Pos83a] J. Postel and J. Reynolds, "TELNET Protocol Specification," RFC 854, University of Southern California, Information Sciences Institute (May 1983).

[Riv92a] R. Rivest, "The MD4 Message Digest Algorithm," RFC 1320, MIT Laboratory for Computer Science (April 1992).

[Riv92b] R. Rivest, "The MD5 Message Digest Algorithm," RFC 1321, MIT Laboratory for Computer Science (April 1992).

[Riv78a] R.L. Rivest, A. Shamir, and L. Adleman, "A Method for Obtaining Digital Signatures and Public-Key Cryptosystems," *Communications of the ACM*, **21**, 2, pp. 120-126 (February 1978). See also U.S. Patent 4,405,829.

[Sta87a]   International Organization for Standardization, "Information Processing Systems Open Systems Interconnection — Specification of Basic Encoding Rules for Abstract Syntax Notation One (ASN.1)," IS 8825 (November 1987). First Edition.

[Sta87b]   International Organization for Standardization, "Information Processing Systems — Open Systems Interconnection — Specification of Abstract Syntax Notation One (ASN.1)," IS 8824 (December 1987). First Edition.

[Sta77a]   National Bureau of Standards, U.S. Department of Commerce, "Data Encryption Standard," *Federal Information Processing Standards Publication 46*, Washington, DC (1977).

[Sta80a]   National Bureau of Standards, U.S. Department of Commerce, "DES Modes of Operation," *Federal Information Processing Standards Publication 81*, Springfield, VA (December 1980).

[Ste88a]   J.G. Steiner, B.C. Neuman, and J.I. Schiller, "Kerberos: An Authentication Service for Open Network Systems," in *Usenix Conference Proceedings*, pp. 191-202, Dallas, Texas (February, 1988).

[Stu92a]   Stuart G. Stubblebine and Virgil D. Gligor, "On Message Integrity in Cryptographic Protocols," in *Proceedings of the IEEE Symposium on Research in Security and Privacy*, Oakland, California (May 1992).

[Tar91a]   Joseph J. Tardo and Kannan Alagappan, "SPX: Global Authentication Using Public Key Certificates," in *Proceedings of the IEEE Symposium on Research in Security and Privacy*, Oakland, California (May 1991).

Author Information

Kohl may be reached at Digital Equipment Corporation, 110 Spit Brook Road, Mailstop ZKO3-3/U14, Nashua, NH 03062, USA. Email: jtkohl@zk3.dec.com.

Neuman may be reached at USC/ISI, 4676 Admiralty Way, Marina del Rey, CA 90292-6695, USA. Telephone +1 (310) 822-1511. Email: bcn@isi.edu.

Ts'o may be reached at MIT Room E40-342b, 77 Massachusetts Avenue, Cambridge, MA 02139, USA. Email: tytso@mit.edu.

Project Athena, Athena, Athena MUSE, Discuss, Hesiod, Kerberos, Moira, and Zephyr are trademarks of the Massachusetts Institute of Technology (MIT). No commercial use of these trademarks may be made without prior written permission of MIT.

X Window System is a trademark of MIT.

Fault-Tolerant Programming Using Process Groups*

Robbert van Renesse   Ken Birman

Computer Science Department
Upson Hall
Cornell University
Ithaca, NY 14853

1 Introduction

ISIS [2,3], developed at Cornell University, is a system for building fault-tolerant applications consisting of cooperating, distributed processes. Group management and group communication are two basic building blocks provided by ISIS. ISIS has been very successful, and there is currently a demand for a version that will run on many different environments and transport protocols, and will scale to many process groups. Furthermore, performance is an important issue. For this purpose, ISIS is being redesigned and rebuilt from scratch [4].

The new ISIS system has several well-defined layers. We will discuss each layer in turn. The lowest layers, which implement multicast transport and failure detection, are near completion and currently run on SUN OS using SUN LWP threads, on MACH using C Threads, and on the x-kernel [5]. This system can use several different network protocols at the same time, such as IP, UDP, Deering multicast [6], and raw Ethernet. This enables processes on SUN OS, on MACH, and on the x-kernel to multicast among each other, even though the environments are very dissimilar.

The system makes use of available hardware multicast if possible. It also queues messages if a backlog appears, so that multiple messages may be packed together in a single packet. Using this strategy, the number of messages per second can become very large, and in the current (simple) implementation about 10,000 per second can be sent between distributed SUN OS user processes, a figure that approaches the speed of local light-weight remote procedure call mechanisms. The round-trip communication time on SUN OS over Ethernet is currently under 3 milliseconds.

---

* This article is based on a paper published in the *Proceedings of the USENIX Workshop on Micro-Kernels and Other Kernel Architectures*[1]. The authors were supported under DARPA/NASA grant NAG-2-593, a grant of the Dutch Royal Academy of Sciences (KNAW), and by grants from IBM, HP, Siemens, GTE, and Hitachi.

In Section 2 we will present the new ISIS system. In Section 3 we will describe some distributed applications that use ISIS for fault tolerance and enhanced performance. We will describe the design of the new ISIS implementation in Section 4, and present some of the protocols in Section 5. In Section 6 we will describe how ISIS deals with multi-threading. Section 7 deals with how ISIS may be integrated in modern microkernel operating system technology. In Section 8 we will present a new concept, called Light-Weight groups that make it possible to manage thousands (or more) of process groups. In Section 9 we briefly go into the repercussions on old ISIS applications. Section 10 describes the current status of the new ISIS system, and Section 11 concludes.

2 The new ISIS system

The ISIS system, as it is currently distributed and supported, is the result of a long evolution. As such, it supports many different applications, and has grown rather complex. The time has come to re-implement the system using the experience gained. It appears that a design strategy such as that used in microkernel-based operating systems is applicable here: a lean core system provides the basic functionality, on which more complicated services can be built. For example, much as a pager can be implemented as an external server using basic mechanisms in the kernel, so can a failure detector run in user space as a service for a communication system. The advantage of this approach is that it makes it possible to experiment with new failure detection mechanisms without major disruption of the system. Moreover, in contrast to an external pager (which might see extremely heavy, performance-critical traffic), the modules external to our new system are infrequently used ones that are off the critical path for the most common communication patterns.

The basic functionality that we plan to put in the core of the system is most easily illustrated through comparison with the USENET news service. The new system will support "ISIS news groups," to which processes can subscribe. Unlike USENET, ISIS news groups may be created dynamically, and, as will be seen, they have stronger semantics. Processes may post messages to news groups, which will be reliably delivered to all subscribing processes. The facility presents the same interface in local-area and wide-area settings. It is possible to reply to messages or to follow-up on messages, just like in USENET. Unlike USENET, it is impossible to receive a follow-up before the original message (an annoying feature of USENET). This guarantee is known as *causality* (see Figure 1). This causality guarantee works even across multiple news groups.

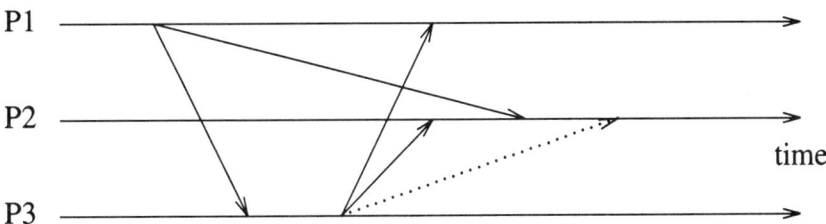

Figure 1. Causal ordering. In this case we have a news group with 3 subscribers. Subscriber P1 posts a message which is sent to P2 and P3. P3 picks up the message and follows up on it. Due to unexpected network delays, it is possible that P2 receives the follow-up message before the original message from P1. ISIS guarantees that this reversal does not happen, so that the message from P3 to P2 follows the dotted path.

An important distinction from the USENET model is that ISIS news supports a way to track membership in "news groups." If so desired, membership changes will be posted to the news group just like other messages. These changes include processes subscribing, unsubscribing, failing, or becoming unreachable. Notification of these changes is causally ordered with respect to normal messages. Therefore, after the notification that a process has unsubscribed or failed, it is impossible to receive messages from it. All subscribers see exactly the same history of membership changes. In particular, all subscribers know how many members there are in the group, and their own *rank* in the group. The ranking is based on age. The oldest member has rank 0, whereas the youngest member has a rank which is one less than the number of members in the group. In addition, it is possible, using cryptographic protection, to preclude processes from subscribing or posting to groups [7]. This kind of functionality simplifies the development of secure, fault-tolerant tools and applications.

Another distinction from the USENET news model is that the ISIS news service does not log every message it receives. Instead, logging is under control of the programs that post and subscribe to a news topic. A service can be unlogged (in which case a message is only seen by the processes subscribing at the time it was posted), temporarily logged (new subscribers see a replay of any temporarily logged messages; these are deleted under criteria controlled by the posting program), or spooled (in which case deletion only occurs under control of the subscribers). The spooling option is the most costly, and is only used when a message is critical and it cannot be predicted when the subscriber will execute, or when the news group includes members on a remote LAN accessible only intermittently.

The ISIS news interface is sketched in Figure 2. *Ng.create* creates a new news group. The options specify the kind of ordering required (unordered, FIFO, causal, or total), whether or not membership information need be posted, the degree of fault tolerance (e.g., whether logging is desired or not), which network transport mechanism to use, and possibly more. *Ng.subscribe* subscribes to a news group, and specifies an upcall interface to be invoked when messages arrive for a news group. The new ISIS system includes a complete pre-emptive multi-threading facility for upcalls and other activities, and appropriate synchronization primitives for maintaining ordering of events.) *Ng.post* multicasts messages to all subscribers of a news group. When invoked in an upcall, it is assumed to be a follow-up message, and causally ordered as such. *Ng.reply* is invoked from an upcall, and sends a point-to-point reply message back to the originator of the posting. *Ng.unsubscribe* undoes the effects of ng.subscribe, and *ng.destroy* releases the resources of the specified news group.

In current ISIS applications, groups are used heavily. For example, replicated object repositories generally use a group per object. The subscribers of each group are the servers that store a replica of the object, or have a cached copy, since each server is interested in updates to the object. The ordering semantics on messages and group membership make it easy to maintain consistency among the copies and to divide work over the servers to enhance performance. Unlike RPC, every process has the same view of failures. Unlike atomic transactions, ISIS does not provide the illusion of local operations on actually remote objects, but provides instead an efficient, straightforward, message interface. However, RPC and atomic transactions may be supported easily using ISIS groups, and thereby will integrate better in a single, uniform system, and have simpler and more consistent error semantics than is usually the case in distributed computing environments. Thus ISIS news groups should be seen as an independent, orthogonal paradigm which provides a simple (optionally secure) message interface with a consistent view of failures.

procedure	arguments	result
ng.create	options	news group
ng.subscribe	news group, upcall	
ng.post	news group, message	
ng.reply	message	
ng.unsubscribe	news group	
ng.destroy	news group	

Figure 2. The basic interface to ISIS news groups.

Interestingly, we think that we can achieve performance comparable to systems that provide straightforward, unordered communication, since messages usually arrive in causal order, so no delay is necessary. If failures are infrequent, our protocols rarely introduce extra messages. In fact, since the ISIS interface is asynchronous in nature, we can make use of pipelining and provide a much higher message throughput (messages/time unit) than other communication mechanisms, simply by packing multiple messages into a single packet.

3 Examples

Before going into the design of the new ISIS system, we will illustrate the use of process groups by means of two simple examples. The first example is a distributed chess algorithm, and the second an implementation of distributed shared memory.

3.1 Distributed chess

In this example we will illustrate the use of process groups using a simple implementation of game tree search. Each node in the game tree presents a position in the chess game, and each of its children the position following a move. By having the child nodes evaluated in parallel, possibly recursively, we may achieve a speed-up. In our implementation we implement each node in the tree by a process group.

Naively, a process evaluating a node would generate all the moves, and send each move separately to another member for evaluation. This would generate a lot of messages. Better is to multicast the list of moves. Each member knows the number of members in the group, and its rank in the group. Based on this information it can select which moves in the list it should evaluate. For example, if the number of members is n, a member with rank r would evaluate all entries in the list with index i for which $i \bmod n = r$.

If one of the processors crashes, all members will receive this event. The members know which moves it was evaluating, so each member can run a select function that will decide which moves it should take over. For example, if member s crashed, a member r might inherit all entries in the list for which the index i satisfies $i \bmod n = s$ and $(i \text{ div } n) \bmod (n-1) = r$.

It will be clear that much fancier alpha-beta algorithms will need more complex interactions, especially if failures need be tolerated. Updates to alpha-beta windows, which can be multicast, may make it necessary to abort the evaluation of a particular position, and to evaluate a new position which was originally assigned to a different member [8].

3.2 Distributed shared memory

Consider a fault-tolerant distributed shared object, where writes occur in a total order. Reads are always done locally, whereas writes are propagated asynchronously (but ordered). Only one process is allowed to write at a time. In spite of this, the implementation allows writer processes to crash without blocking other writers. The algorithm described here can also be used to maintain consistent shared caches for objects. (Note that we are not implementing atomic transactions here. Multiple read and write operations are not grouped into serializable units of execution. However, atomic transactions may be implemented conveniently on top of ISIS as well.)

To implement the specified behavior, we use two groups. The first group, called the *reader group* contains all processes. The other group, the *writer group* contains all processes that are interested in writing the shared object. This group is a subgroup of the reader group. Only the oldest member in the writer group, the member with rank 0, is allowed to update the object. A write operation thus follows the following lines:

> subscribe to the writer group
> wait to get rank 0
> post the update to the reader group
> unsubscribe from the writer group

The required semantics are achieved using the causal ordering guarantees. As there can only be one oldest member in the group, there can only be one writer. As subscribing, posting, unsubscribing are causally ordered with respect to each other, it is never possible that a process can deliver updates to other processes before previous updates have been delivered there as well. If the current writer were to crash, the next writer will automatically get rank 0, and will be able to proceed. Also, ISIS guarantees that a message is either delivered to all surviving members, or to none. Thus, if a writer crashes during the posting of an update, either all members receive the update, or none do.

For example, say that two processes P1 and P2 decide to update the shared object at the same time, and P3 is a third process reading the updates. As P1 and P2 are subscribing to the group, ISIS guarantees that either P1 or P2 will get rank 0, and the other rank 1. Assume that P1 got rank 0. P1 can now post the update and will then unsubscribe. P2 will then receive first the update, and then the unsubscribe event message. The unsubscribe event changes the rank of P2 to zero, so that P2 can now post its update. Without the causal ordering guarantees, it may happen that this second update is received by P3 before the update of P1. However, as the posting by P2 causally follows the unsubscription of P1, and the unsubscription of P1 follows the posting of P1, P3 will delay the delivery of the posting by P2 until the posting by P1 has been received and delivered.

Note that the causal guarantees of ISIS would also make updates on multiple objects in that shared memory ordered with respect to each other. The new ISIS system has a notion of causality domains if this is overly restrictive. Multiple group ordering is only enforced within a single causality domain.

This implementation allows all but one member in the group to crash. The ISIS system also has a logging facility that allows checkpointing, which would allow recovery from a total failure where all members crash. This facility will be further described in the next section.

4 Design

The new ISIS implementation, now under development, follows the design principles of microkernel operating systems closely. It consists of a small core that implements the basic protocols. More policy-oriented matters, such as the determination of what constitutes a failure and how to detect one, or how to log messages in fault-tolerant settings, are implemented externally. This compares to similar concepts in microkernel designs, such as external pagers and schedulers. In this section we will describe the new design inside-out (see Figure 3). Usually, this would correspond to bottom-up, as the core would be implemented near the microkernel, and the external services in user space.

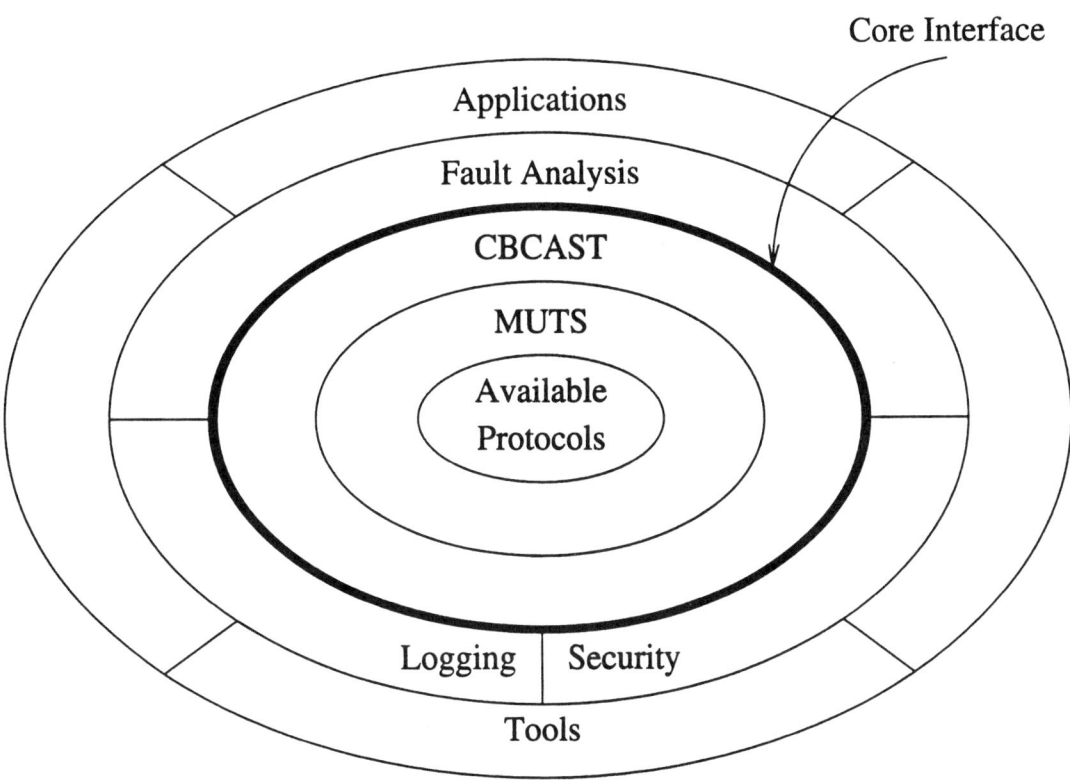

Figure 3. Structure of the new ISIS implementation.

At the very core of the new system are the network protocols that are available for the host system. Typically, these would include IP and UDP, optionally extended to include the Deering multicast facilities. In addition, there may be access to the raw network hardware, or to more sophisticated protocols that may implement forms of reliable multicast.

At the first ISIS shell, we provided a layer called the Multicast Transport Service (MUTS) [1,4]. MUTS provides a simple, reliable multicast service that runs on one or more lower level protocols. It does not implement any group membership services, and only provides FIFO ordering. Thus "follow-up messages" from a third party may still arrive at a particular destination before the original message. MUTS detects communication problems, but does not act upon them other than reducing the retransmission rate to a problematic member. Instead, it passes error statistics up, in the hope that external layers will decide to delete the member from the group. Finally, it supports optional encryption and signing of messages to support security.

The second shell is the Causal Broadcast (CBCAST) layer. It implements group membership protocols and guarantees causal ordering of messages. Causal ordering is achieved, in principle, by attaching a simple vector of sequence numbers to each message that allows receivers to detect if they have missed any messages [9]. If so, they will delay the delivery of the message. In practice it is usually unnecessary to attach the whole vector, since changes are mostly minimal. CBCAST does not actually decide on failures, but relies on an incoming stream of failure notifications from an external source. CBCAST merges this stream with the message stream, and uses it to provide a consistent view of the group membership. The CBCAST interface is the core interface, and both MUTS and CBCAST will usually be located near the network interface for efficiency.

The next shell contains the external services, which implement policies rather than mechanisms. These services may use the core mechanisms, but need to be careful not to create infinitely recursive dependencies. Other than the core services, they can make use of local operating system facilities such as disk storage. The first external service, the Failure Detector (FD), performs fault analysis [10]. FD is a distributed service that uses information passed up by MUTS, in addition to information made available by the host operating system, to determine the sites that have become unreachable. As its output, it provides a stream of failure notifications. Each member site of FD will provide the same stream, and feed it to its local CBCAST shell. As it is an external service, users may plug in their own failure detectors for special applications.

A second external service is the logging facility. As discussed earlier, this facility logs messages that have been posted to a news topic on stable storage. The facility is only needed in applications that desire long-term stability of messages.

The last external service assists in providing security. MUTS can encrypt and sign messages, but is not involved in key distribution itself. Instead, this is done with the help of an authentication service [7]. When security has to be provided right from a cold start, this service also assists in bootstrapping the system.

The outermost shell consists of the applications, and standard tools for implementing distributed applications. ISIS provides a set of those tools, such as RPC, atomic transactions, monitoring and control facilities, and resource management, which will be described briefly in Section 9. Additionally, this layer provides a light-weight group mechanism which simplifies resource allocation and provides a portable interface to heterogeneous systems. This light-weight group mechanism is the subject of Section 8.

5 Protocols

In this section we will have a look at the protocols that are used for implementing this system. In particular, we will look at the protocols that are used for reliable delivery (MUTS), the protocols for failure detection, and the protocols that provide causal ordering (CBCAST). We have only described part of these protocols for brevity. For example, details on subscription to news groups have been omitted.

5.1 MUTS

MUTS implements one-to-many communication and guarantees no more than FIFO ordering [1]. For this it applies a simple *sliding window* protocol [11], extended to handle multicast communication. Sliding window protocols handle packet loss, duplication, and re-ordering, and at the same time provide some form of flow control. In our particular implementation, packets are numbered from 0 to virtually infinity. The sender and all receivers maintain a range (window) of acceptable sequence numbers (see Figure 4 for an example). The sender's window is variable in size, but limited, and represents the outstanding (unacknowledged) packets. The low edge of the sender's window is advanced when acknowledgments have been received from all receivers. The high edge of the sender's window is advanced when more packets need be sent.

A receiver's window is fixed in size, starting at the next packet that it is expecting, and ending at the last packet that it is willing to receive, and should be at least as large as the maximum size of the sender's window. Once every while the receiver sends an acknowledgment, in particular when the receiver's window has been advanced by the maximum size of the sender's window. An acknowledgment contains the sequence number of the next packet that the receiver is expecting, and acknowledges *all* packets that precede it. Messages out-of-order, but within the receiver's window, are accepted but not delivered until all messages in front of it have been received as well.

The sender maintains for each receiver how many packets that receiver has acknowledged, and advances the low edge of the send window to the minimum acknowledged packet. In particular, if there is a faulty receiver that does not acknowledge the outstanding packets, the protocol may block since the send window is limited in size. MUTS will then report the faulty receiver to the higher-level protocols. When, subsequently, the receiver is removed from the group or receivers, the send window may be advanced.

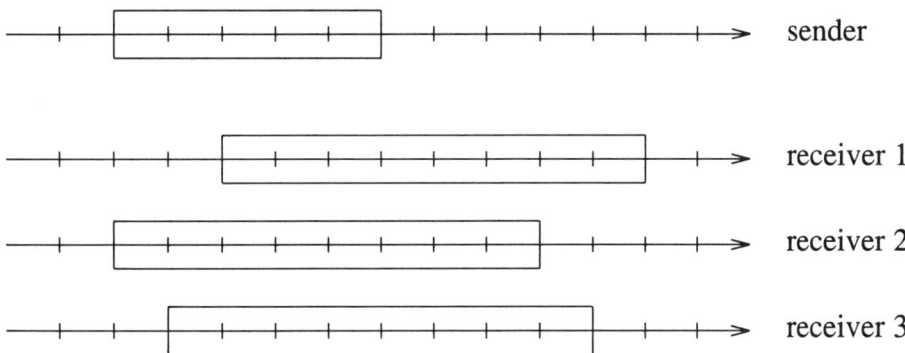

Figure 4. The multicast sliding window protocol. The receiver's window size is 8 messages, while the sender has 5 messages outstanding. Receiver 1 has received the first two packets in order, receiver 2 has not received the first packet yet, and receiver 3 has received only the first packet in order so far.

Because the MUTS interface is asynchronous, the bandwidth of messages may be higher than the underlying protocols can handle. This is detected when the send window fills up. At that time, MUTS will start queuing up messages. When a slot becomes available in the send window, MUTS fills up the packet with as many messages as possible. This way, the number of messages can become much larger than in conventional, synchronous systems.

5.2 Failure Detector

The Failure Detector (FD) is a replicated service that is implemented on top of MUTS [10]. It takes the monitoring information as generated by MUTS, and multicasts a totally ordered stream of crashes to the CBCAST instances on every site. We assume an asynchronous system:

there is no global clock, and there is no way to differentiate between a slow site and a crashed site. Therefore, the failure detector may incorrectly decide that a site has crashed, but all "surviving" sites will still be consistent with respect to each other. The slow site, in that case, will fail to communicate with the other sites and will attempt to resubscribe.

FD is replicated on a subset of the MUTS sites. We call these sites the *members* of the FD. The members are ordered by their age in the FD group. The oldest member of FD is special, and is called the *manager*. The manager coordinates the updates using a two-phase commit protocol. In the case where the manager crashes, or is slow to respond, the rest of the FD uses a three-phase protocol to elect a new manager.

All failures are propagated to the current manager. In phase one the manager broadcasts a *removal invitation* message, and waits for all other members to respond or to be removed from the FD (due to their crash or slowness). The manager then broadcasts a commit message (see Figure 5 (a)). As only one process decides on the commit, the order and consistency of the notification is assured.

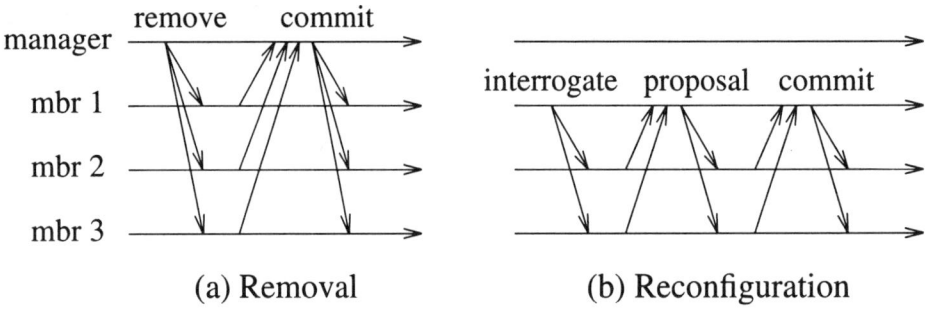

Figure 5. The two-phase (a) and three phase (b) protocols. In (b), the manager is believed to have crashed, and member 1 is the *reconfigurer*.

If a member, henceforth called the *reconfigurer*, believes that all those members older than itself have crashed, it will broadcast a *reconfiguration interrogation* message to the younger members and await their responses (see Figure 5 (b)). A response will include whether the member goes along with the reconfiguration, whether it was awaiting a commit message from the manager or not, and, if so, for which entity. If a majority responds positively, the reconfigurer will broadcast a *reconfiguration proposal* message based on the responses in the first phase. This proposal will try to complete any outstanding commit phase. (It is for this reason that the protocol requires a majority, so that multiple reconfigurers agree on the same state.) After the reconfigurer has received another majority of responses, it will broadcast a commit message and becomes the new manager.

Clients of the FD (the CBCAST instances) register with the failure detector. This registration is carefully recorded with all members of the FD using commit protocols. Any member of FD may be responsible for propagating the failure events to the clients. As any such member may crash, another member may take over and repeat the failure notification. Therefore, clients have to be prepared to filter out duplicate notifications. The order of notifications is still well-defined.

Note that this section described one particular implementation of a failure detector. However, since the failure detector is a user-level service, other failure detectors may be substituted in its place (or even run next to it). Such failure detectors may be faster, or deal better with, say, network partitions.

5.3 CBCAST

CBCAST guarantees causal delivery of messages, and merges the failure stream coming from the Failure Detector with the message stream [9]. Each site has its own copy of the CBCAST implementation to deal with these problems. In this section we will look at each of this in turn. First we will assume that there is one fixed set of MUTS instances, called processes in this section, that communicate using multicast to all members in the set only. Later we will look in particular at how to deal with point-to-point communication.

5.3.1 Causal ordering

Each message m is labeled with a timestamp vector $VT(m)$, with an entry $VT(m)[k]$ for each process P_k in the set. $VT(m)[k]$ describes exactly how many messages the sender of m has received from P_k. Any recipient of the message will wait until it too has received $VT(m)[k]$ messages from P_k. For this, each process P_i maintains how many messages it has received from each other process in $VT(P_i)$. The protocol may be described more formally as follows:

(1) Before sending message m, process P_i increments $VT(P_i)[i]$ and timestamps m with the result: $VT(m) := VT(P_i)$.

(2) When process P_j receives m ($j <> i$), it delays delivery of m until

$$\begin{cases} VT(m)[i] = VT(P_j)[i]+1 \\ VT(m)[k] < VT(P_j)[k] \quad \text{for all } k <> i \end{cases}$$

By FIFOness of MUTS, the first condition is automatically satisfied. Messages "received from itself" ($j = i$) may be delivered immediately in all cases.

(3) When m is delivered remotely, $VT(P_j)[i]$ is incremented.

5.3.2 Failure handling

When a process receives a failure notification from the Failure Detector, it broadcasts this event to all other processes. As all processes receive this notification, all processes will receive a message from all other that have not failed. When a process has received all flush messages, it knows that it has also received all multicasts (by FIFOness of MUTS), and that all other processes will arrive in the same state. Therefore it can start fresh, with a new, zeroed timestamp and a new (smaller) set of processes. During the flush protocol the processes do not initiate new multicasts, but they do receive and deliver messages. (This protocol has been optimized in our implementation to using only $2n$ messages.)

There is one problem that need be solved still, which is *delivery atomicity*. The process that failed might have been in the process of transmitting a message to the other processes. Therefore, some of the processes may not have received this message. Worse, the processes that did receive the message may have delivered the message already, and ISIS guarantees that in that event all surviving processes will deliver the message.

To solve this problem, all processes retain a copy of each message they deliver until they know for sure that each (surviving) process has delivered the message. A process may learn that all other processes have delivered a message by inspecting the timestamps on arriving messages. If so, the message may be removed from the store. To keep the store of messages within bounds, each process that has not sent a message for a while sends a dummy message containing its timestamp. After a failure, the message store is piggybacked on the flush message so that all processes will receive any messages they have not delivered yet. Moreover, at the end of the flush protocol (when all acknowledgments have been received) the store may be cleared altogether.

5.3.3 Point-to-point messages

So far we have assumed that all communication is through multicast to all members in the group. Another common form of communication is point-to-point messages, particularly used for RPC and, more generally, replies to multicast requests. It is undesirable to multicast these messages as that would induce unnecessary overhead at all processes but the destination.

Instead, we inhibit the sender of the point-to-point message m from sending other messages until m has been acknowledged (either by a reply message, or by a separate acknowledgment packet). The sender piggybacks the vector timestamp as usual, but does not increment its own vector timestamp prior to transmission. Thus causality is maintained without affecting the cost of point-to-point transmission. Experience with the old ISIS system has shown that this is a satisfactory solution.

6 Multi-threading and ordering

The current ISIS system is multi-threaded. For each arriving message, a new thread is created. ISIS was one of the first available systems under the UNIX system that provided multi-threading, and this was one of the reasons for its success. Now that microkernels provide their own multi-threading, we wish to adopt the available threading mechanisms, rather than impose our own. Yet there is a problem to be resolved.

If multiple messages become available at once, several threads will get started, one for each message. The threads will process the messages in parallel, and, as a consequence, ordering is lost. In the current ISIS this is solved by scheduling threads non-preemptively and in the correct order. However, if we want to be able to take full advantage of real parallelism, this approach no longer suffices.

The new ISIS system attaches a sequence number to each message to be delivered. Any ordering issues are now left to the application. To support this, the ISIS library provides a construct called *event counters*, based on Reed and Kanodia's work on synchronization [12]. An event counter is basically a lock, which can be acquired only in a certain order. The interface is presented in Figure 6.

procedure	*arguments*	*result*
ec.create		event counter
ec.acquire	event counter, sequence number	
ec.release	event counter	
ec.destroy	event counter	

Figure 6. The event counter interface.

Ec.create creates a new event counter, and initializes it to zero. To acquire the event counter, a thread calls *ec.acquire* with a sequence number. If the sequence number does not correspond with the event counter, the procedure will block until the value of the event counter has reached the given value. *Ec.release* will release the event counter, and increment its associated value. *Ec.destroy* will destroy the event counter, and release the associated resources. Figure 7 demonstrates how an event counter may be used. Basically, an event counter implements a critical region for processing messages, so that the messages are processed in the right order.

>
> upcall (*message, sequence number*) {
>
>   initial processing on *message*;
>
>   **ec.acquire** (*event counter, sequence number*);
>
>   main processing on *message*;
>
>   **ec.release** (*event counter*);
>
>   final processing on *message*;
>
> }

Figure 7. How event counters are used. Several of these threads may run in parallel, yet the main processing on messages happens in a strict order.

This simple interface is consistent with the microkernel philosophy underlying our work. Other researchers have proposed more elaborate interfaces for this type of event ordering. For example, the PSYNC system allows programs to detect and act upon very complex message ordering properties [13], and the work of Liskov and Ladin also supports user-implemented message delivery orderings [14]. Experience with ISIS, however, leads us to believe that while causal delivery is vital, other sorts of delivery orderings are rarely needed. The approach described above, which forces users to process messages in a fixed order consistent with causality is less powerful than these other schemes, but it has the benefit of being simple and highly concurrent. Single-threaded application may ignore event counters altogether.

7 Customizing ISIS to a port interface

The original ISIS runs as a UNIX application. Of particular importance to us is getting the new ISIS system to run well on modern microkernel technology, notably MACH[15] and Chorus [16,17]. These systems provide their own communication mechanisms on top of an interface based on ports and messages. We wish to integrate the ISIS system within this framework. The basic reasoning behind these plans is that microkernels appear to offer satisfactory support for memory management and communication between processes on the same machine, but that support for applications that run on multiple machines is weak. The current IPC mechanisms, with Remote Procedure Call as the most popular one, are adequate only for the simpler distributed applications, as they do not address any of the internal management issues of distribution [18,19,20].

Our goal is to add stronger functionality and semantics to the existing MACH and Chorus message interfaces, rather than defining a new interface. This functionality and semantics will take the form of ISIS news groups. In this section we will first look at the existing MACH and Chorus port interfaces, and then discuss how we wish to integrate ISIS within these interfaces.

7.1 Ports

Modern operating systems support ports with a wide range of semantics. As a minimum, as in the Amoeba system [21], a port is an address to which messages can be sent. In Chorus and MACH, a bounded queue is associated with the port, so the process holding the port need not listen continuously (in Amoeba this is done by having several threads wait for messages simultaneously). In MACH, the messages are reliably delivered, and the sender may block if the port queue is full. Chorus messages to ports are unreliable, although a reliable port-level RPC interface is supported. MACH and Chorus allow only one receiver process on a port (although possibly multiple threads within that process), but the port may be migrated to a new receiver process.

MACH ports do not have user-visible global names, and have, in reality, no global access. The ports, instead, are accessed using so-called rights, which can be compared to file descriptors or capabilities. Global access is simulated through a user space server, the NetMsgServer. This server acts as an agent for remote ports: it creates a local proxy port, and forwards messages sent to the port to the remote NetMsgServer using TCP or another conventional protocol. Similarly, it delivers messages received from remote NetMsgServers to the local port. MACH users do not notice this, and, in principle, local semantics are transparently maintained (currently, however, this is not the case). Chorus ports, on the other hand, do have global names and a corresponding global implementation.

Chorus provides a port group concept, with weak semantics. It is possible to allocate a group, and add (local) ports to it. Messages can be sent to the group in the same way as to ports, and are unreliable. There is no membership information available. (Note: the MACH "port set" is a mechanism that allows receiving on multiple ports at once, much like UNIX *select*, and has no group communication role. MACH currently does not provide a group mechanism.)

7.2 Integrating ISIS into a port interface

The news interface will look similar on both Chorus and MACH. Rather than having processes subscribe to news groups, ports may subscribe. Henceforth, messages sent to the port are multicast to the corresponding news group, and messages received on the news group are delivered through the port. We also want to extend the basic Chorus and MACH system calls so that we can transparently replace a conventional Chorus or MACH application with one that has been replicated for fault tolerance. The users of such an application would continue to use the original application interface, but all communication would transparently be sent to a group, and processed cooperatively by the group members. This raises the question of how to integrate the ISIS news group mechanisms into the Chorus and MACH microkernel interfaces.

As described, Chorus currently provides an unreliable group interface. The Chorus group-allocate function will be implemented by creating an ISIS news group. A new option will indicate if membership information should be posted to the group or not. Adding a port to the group will be the same as subscribing the port to the news group [22].

MACH does not currently have a group concept. (As noted before, the "port set" provides only a select functionality, with no global semantics.) We intend to use the NetMsgServer to simulate a global port with multiple receivers, much in the same way as MACH already uses the NetMsgServer for simulating global ports. Instead of TCP, the NetMsgServers will use ISIS to do their group communication (see Figure 8). Each application task will have two ports: one to receive incoming messages, and another to which it sends outgoing messages. The NetMsgServer forwards messages it receives from ISIS to the first port. Messages sent to the second port are received by the NetMsgServer and forwarded to the corresponding news group [23].

It may be useful to walk through this architecture in the case where a pre-existing application is replaced with a fault-tolerant group. This will work roughly the same way under MACH and Chorus. Under MACH, when a client thread looks up the name of a server to find the port, this request is sent to the NetMsgServer. The NetMsgServer can now generate a local port and return the send right to the client. The NetMsgServer subscribes the port to the ISIS news group that implements the fault-tolerant service. When the client sends a request message to the port, the NetMsgServer will post this to the news group, the members of which cooperate to respond fault-tolerantly using one of several methods supported by ISIS. After the NetMsgServer receives a reply to the request, it forwards it back to the client. The client can be kept completely unaware of this change. (Details of the comparable algorithm in Chorus are omitted for brevity.)

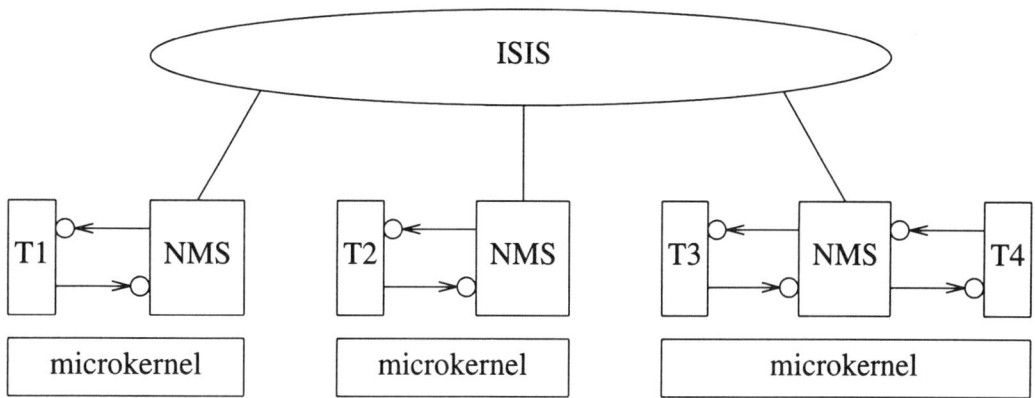

Figure 8: Structure of the MACH/ISIS implementation with four tasks, showing the microkernels, the NetMsgServers (NMS), and the ports.

8 Light-weight groups

As mentioned earlier, ISIS users have found it convenient to implement small, single objects as separate groups, rather than having one group that manages a complete service with a large set of objects. For example, in a replicated file system, a file would be a group with a member on every server that stores the file. For each open file, there would be a group that includes not only the servers, but also the clients that maintain cached copies of the file. To deal with the resulting proliferation of groups, we saw a need for a light-weight version of the group mechanisms.

Again, we were influenced by microkernel design concepts, in which several light-weight mechanisms are provided in user space. The most obvious of these is the lightweight process or thread abstraction. Another well-known, older abstraction is memory allocation. These abstractions not only allow easier resource management by sharing most of a core environment, but also provide a portable interface across different environments. For example, POSIX threads and *malloc* provide a portable, light-weight execution and memory allocation facility which may be used for applications that need to run on several different platforms.

In the new ISIS system we have designed a portable, light-weight news group (LWG) mechanism. The basic idea is that many LWGs will be mapped to a single news group as implemented by the core ISIS system. Thus, these LWGs will share the same security environment, and have the same failure model, as their messages will be multiplexed over a single core news group. The benefit of this approach is that membership changes to the core news group will now automatically affect a potentially large number of LWGs, allowing us to amortize the cost of maintaining membership information over what the application thinks of as being a large number of independent groups. (In particular, the flush protocol of Section 5.3.2 need be run only once.) The old ISIS system lacked such a facility, forcing many application programmers to develop equivalent mechanisms on their own.

The interface to light-weight groups, almost identical to that in Figure 2, is the same in MACH, Chorus, or any other system that supports ISIS. The difference to the interface in Figure 2 is that the light-weight group create function takes an argument that names the core news group to be used (initially). Applications using this interface, along with a standard thread interface (also provided in the ISIS library) and the UNIX interface, should run equally well under MACH or Chorus. As there is nothing that prevents MACH and Chorus processes from subscribing to the same ISIS group, applications should even be able to run on a mixture of these systems. There is a complication though, since the network message formats for MACH and Chorus are different (MACH messages are self-describing). To make this work, we intend to provide an option to the create function of core news groups that results in "raw" mode: in this mode, messages pass through the port interface unchanged as byte arrays. (In MACH, it would not be possible to distribute port rights through this type of group, although rights could still be sent through separate "pure Mach" groups.)

9 The ISIS toolkit

Readers familiar with the ISIS system will have noticed that several aspects of the system have not been described yet, in particular the tools. The current ISIS system comes with a *toolkit* containing tools for applications that use RPC, atomic transaction, primary-backup replication, resource management, and monitoring and control [24]. The new system will continue to support these tools, but they will be implemented entirely as a set of user libraries and services. Other old ISIS applications will continue to be supported through a compatibility library that offers the old interface. For brevity, we will not present details of this mapping. The key point, however, is that the CBCAST and group membership layer of our new system is sufficiently powerful to let us support the full range of functionality implemented by the old ISIS system.

10 Status of the implementation

The new ISIS system is in a fairly advanced stage of implementation. The MUTS shell has been completed, and currently runs on several different platforms, namely SUN OS in user space (using SUN LWP threads), MACH 2.5 and 3.0 in user space, and the x-kernel in kernel space [5]. This implementation uses IP or UDP, optionally extended with the Deering multicast facilities [6], or raw Ethernet. A simple version of the CBCAST shell has been implemented, but does not fully support multiple groups and failure handling yet. We also have an initial version of the failure detector running.

In our initial implementation, we achieve 10,000 (1-byte) messages per second from SUN OS user process to user processes on different SPARCstation 2s connected by Ethernet, and about 5,000 parallel RPCs per second using a simple RPC implementation on top of the MUTS interface. The complete round-trip time of a single RPC is a little under 3 milliseconds. The maximum data bandwidth is about 800,000 bytes per second, using larger messages (which may be up to 2 Gigabytes). These numbers are very respectable for this kind of hardware and software. Initial results on the light-weight group mechanisms (on the old ISIS system we achieved a speed-up of about 9 for the group create operation and even higher speedup factors for other operations) lead us to believe that we will be able to produce a fast system.

In the MACH and Chorus systems, the plan is to run both MUTS and CBCAST as x-kernel protocols. In MACH, the NetMsgServer will be reimplemented to use the x-kernel, so that the core of the ISIS system will run within the NetMsgServers. In Chorus, the x-kernel will be made part of the microkernel itself. We believe that we will see significantly better performance for these systems. We expect to provide the first releases of these implementations by the end of 1992.

11 Conclusion

Process Groups are an important paradigm for fault-tolerant distributed applications, which should be seen as a management paradigm orthogonal to RPC and atomic transactions. ISIS news groups are an implementation of process groups that provide asynchronous, one-to-many message passing, but with the ordering of messages arranged as if the system was synchronous. This increases the performance, while maintaining simplicity. All processes in a process group have the same view of which processes are running, and which have failed. A news group can be made secure, which restricts who can post messages to the group, and who can subscribe to the group to receive messages. RPC and atomic transactions can be integrated into a single system by building them together on top of ISIS news groups.

Acknowledgments

We would like to thank Aleta Ricciardi, Barry Gleeson, Brad Glade, Carlos Almeida, Micah Beck, Mike Reiter, Patrick Stephenson, and Robert Cooper, not only for their helpful comments on this text, but also because we have borrowed heavily from their work.

References

1. R. van Renesse, K. Birman, R. Cooper, B. Glade, and P. Stephenson, "Reliable Multicast Between Microkernels," *Proc. of the USENIX Workshop on Micro-Kernels and Other Kernel Architectures*, pp. 269-283, Seattle, Washington, April 27-28, 1992.

2. K. Birman and R. Cooper, "The ISIS Project: Real Experience with a Fault Tolerant Programming System," *Operating Systems Review*, pp. 103-107, April 1991.

3. K.P. Birman and T.A. Joseph, "Exploiting Virtual Synchrony in Distributed Systems," *Proc. of the 11th ACM Symp. on Operating Systems Principles*, pp. 123-138, Austin, TX, November 1987.

4. The ISIS Group, "The Restructuring of ISIS for Modern Distributed Operating Systems," Internal Cornell Report, September 1991.

5. N. Hutchinson and L. Peterson, "The x-Kernel: An Architecture for Implementing Network Protocols," *IEEE Transactions on Software Engineering*, Vol. 17, No. 1, January 1991.

6. S.E. Deering and D.R. Cheriton, "Multicast Routing in Datagram Internetworks and Extended LANs," *ACM Transactions on Computer Systems*, Vol. 8, No. 2, May 1990.

7. M. Reiter, K. Birman, and L. Gong, "Integrating Security in a Group-Oriented Distributed System," *IEEE Symposium on Research in Security and Privacy*, Oakland, CA, May 4-6, 1992.

8. H.E. Bal and R. van Renesse, "A Summary of Parallel Alpha-Beta Search Results," *Int. Computer Chess Assoc. Journal*, Vol. 9, No. 3, pp. 146-149, September 1986.

9. K. Birman, A. Schiper, and P. Stephenson, "Lightweight Causal and Atomic Group Multicast," *ACM Transactions on Computer Systems*, Vol. 9, No. 3, pp. 272-314, August 1991.

10. A. Ricciardi and K. Birman, "Using Process Groups to Implement Failure Detection in Asynchronous Environments," *ACM Symp. on Principles of Distributed Computing*, pp. 341-353, Montreal, Quebec, Canada, August 19-21, 1991.

11. A.S. Tanenbaum, *Computer Networks*, Prentice-Hall, Englewood Cliffs, NJ, 1981.

12. D.P. Reed and R.K. Kanodia, "Synchronization with Eventcounts and Sequencers," *Comm. of the ACM*, Vol. 22, No. 2, pp. 115-123, February 1979.

13. L. Peterson, N. Bucholz, and R. Schlichting, "Preserving and Using Context Information in Interprocess Communication," *ACM Transactions on Computer Systems*, Vol. 7, No. 3, pp. 217-246, August 1989.

14. B. Liskov and R. Ladkin, "Highly-Available Distributed Services and Fault-Tolerant Distributed Garbage Collection," *Proc. of the Fifth ACM Symp. on Principles of Distributed Computing*, pp. 29-39, Calgary, Alberta, August 1986.

15. M. Accetta, R. Baron, W. Bolosky, D. Golub, R. Rashid, A. Tevanian, and M. Young, "Mach: A New Kernel Foundation for UNIX Development," *USENIX Summer '86 Conf. Proc.*, pp. 93-112, Atlanta, GA, June 9-13, 1986.

16. F. Armand, M. Gien, F. Hermann, and M. Rozier, "Revolution 89, or Distributing UNIX Brings It Back to Its Original Virtues," *Proc. of the Workshop on Experiences with Building Distributed (and Multiprocessor) Systems*, pp. 153-174, Ft. Lauderdale, FL, October 5-6, 1989.

17. M. Rozier et al., "Chorus Distributed Operating System," *Computing Systems*, Vol. 4, No. 1, 1988.

18. K.G. Hamilton, "A Remote Procedure Call System," Ph.D. dissertation, Tech. Rep. No. 70, Computing Laboratory, University of Cambridge, Cambridge, England, December 1984.

19. H.E. Bal, R. van Renesse, and A.S. Tanenbaum, "Implementing Distributed Algorithms using Remote Procedure Call," *Proc. of the 1987 National Computer Conf.*, pp. 499-506, Chicago, IL, June 15-18, 1987.

20. A.S. Tanenbaum and R. van Renesse, "A Critique of the Remote Procedure Call Paradigm," *Proc. of the EUTECO 88 Conf.*, pp. 775-783, Vienna, Austria, April 20-22, 1988.

21. A. Tanenbaum, R. van Renesse, H. van Staveren, G. Sharp, S. Mullender, A. Jansen, and G. van Rossum, "Experiences with the Amoeba Distributed Operating System," *Comm. ACM*, Vol. 33, No. 12, pp. 46-63, December 1990.

22. M. Beck, K. Birman, R. Cooper, and S. Toueg, "A Fault Tolerant Extension of the Chorus Nucleus," Internal Cornell Report, January 1991.

23. R. van Renesse, K. Birman, B. Glade, and P. Stephenson, "Options for Adding Group Semantics to Ports," Internal Cornell Report, January 1992.

24. K. Marzullo, R. Cooper, M. Wood, and K. Birman, "Tools for Distributed Application Management," *IEEE Computer*, Vol. 24, No. 8, pp. 42-51, August 1991.

Tools for Monitoring and Controlling Distributed Applications

Keith Marzullo*
marzullo@cs.cornell.edu

Mark D. Wood**
wood@cs.cornell.edu

Cornell University
Department of Computer Science
Ithaca, New York 14853
May 22, 1992

Abstract

The Meta system is a UNIX-based toolkit that assists in the construction of reliable reactive systems, such as distributed monitoring and debugging systems, tool integration systems and reliable distributed applications. Meta provides mechanisms for instrumenting a distributed application and the environment in which it executes, and Meta supplies a service that can be used to monitor and control such an instrumented application. The Meta toolkit is built on top of the ISIS toolkit; they can be used together in order to build fault-tolerant and adaptive distributed applications.

1 Constructing reactive systems

In a *reactive system* architecture, the system is partitioned into two pieces: an environment that follows a basic course of action, and a control program that monitors the state of the environment in order to influence the environment's progress. This architecture is very general. For example, process control systems, system monitors and debuggers, and tool integration services all have a reactive system structure.

Another application of the reactive system architecture is the structuring of distributed applications. For example, many distributed applications are constructed by taking off-the-shelf programs and connecting them with some communication subsystem. Such an application can be thought of as an "environment" with a state including the properties of machines running the application, current performance of the component programs, and the state of the communication

---

* This work was supported by the Defense Advanced Research Projects Agency (DoD) under NASA Ames grant number NAG 2-593, Contract N00140-87-C-8904. The views, opinions, and findings contained in this report are those of the authors and should not be construed as an official Department of Defense position, policy, or decision. This work was also partially supported by a grant from Xerox.

** This author was also partially supported by a G.T.E. Graduate Student Fellowship.

An earlier version of this paper was published in *Proceedings of EurOpen Spring '91 Conference*, 1991, Tromsø, Norway.

subsystem. The job of the control program is to monitor the state of the application in order to guarantee that the system operates efficiently in spite of changing load and failures. The control program can also be used to interconnect the application's components in a more loosely bound manner than conventional RPC mechanisms.

The Meta system, described in this paper, is a UNIX-based toolkit that provides the basic primitives needed to build a non-real-time reactive system. Using the toolkit, a distributed program can be instrumented with sensors and actuators in order to expose its state for purposes of control. Meta provides mechanisms that allow a control program to query the state of the instrumented application and to respond by invoking actuators when some condition of interest occurs. The toolkit includes facilities for structuring individual components into collections of components for fault tolerance. In addition, Meta guarantees that the monitoring and reaction is done atomically.

Meta itself is built on top of another toolkit, the ISIS system. The application designer can use ISIS for fault-tolerant communication and Meta for distributed control. In fact, the Meta project was started when four of us in the ISIS project worked on integrating a distributed application constructed from off-the-shelf components [MCWB91]. The facility we found lacking in ISIS was support for distributed control, which Meta provides.

The next section introduces the architecture of an application managed by Meta. Section 3 presents how applications are instrumented, and Section 4 discusses how the resulting application is controlled. Finally, Section 5 presents the current status of Meta and discusses our future plans.

2 The Meta architecture

The architecture of Meta can be illustrated through an example of managing a distributed application. Consider an application that includes services and clients making use of the services. A given service consists of a set of identical servers replicated both for fault tolerance and for coarse-grained parallelism. Meta will be used to manage the services; in particular, if the load on a service is too large or the number of servers becomes too small due to crashes, then a new server is to be started and added to the service. Additionally, if a server's queue becomes too long, then waiting requests are to be migrated to less-loaded servers in the service. There are other conditions that would probably need to be maintained as well, such as reducing the number of servers when appropriate, but for sake of brevity we will keep our example limited.

Meta structures a distributed application using a data model based on the entity-relation data model [Che76], with each instrumented component (i.e., a program equipped with sensors and actuators) being viewed as an *entity* and its sensors and actuators being viewed as the *attributes* of that entity. For example, a server in the above example could be instrumented with sensors that give the server's load and the queue of waiting requests. Entities of the same type, that is, having the same set of sensor and actuator attributes, form an entity set.

Subsets of an entity set may be grouped together to form *aggregates*. Aggregate structures provide control programs with a way of grouping related entities together and limiting actions to members of that group. For example, the servers comprising a service can be grouped into an aggregate representing the service. Aggregates are themselves entities, and the system architect can define sensors and actuators on aggregates. An aggregate sensor is a function over the state of all the members of the aggregate. For example, a service aggregate could have a sensor that gives the average queue length of the servers in the service. An aggregate actuator causes an action to be performed on some subset (from one to all) of the current members.

A distributed application is managed through the use of guarded commands; that is, through a set of (*condition, action*) pairs that reference the sensors and actuators of the instrumented application. These commands are executed by interpreters that reside in *stubs* (somewhat like RPC stubs) coresident with the instrumented programs, thus allowing for fast notification and reaction. Each condition is a proposition on the state of system; references to both local sensors within the entity to which the stub is attached and nonlocal sensors are allowed. The action portion is a sequence of actuator invocations that are executed atomically. Actions may enable guarded commands on another Meta stub; this facility allows one to write control programs that span multiple components.

Since guarded commands are evaluated in the same address space as an instrumented program, their impact on the performance of the application is a concern. The syntax of the guarded command language (a postfix language called NPL) is tailored for fast and efficient evaluation, and so we do not expect programs to be written directly in this language. We are designing an object-oriented control language called *Lomita* [MCWB91] that can be used to describe the structure of the application and to specify its control behavior. A Lomita program contains a schema specifying the entity and aggregate structure along with their sensors and actuators. The control behavior of the application is specified in Lomita through the use of rules, where the conditions for the rule may include real-time interval logic expressions [SMSV83]. Such temporal expressions are compiled into finite state automata, where the state transitions are implemented using Meta guarded commands.

Figure 1 illustrates the use of stubs. The machine M_1 is running a server that has been instrumented, so there is a stub running in the same address space as this server that can directly access the sensors and actuators of the server. The machine is also running a separate Meta-supplied program accessing the various properties of the machine and its operating system, such as the amount of available memory and the processor load. This program is instrumented, and so has a stub that supports a set of sensors and actuators over the machine and operating system state.

3 Application instrumentation

An application first must be instrumented before it can be controlled. This is accomplished by inserting into the application a small amount of code, and then linking the application with a Meta library. This section describes the instrumentation process in more detail.

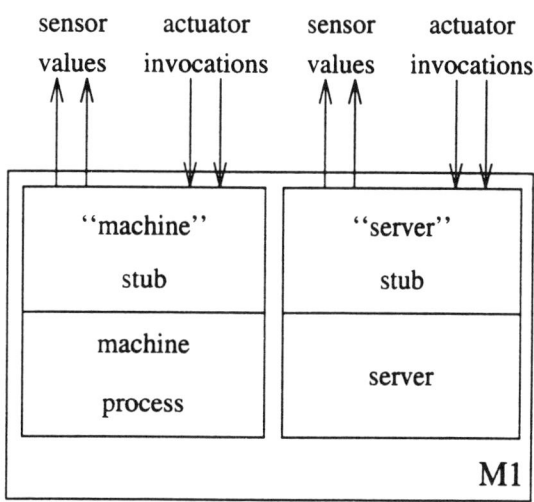

Figure 1. An instrumented component.

3.1 Access to base values

A sensor provides access to the value of some underlying system variable. An application defines a sensor with a Meta library routine:

```
meta_new_sensor(svr_q_length, "load", TYPE_INTEGER, min_period);
```

This routine creates an integer-valued sensor named "load". When this sensor is referenced, the function `svr_q_length` in the instrumented program is called, which presumably returns the number of entries on the server's work queue.

In a reactive system, the fact that a sensor's value has changed is as important to know as the current value of the sensor. There are two methods by which an application can alert its stub that a sensor's value has changed. In some cases, a sensor's value changes either slowly or regularly, in which case a lower bound on the time between changes in its value can be determined. The application tells the stub this lower bound as the fourth parameter of the `meta_new_sensor` call. This value states how long that sensor's value can be cached before repolling is needed. In other cases, it would be very hard to determine such a lower bound. In this case, the fourth parameter of the `meta_new_sensor` call is NEVER_POLL, and the stub will then obtain a fresh value only when the application makes an upcall to the stub. Such upcalls never block and can be made even when a nonzero polling period has been specified.

Actuators provide the means through which Meta acts upon the system. Like sensors, actuators are implemented by function calls in the application program. Actuators can be parameterized and can return either *success* or *failure*.

3.2 Functional composition

A control program may wish to monitor a sensor whose value is a function of an existing sensor or sensors. For example, the control program may wish to monitor the maximum load of a server or the difference between two queue lengths supported by a server. Such sensors can be easily defined using Meta. A stub can construct functions of the sensors it supports and can define additional sensors in terms of these functions. The stub ensures that the sensors comprising such a sensor are sampled atomically. A extensive collection of pre-defined functions are available, and this collection can be augmented with user-defined functions.

3.3 Aggregates

An aggregate has, as predefined sensors, set-valued versions of the sensors on the components comprising the aggregate. For example, if a component has an integer sensor named `load`, then an aggregate of this component has a group sensor named `load` whose type is "set of integers" and whose value is the set of loads of the components. Other aggregate sensors can then be defined as functions of group sensors.

Just as an aggregate inherits the sensors of its components, an aggregate also inherits the actuators of its components. For example, if a component has an actuator named `run`, then an aggregate of this component has a group actuator named `run`. An invocation of the group actuator `run` invokes all of the component `run` actuators.

3.4 Fault tolerance

When necessary, sensor fault tolerance is achieved through replication. The process containing the sensor to be made fault-tolerant is replicated, and the replicas are grouped into an aggregate; the value of the fault-tolerant, aggregate sensor is then a function of the members' sensor values [Sch90]. The severity of sensor failures that can be tolerated depends on the choice of aggregate function. For example, to provide tolerance to crash failures, the aggregate function need only pick one of the member's values to return as the sensor value. In this case, the availability of the sensor is the same as the availability of any member of the aggregate. In process control systems, however, a real-world sensor such as the temperature of a reaction vessel can be represented as an interval bounding the actual value of the quantity being measured. In this case, a fault-tolerant intersection function can be used to mask arbitrary failures of sensors [Mar90, CM91].

Actuator fault tolerance is achieved by grouping actuator replicas into an aggregate and using *preference-list* based actuation. Two additional parameters are specified when an aggregate actuator is invoked: an integer n giving the number of aggregate members who are to perform the action, and the preference list, which gives the order in which aggregate members are to be tried. The aggregate action is carried out by invoking the actuator on the first n members on the preference list. If any of those members should crash while carrying out the actuation, then additional members are chosen from the preference list. This continues until n members have performed the actuation; the actuation fails if the preference list is exhausted before n aggregate members have carried out the actuation. An alternative form for group actuation invokes the actuation on all currently active members of the aggregate.

4 Control

Once an application is instrumented, a control program can be written. The basis for controlling applications in Meta is a language of guarded commands that reference the state of the instrumented application.

4.1 Interpreting guarded commands

Each Meta stub implements a guarded command interpreter that has direct access to the sensors and actuators of the component to which the stub is attached. A stub can reference sensors and actuators not local to the component by communicating with the interpreter that does have direct access. The name of a sensor or actuator is sufficient for the Meta system to resolve which interpreter has direct access. So, a guarded command can be executed by any stub, although some stubs will provide better performance than others, because of improved locality.

Fault-tolerant execution of guarded commands is provided for by the use of special "Meta servers." A Meta server is just a Meta stub instrumenting a dummy process, i.e., one containing no local sensors of its own. One advantage to Meta servers is that they may be run in a replicated mode; running n replicas of a Meta server provides resiliency to $n-1$ crashes of individual replicas. The replicas use an optimized form of active replication to execute the guarded commands; the exact details may be found in [Woo91].

Since the aggregate structure is not directly represented by a component in the application, some stub must be selected to maintain the definitions of a given aggregate's sensors and actuators. Exactly which stub implements the aggregate is up to the application designer; either an existing stub or a Meta server can be designated to do so. Using a replicated Meta server provides a fault-tolerant way to implement the aggregate. The approach of designating a specific stub or service to implement the aggregate centralizes the computation of aggregate values, which in turn facilitates providing consistent views of the aggregate's state.

In our client-server example, the servers of a service are grouped into an aggregate. Each member of the aggregate (a server) has been instrumented, as described previously in Section 3, with a sensor that gives the load of the server. An aggregate sensor can then be defined that provides some measure of the service load, such as the average load of all the servers. If each server is equipped with an actuator that accepts a request for migration, then reliable migration can be implemented by invoking the set-valued aggregate actuator with the number of actuations specified as one and the preference list selected, for example, from the servers' loads. The stub that implements the aggregate sensors and actuators could be one of the servers in the service or a separate Meta server.

4.2 Atomic Guarded Commands

Recall that a guarded command consists of a set of (*condition, action*) pairs. A condition is a propositional expression over the sensor values, and an action is a sequence of parameterized actuator invocations. Ideally, Meta would ensure that the action is executed as an *atomic command*, that is, atomically and consistently with respect to its triggering condition [LS84].

When a predicate becomes true, the action should be executed in the same state in which it was triggered, but due to the asynchrony in the environment this can not be done without introducing blocking. Instead, Meta guarantees that any reference to sensor values during the action sequence obtains the same value as when the condition was triggered. Another property of atomic actions is that either all of the action is executed or none of it is executed. Providing this property requires a transactional facility with the ability either to undo the effects of partial actions or to invoke a forward recovery mechanism. Additionally, to provide consistent execution, the intermediate states of the action should not be visible to other guarded commands.

Meta currently provides only a limited amount of atomicity. For example, if a guarded command references only the sensors and actuators of a single component (either simple or aggregate), then its execution will be atomic. This amount of consistency is all that is needed for our client-server problem. For example, Meta will guarantee that if a machine is selected and removed from a *free-machine* aggregate when starting a new server, then the selection and removal will be done atomically. Other applications will require stronger guarantees of atomicity, however, so we are currently examining mechanisms that will enforce stronger guarantees of atomicity when necessary.

4.3 Example

Figure 2 shows part of a Lomita description of our client-server application. The description first defines the schema for server entities. In this simplified presentation, a server contains separate actuators for starting and stopping a job, with jobs being named by a string. For the sake of discussion, we assume that a job may be started and stopped repeatedly. The service aggregate has the sensor *sload* which is defined to be the average load of the individual sensors. The *run* actuator starts a job on some member of the aggregate, and the preference list specifies that the member should be selected on the basis of its load.

The two rules shown in this figure are compiled into NPL programs. The first rule states that a job should be migrated from a server whose load is too high. This rule can be translated into a single guarded command that can run in the server's stub. The second rule is more complex; it states that if the size of a service is too small or the load remains high for too long, then a new server should be started. The Lomita compiler would translate this rule into a finite state automaton, which in turn would be implemented by a set of Meta guarded commands.

```
server: entityset
    attributes
        key name : string;
        sensor load: integer;
        sensor jobs: {string};
        actuator stop(string);
        actuator start(string);
    end
end

service: server aggregate
    attributes
        key port : string = "JobService";
        sensor sload : integer = median(load);
        actuator run(job : string) = start(job)[load,1,"<="];
        actuator create = ...;
        ...
    end
end

when server(Name).load > 5 do
    job = First(server(Name).jobs);
    server(Name).suspend(job);
    service("JobService").run(job);
end

when SIZE(service("JobService")) < 3 or
    during service("JobService").sload > 5 for 60
        always service("JobService").sload) > 5
do
    create(...);
end
```

Figure 2: Job service

5 Discussion

The Meta project has explored the feasibility of toolkit-based architecture for building reactive systems and has applied this approach to distributed application management. Meta provides a uniform way of interconnecting disparate components, facilitating both the design of new systems and the construction of systems glued together from existing applications. Our approach has the benefit of separating management policies from their implementation that is, how those policies are carried out.

5.1 Related Work

Although much work has been done on system monitoring, our work differs in that it combines control with monitoring to provide the general architectural support needed to construct a class of reactive systems. A prominent example of a system designed strictly for monitoring is the work of Snodgrass [Sno88]; in his work, the system state is cast as a temporal database. Systems for debugging (especially those for debugging distributed systems), are a specialization of general monitoring systems. These systems provide a way to access the system state and to watch for certain predicates to be satisfied through the use of breakpoints [MH89, Bat88]. Of particular interest is the system IDD [HHK85] that permits interval logic expressions in specifying breakpoints.

Lomita is a rule-based language built on a real-time extension of interval logic. The rule-based language we have found most similar to Lomita is L.0 [CCNS90]. However, this executable language does not deal with the problem of instrumenting existing applications nor does it use a sensor-actuator data model. Configuration systems such as Conic [JKS89] overlap with the use of Meta for distributed application management in that they facilitate interconnecting components, but they lack the means for specifying reactive behavior.

5.2 The ISIS System

Much of Meta depends upon facilities provided by the ISIS toolkit. One such facility is the notion of a *group*. An ISIS group is a named dynamic set of processes. Each member of the group has the same view of which processes are currently in the group despite other processes asynchronously joining the group, leaving the group and crashing. Among other uses, Meta uses ISIS process groups to implement atomicity of aggregate invocation and to organize the members of an aggregate.

Providing consistent behavior in Meta relies heavily upon the notion of *virtual synchrony* provided by the ISIS system [BJKS88]. The ISIS system makes asynchronous events such as message receipts and group membership changes appear to happen synchronously. This property greatly facilitates reasoning about system behavior and constructing a system that behaves in a consistent manner. Fundamental to this property is the notion of an ordered broadcast. ISIS provides two important broadcast primitives [BSS91]: *abcast*, which totally orders the broadcasts to a group, and *cbcast* which partially orders the broadcasts to a group dependent on the causal order of the broadcasts. For example, if two apparently concurrent events occur in the instrumented application, Meta can impose a global total order on these events by using *abcast*.

5.3 Status

The current version of Meta as of this writing (Spring 1992) is Version 2.1, which is publicly available via anonymous ftp from Cornell University. This version provides the low-level Meta facilities but does not yet include the Lomita language.

A detailed discussion of Meta's performance appears in [Woo91]. We summarize here the execution times for executing a simple guarded command of the form when A do B for both the case when A and B are local to the stub executing the rule and for the case where they are accessed via a remote stub. These benchmarks were obtained by running Meta version 2.1 on Sun 4/60s connected via a 10 Mbps Ethernet with the interprocess communication handled by ISIS. The time to execute when A do B with trivial local sensor A and trivial local actuator B is 127.1 ±0.8 microseconds. This implies approximately 8,000 guarded commands can be executed a second. Much of the time required to execute this guard is consumed in reevaluating the value of the local sensor A and updating the stub's sensor cache. The bulk of the time for remote actions is of course in the message delivery.

Running the previous simple guarded command at a remote interpreter takes 25.4 ±0.5 milliseconds. This time includes the cost of sending the sensor value to the remote interpreter, and the cost of the interpreter carrying out an RPC to perform the actuation. The cost of remote communication is determined by the cost of the underlying communications system, in this case, the ISIS toolkit running on top of UNIX.

5.4 Directions

Meta, as it stands, is somewhat awkward to use, and so we are currently concentrating on supplying a better environment for writing control programs. A major part of this effort is the Lomita language that was mentioned in this paper. We also have been developing a Lomita runtime and have a basic version operational. This program is a distributed service that reads object files produced by Lomita, manages the distribution and placement of rules, and supplies a basic set of NPL debugging commands.

The current Meta toolkit is adequate for use in systems in which timing is not crucial. Although guarded commands can make temporal assertions, given the potentially unbounded latencies in the underlying UNIX and ISIS platforms, such assertions can only be viewed as approximate upper bounds. However, the structure that Meta provides is general enough that we should be able to extend it to real-time reactive systems as well.

There are two main obstacles we see to extending Meta to real-time systems. The first has to do with the underlying ISIS toolkit; to guarantee bounded reaction time, the underlying causal broadcast and group membership protocols must provide some real-time guarantees. A companion project in the ISIS group is currently looking into structuring ISIS under Mach to provide these two protocols. The second obstacle has to do with the semantics of guarded commands. Guarded commands currently have the semantics of atomic actions; if a guarded command is continuously enabled, then it will eventually execute. We need to add an upper bound on how long the command can be enabled without executing, and then build a scheduler that either guarantees the command will be executed within its deadline or aborts the command if it cannot be executed within its deadline.

Acknowledgments

Several people have contributed to the Meta project. Nancy Thoman designed and wrote the first version of the guarded command language, and Wanda Chiu designed a reactive relational database that provided a testbed for earlier versions of Meta. Kenneth Birman and Robert Cooper have contributed much to the design of the overall system. We would also like to thank Robert Cooper and Laura Sabel for their helpful comments on earlier drafts of this paper.

References

[Bat88] Peter Bates. Debugging heterogeneous distributed systems using event-based models of behavior. In *SIGPLAN/SIGOPS Workshop on Parallel and Distributed Debugging*. ACM, 1988.

[BJKS88] Kenneth P. Birman, Thomas A. Joseph, Kenneth Kane, and Frank Schmuck. *ISIS — A Distributed Programming Environment User's Guide and Reference Manual*. Department of Computer Science, Cornell University, second edition, June 1988.

[BSS91] Kenneth Birman, Andre Schiper, and Pat Stephenson. Lightweight causal and atomic group multicast. *ACM Transactions on Computer Systems*, 9(3):272-314, August 1991.

[CCNS90] E.J. Cameron, D.M. Cohen, L.A. Ness, and H.N. Srinidhi. L.0: A language for modeling and prototyping communications software. Technical Report ARH-015547, Bellcore, April 1990.

[Che76] P.P.-S. Chen. The entity-relationship model — toward a unified view of data. *ACM Transactions on Database Systems*, 1(1):9-36, March 1976.

[CM91] Paul Chew and Keith Marzullo. Masking failures of multidimensional sensors. In *Proceedings of the Tenth Symposium on Reliable Distributed Systems*, pages 32-41, October 1991.

[HHK85] Paul K. Harter, Dennis M. Heimbigner, and Roger King. IDD: An interactive distributed debugger. In *Proceedings of the Fifth International Conference on Distributed Computing Systems*, pages 498-506, 1985.

[JKS89] Jeff Magee, Jeff Kramer, and Morris Sloman. Constructing distributed systems in Conic. *IEEE Transactions on Software Engineering*, 15(6):663-675, June 1989.

[LS84] Leslie Lamport and Fred B. Schneider. The "Hoare logic" of csp, and all that. *ACM Transactions on Programming Languages and Systems*, 6(2):281-296, April 1984.

[Mar90] Keith Marzullo. Tolerating failures of continuous-valued sensors. *ACM Transactions on Computer Systems*, 8(4):284-304, November 1990.

[MCWB91] Keith Marzullo, Robert Cooper, Mark Wood, and Kenneth P. Birman. Tools for distributed application management. *IEEE Computer*, 24(8):42-51, August 1991.

[MH89] Charles E. McDowell and David P. Helmbold. Debugging concurrent programs. *ACM Computing Surveys*, 21(4), December 1989.

[Sch90] Fred B. Schneider. Implementing fault-tolerant services using the state machine approach: A tutorial. *ACM Computing Surveys*, 22(4):299-319, December 1990.

[SMSV83] R.L. Schwartz, P.M. Melliar-Smith, and F.H. Vogt. An interval logic for higher-level temporal reasoning. In *Proceedings of the Second Symposium on Principles of Distributed Computing*, pages 173-186. ACM SIGPLAN/SIGOPS, 1983.

[Sno88] Richard Snodgrass. A relational approach to monitoring complex systems. *ACM Transactions on Computer Systems*, 6(2):157-196, May 1988.

[Woo91] Mark D. Wood. Fault-tolerant management of distributed applications using the reactive system architecture. PhD thesis, Cornell University, December 1991.

Distributing Objects

Andrew Herbert
Architecture Projects Management Limited
Cambridge, England
ajh@ansa.co.uk

Abstract

Similar concepts, called objects, have appeared in several areas of computing, from object-oriented databases, object-oriented programming languages, application environments and graphical user interfaces. These concepts have been reviewed by Alan Snyder of HP in a technical report called "The Essence of Objects." This paper builds upon Snyder's analysis and presents the requirements for adding distribution to the object concept. It is written for an audience who understand object orientation, accept Snyder's principles, and want to know how distribution might modify them.

What are objects?

Similar concepts, called objects, have appeared in several areas of computing, from object-oriented databases (such as Iris [Fis87a]); object-oriented programming languages (such as C++ [Str86a]), and Smalltalk [Gol83]; application environments (such as MacApp [Sch86a], ET++ [Wei88a], HP New Wave Environment [Hew89a]); and graphical user interfaces (such as the HP New Wave Desktop).

These concepts have been reviewed by Alan Snyder of HP in a technical report called "The Essence of Objects," [Sny89a] (a revision of which is scheduled for publication by *IEEE Software* during 1991). This paper builds upon Snyder's analysis and presents the requirements for adding distribution to the object concept. It is written for an audience who understand object orientation, accept Snyder's principles and want to know how distribution might modify them.

Definitions and commentary taken from Snyder's report are shown in italics.

The essentials of objects

Snyder characterizes the essential principles of objects as follows:

1. *An object is not just bits*

    1.1 An object embodies an **abstraction**

    1.2 An object provides **services**

2. Clients **request** services from objects

    2.1 Objects are **encapsulated**

    2.2 Clients issue requests

An earlier version of this paper was published in *Proceedings of EurOpen Spring '91 Conference*, 1991, Tromsø, Norway, and as an Architecture Projects Management, Ltd. technical report.

2.3 Requests are named

   2.4 Requests identify objects

   2.5 Requests may take arguments and produce results

   2.6 Services can be described

3. Requests can be *generic*

4. Objects may be organized *hierarchically* in terms of the services they provide

5. Objects may be organized *hierarchically* in terms of the degree to which they share a common implementation

   5.1 Objects may share a common implementation (multiple *instances*)

   5.2 Objects may partially share a common implementation (*implementation inheritance*).

The following sections explore the effect of distribution upon these principles.

1 An object is not just bits

*An object is not just a data structure. It embodies an abstraction that is meaningful to its clients (users or programs). The purpose of the data is to represent abstract information. An object is more than just information: it provides a set of services to its clients. These services correspond to the embodied abstraction — they do more than just read and write data. The services are carried out by executing code that accesses or manipulates the actual data. The set of services provided by an object is called the **behaviour** of the object.*

This principle shows the benefit of object-orientation in **heterogeneous** systems since it separates the service provided by an object from the implementation of that service.

> *Benefit:* Objects provide application independence — different implementations of a service can be provided for different environments based on different programming languages, operating systems or hardware, provided that a uniform way of interworking with services is provided.

> *Benefit*: Objects enable controlled, incremental evolution of a system — the implementation of a service can be changed **transparently** to all the clients of that service.

2 Clients request services from objects

Clients respect the intent to use data to represent abstractions. Instead of directly accessing the data, clients issue requests for service that are carried out by objects.

2.1 Objects are encapsulated

This principle is the basis for using objects in distributed systems: since objects are encapsulated they need not be in the same place as their clients provided that some means is provided for clients to identify and remotely access an object's services. Approaching the principle from the opposite direction, distribution — in the sense of separate location — enforces the encapsulation of objects and prevents direct access to data.

In non-distributed systems, the benefit of encapsulation is to guarantee that an object satisfies application-defined integrity constraints since there is no direct client contact with the data. The encapsulation property of objects equates two notions — objects as:

1. A unit of *service*, or unit of representation. This is an object in the sense of a design, or a representation of a part of a system. Within the object the design or representation can change without affecting the rest of the system.

   Benefit: Objects provide strong modularity in design and permit incremental development and evolution of designs.

2. A unit of *programming*: an object in an object-oriented programming language, for instance. A unit of service would be made up of one, or more, units of programming.

   Benefit: Objects in programs can be subject to scope-checking to ensure that a program maintains the modularity of the design it implements and that the objects are separately compiled and linked into multiple programs.

In distributed systems there are further integrity constraints which have to be met by encapsulation: the different types of encapsulation needed are:

3. A unit of *distribution* — encapsulation for objects that may migrate around a distributed system independently from other objects, but must remain integral within themselves.

   Benefit: Objects can migrate from one computer to offload functionality from a processor being taken out of service, to balance load between processors, to bring data to the processor where it is being used to reduce latency, to move data out to storage services when it is not in current use without involving the object's clients.

4. A unit of *failure* — encapsulation for objects such that all of an object fails, or none of it does. This is usually achieved by keeping the whole object on the same processor.

   Benefits: Replication techniques can be used to make fault tolerant implementations of critical objects; distributed applications can be written to provide "graceful degradation" in the presence of object failures.

5. A unit of *security* — encapsulation such that all of the components of an object are subject to the same access control rules. This usually means the components belong to the same principal and that interaction within the components of the object is not subject to access control.

   Benefits: Hardware protection mechanisms can be used to physically enforce object encapsulation; encipherment can be used to physically protect request and responses between objects.

In a distributed system, the boundaries of these units are not identical; but in modelling and discussing object-oriented distributed systems each of these different units is collectively known as an "object." All of these units exist in an object-oriented programming system, but they are implicit and implicitly bound to the program unit. Consequently, the object-oriented programming concept of an object can be seen as a simplification of the more general concept of object which arises in object-oriented distributed systems.

The challenge in a distributed system is to manage the different units (objects) at run-time with a mixture of programming language and configuration tools; but without the simplifications of a single programming environment and recompilation assumed by object-oriented programming systems.

2.2 Clients issue requests

Clients issue requests for services that are carried out by objects. A request causes code to be executed to perform the requested service. The details of where and how this code runs are intentionally not of concern to the client.

In a distributed system there may be many clients on separate processors simultaneously requesting the same service and therefore a server object must be able to exercise concurrency control over requests. Concurrency control takes two forms:

1. *Ordering and synchronization*: the server may require that requests be processed one at a time, or that only certain sequences of overlapped execution are possible (for example, producers and consumers can both access a finite buffer while there are free slots in it), or that only a certain number of requests be executed at once to limit the consumption of resources.

2. *Separation*: the server may require that sequences of requests from separate clients be scheduled in an order that avoids conflicting updates to the data contained in the object (for example conflicts between reads and write to the records of a data base object). A client may wish to abandon a sequence of requests if an intermediate request produces a particular result (e.g. a debit on an empty account), or if an object to be invoked as part of the sequence fails. This requires that the execution model support the notion of *committing* and *aborting* sequences of requests and the correct interplay of *commit* and *abort* with the scheduling mechanisms for separation (i.e. transaction processing capabilities).

In a distributed system objects may be remote from their clients, introducing a latency due to the overheads of communication. A client may be able to reduce latency by making concurrent requests to different objects (or even the same object if its concurrency controls permit). It must be possible to indicate that a concurrent request is either part of a transaction or starting a new independent transaction.

2.3 Requests are named

Requests are typically named. To make a request, the client identifies the request by name.

2.4 Requests identify objects

To make a request a client must identify one or more objects to perform the requested service. An object can be identified directly or reliably. Object reference is direct in the sense that one is naming the object not describing it. Object reference is reliable in that, within certain limits of time and space, repeating reference to an object will reliably access the same object.

Requests are directed towards objects which are units of service; it may be that an object which is a unit of distribution encapsulates several units of service. The latter can be conveniently termed the *interfaces* of the distributed object (and thus objects in object-oriented programming languages can be equated with distributed objects containing just one interface). For example, there may be some data which is encapsulated in a single object for reasons of security, but for which there is the notion of both "user" services and "manager" services. The two forms of service can be readily distinguished by putting each in a separate interface. In a distributed system requests identify **interfaces**.

In many distributed systems there is no notion of "system restart" and so an object (i.e. interface) reference has to retain its meaning for all time. Nor can it be assumed that separate distributed systems will never become joined (for example when the organizations merge or do business with one another) and so an interface reference has to retain its meaning throughout space.

It may not be possible in a distributed system to distinguish between an object which cannot be accessed because of disruption of communications and an object which has become lost from the system because it did not take steps to ensure its reliability. Clients must be prepared to cope with the failure of communication, and objects which use replication to increase their stability must take steps to ensure the replicas present a consistent service to their clients even if replicas are unable to communicate with one another.

Since objects may migrate in a distributed system, interface references must be **location independent** names. A distributed system must include a **location service** for discovering the current location — i.e. address — of objects which have migrated so that requests can be delivered to the correct place. (For objects which will never migrate the interface reference can include an address for the interface to save on the time overheads of name to address resolution and the potentially vast overhead of storing name to address translations for all interfaces).

Client to server binding can be **early** or **late**. In early binding client and server are made together and an interface reference for the servers embedded in the client. Late binding is a dynamic process, called **trading**. A server object providing a service registers (or has registered on its behalf) a description of the service provided and its interface identifier with a **trading service**. A client object wanting to use a service queries the trading service, and if a matching service offer is found its interface reference is returned. The client can then use the interface reference to make requests.

Both location and trading services may be built upon **name services** which provide name-to-name translations.

Service descriptions given by servers and clients must necessarily describe the range of services available at the interface so that the client gets access to an object providing at least the service required. There may be many objects providing a suitable service and therefore service descriptions may involve names and attributes to permit disambiguation between service offers. For example a service may be further qualified by its location, who owns it, how secure it is, how fast it is, how robust it is against failures, and so on.

If a client makes purely functional use of a service (i.e. does not require that the service keep state on its behalf), the client may elect to rebind on every request rather than retain the interface reference found on the first attempt at trading. Alternatively, a functional client may only rebind if the service it is using becomes inaccessible because of failure or communications problems.

> *Benefit*: Providing a trading service makes a system configuration open-ended — new objects can be added to the system and made accessible to existing clients without

requiring that the clients be rebuilt in any way. Interface references (i.e. addresses) need not be built into programs.

2.5 Requests may take arguments and produce results

Particularly in a computational context (as opposed to a user interface), it is commonly the case that a request may have associated argument values (which may be object references) and the service may return one or more results (which may also be object references) when it completes.

In a distributed system all arguments and results have to be either interface references or immutable data types (i.e. integers, booleans, characters, etc.). It is not meaningful to pass pointers since client and server may not be on the same computer. (Some systems give the illusion of passing pointers by wrapping them up as an interface reference to a service for accessing memory locations, or by copying the data referenced by the pointer).

Passing an interface reference gives the recipient the right to share in the use of a service (hence the need for the concurrency controls mentioned in Section 2.2). Passing an immutable data type requires that a copy of the data type be made at the recipient. In a computational model in which all data types are objects, both these schemes can be viewed as providing sharing semantics, as can other schemes such as migrating the object to the recipient, or replicating the object so that both sender and recipient have local copies kept in step by some sort of consistency protocol.

Benefit: Treating all arguments and results as interface references (i.e. a pure object model of data) provides a clean computational abstraction of a wide range of argument and result passing schemes. Alternative schemes can be substituted without requiring changes to the programs involved.

Many programming languages only permit a request to return a single data type as result. Often what is returned is a memory address for a data structure made by the called service. Since memory addresses cannot be permitted as results in distributed systems, an interface reference to a result object constructed by the service would have to be used instead. But this then imposes a significant latency overhead when the recipient of the reference tries to access the object. Therefore in a distributed system it should always be possible to pass multiple arguments and obtain multiple results.

In a distributed system a request may fail because of some communications problem or resource limitation. This fact has to be conveyed back to the caller as an abnormal outcome of the request. It may also be that the service has several possible outcomes. These could be encoded as a data type — a discriminated union for example; alternatively a general mechanism permitting a request to generate different outcomes could be provided, with facilities for the requester to take different actions depending upon the particular outcome obtained for any given request.

The synchronous request-response style of interaction is well suited to distributed computing. It matches well with the concept of **remote procedure call** found in many distributed systems architectures. It also fits well with the concept of **nested transactions** as a way of providing the kinds of atomicity guarantees given in Section 2.2. Note that a request which returns no results is strictly a request that returns an "empty" response — the response contains no results, but there is an explicit indication of termination. Request-response interactions create chains of dependent nested calls. In 2.2 it was noted that there is a need to establish new independent activities: this can be modelled by a service which can be requested but which produces no response at all — a "fire and forget" style of interaction.

It is useful to compare conventional object-orientation and remote procedure call in terms of the object with the "multiple interfaces, each interface supporting several services" model outlined above. Conventional object-oriented systems merge the concepts of object and interface into the single concept "object" and thereby lose the ability to determine which services are available to which clients and the ability to distinguish clients by giving each one a separate interface and associating client state with the interface used. Remote procedure systems merge the concept of interface and request together into the concept procedure and thereby lose the benefits of encapsulation and abstraction that come from grouping services together. Some remote procedure call systems do provide the notion of interface so that services can be grouped to form an abstraction, but they do not provide means to pass such interfaces as arguments and results, and therefore lack the flexibility of object-oriented systems. The general object / interfaces / services model supports both conventional object-orientation and remote procedure call as a special case.

2.6 Services can be described

The set of services provided by an object to its clients is often made explicit to clients in the form of an **interface description** *that identifies a set of requests that can be made to an object. This interface description is sometimes called a protocol. Often this specification will include information about the expected arguments and results associated with each request. Such a specification is sometimes called a signature.*

(In distributed systems the term protocol usually refers to the means provided by networks to copy data from one computer to another.)

Services must be described by signatures in distributed systems, since clients and servers are often written by different programmers in different locations and at different times. The signature provides a contract between the two programmers, telling them what service is to be provided at an interface to an object. It may be that the two programmers use different languages to write their programs and the programs run on computers with different data representations. The signature provides the information need to automatically generate the data type conversions needed to permit interworking between client and server.

Benefit: Signatures permit decoupling of client and server programs and the use of multiple implementation languages.

As discussed in Section 2.4, there may be many objects providing the same service — i.e. with the same signature. Therefore in a trading system additional attributes beyond signatures must be used to distinguish between different offers of the same service.

3 Requests can be generic

A client can issue the same request to different kinds of objects that provide "similar" (at least homonymous) services. Depending upon which objects are identified by the client, different code may be run to perform the requested service. The selection of code to execute is based on the object identified by the clients in the request. In the general case, the identification of objects is not determined until the request is actually issued, so the selection of code would happen at that time. (In some cases information exists at compile time or link time to statically bind a request to the code that will implement it.) Also in the general case there is no limit on the number of different kinds of object that may support a given request.

The benefit of generic request in distributed systems is that services can be more general, which implies more re-usable, and that users benefit by being able to apply a standard model in many cases. For example all objects can be made to support a common management model by requiring they support a common management interface.

An open system is one in which new objects can be introduced dynamically, such that the new objects can be operated upon by existing clients, without changing the existing clients. The existing clients are able to use the new objects because the new objects support the requests for generic services made by the existing clients.

Benefit: Openness is mandatory requirement for practical distributed systems.

4 Objects may be organized hierarchically in terms of the services they provide

Objects can be classified in terms of the services they provide to clients or equivalently, in terms of the requests that can be made of them. Objects that provide the same set of services would be classified together. This classification may be based on explicit descriptions of services (or requests) called interfaces.

(Note: since the term "interface" has a particular meaning in distributed systems — see 2.4 above — classifications of services will be called **types** in the following discussion.)

An object could provide a subset of the services provided by another object, leading to a hierarchical classification. This interface hierarchy can be used as a type hierarchy in describing permissible values for arguments to procedures in a program, etc.

Benefit: A classification of objects based on their services is a way of organizing objects to make their behaviours easier to understand. A classification of object services can also be used to describe the services expected of an object by a client.

The need for type descriptions — signatures — in distributed systems was discussed in Section 2.6. Organizing types hierarchically eases the burden of writing such descriptions since a complex service can be defined as being an extension of a set of simpler services. This is particularly useful when there are large numbers of generic requests that can be made of an object.

The existence of a type hierarchy means that the model of type-checking in a distributed system should be one of **type conformance** rather than type equality: a client request is acceptable to an object if the object is capable of responding to the request, if the client offers arguments which conform to those expected by the server and if the server returns results which conform to those expected by the client. The use of type conformance increases the genericity of objects and hence the openness to service evolution in a system since it permits an object to incrementally "widen" the type of an interface without disrupting the client.

5 Objects may be organized hierarchically in terms of the degree by which they share a common implementation

Mechanisms are generally provided (in object systems) to allow different objects to share the same implementation. Mechanisms are often provided by which the implementation of one object can not only share the implementation of another object, but also extend or refine it.

5.1 Objects may share a common implementation (instances)

The implementation of an object generally specifies both the format of the data used to represent the information associated with an object and the code used to implement the services it provides. Mechanisms are generally provided to allow different objects to share the same implementation. Objects that share a common implementation have identical data formats and share executable code; however each object has its own copy of the actual data. Objects that share the same implementation would be classified together. Each object can be thought of as an **instance** *of the common implementation.*

It is the sharing of implementations that is of primary interest, not the classification resulting from it. In general clients should be concerned with the services provided by an object, not how the services are implemented, and thus should not be interested in an implementation-oriented classification.

> *Benefit*: Sharing one implementation among many objects has the obvious benefit of reduced source code duplication (which eases maintenance by avoiding the need for manual propagation of changes) and reduced executable code size (where sharing of executable code is possible).

In a distributed system there may be instances of a common implementation on many different computers with different data representations and instruction formats, so sharing of a single execution image and data format is not possible (except in the special case where several instances reside on the same computer).

Some object systems are **reactive** in that a change to the source code for a set of instances is immediately reflected in a change in behaviour of the instances. This is a difficult effect to achieve in a distributed system; it raises many questions about consistency and atomicity since there is not a single copy of the executable code to be updated.

Programmers may wish to exercise control over where an instance is created. This is readily accomplished by providing **factory** services which create new instances upon demand. A factory service embodies a template for the class of which the object to be made is an instance. All the objects made by the same factory may share the same data format and executable code.

If an object is to be able to migrate from one computer to another means must be provided for the object to externalize itself into a representation which can be moved between machines and re-instantiated at the destination. In the general case, the external representation must include information about all the activities that were taking place inside the object at the moment it began migrating. If the source and destination computers are identical, the external representation can be close to the internal representation. If the potential destinations for a migrating object are known in advance the size of the external representation can be reduced by pre-arranging for the code and data formats to exist at the destinations.

5.2 Objects may partially share a common implementation

Mechanisms are often provided by which the implementation of one object can not only share the implementation of another object, but also extend or refine it. (Such mechanisms are generally called **inheritance** *mechanisms.) In this case of partial sharing implementations, the classification of object implementations becomes hierarchical.*

> *Benefits*: In addition to the maintenance and size benefits listed above, partial sharing of implementations extends the benefits of software re-use to cases where implementations are similar but not identical. Partial sharing is a useful technique for encouraging consistent behaviour among related objects.

Inheritance has a number of properties that make it unsuitable for general use in distributed systems [Raj89a] :

1. *Encapsulation is violated* — Inheritance may violate encapsulation in at least three ways: a subclass may (a) refer to data defined in the superclass, (b) request an internal service of the superclass, and (c), refer to the superclasses of its superclasses. The consequence of this in a distributed system is that the locality of objects is lost — inheritance introduces object dependence on unknown, potentially remote, inherited information defeating the major benefits of objects as independent units of migration, failure propagation and security.

2. *Classes are not automatically reusable* — For successful reuse, inheritance requires the use of a set of coding rules and a set of design rules to ensure consistent interpretations. In a distributed context it is not viable to expect all code to be written to the same conventions except in as much as there must be a commitment to the same means of interaction between objects. The internal structure of objects is a local concern guided by the implementor's local rules. (Indeed it cannot be assumed in a distributed system that all implementors are using object-oriented languages, let alone the same language and the same inheritance structure!)

3. *Class organization is not scalable* — Inheritance is successful where software is written by a few people working together with an agreed hierarchy and where the number of classes is hundreds at most; inheritance falls down when there are large numbers of classes involved or where there are large numbers of people involved.

4. *Reactive inheritance is difficult to achieve* — Reactive inheritance requires a consistent, atomic update be made to all members of a class and its sub-classes wherever they are located.

5. *There should be no linkage between typing and implementation* — The desirability of types as a means to permit multiple implementations of the same service has already been discussed. Many object-oriented systems use inheritance as a substitute for type-checking — two objects are deemed to be of the same type if they are made from the same components. This is too restrictive a view for a distributed system. Implementations have no part to play in the classification of services.

Thus implementation inheritance has little part to play in distributed systems. The objectives of maintenance and re-use must be met by techniques for the identification, sharing, and composition of source code components alone. (Only where a same component is referenced several times by objects which are going to be co-located on the same computer is there scope for sharing object code as an optimization.) If maintenance and re-use are conducted at this level, many other tools beyond inheritance become available for classifying and linking together software components. Distributed systems are facilitated by objects whose definition and implementation are fully self-contained.

References

[Fis87a]   D.H. Fishman, "Iris: An Object-Oriented Data Base System," *ACM Transaction on Office Automation Systems*, 5 (1), pp. 48-69, 1987.

[Hew89a]   Hewlett-Packard, "HP New Wave User Guide," Part number 5958-9678, August 1989.

[Raj89a]   R.K. Rajand and H.M. Levy, "A Compositional Model for Software Reuse," Technical Report TR 89-01-04, Department of Computer Science, University of Washington, Washington, 1989.

[Gol83]   A. Goldberg and D. Robson, *SmallTalk 80: The Language and Its Implementation*, Addison-Wesley, Reading, Massachusetts, 1983.

[Sch86a]   K.J. Schmucker, "MacApp: An Application Framework," *Byte,* 11 (8), pp. 189-193, August, 1986.

[Sny89a]   A. Snyder, "The Essence of Objects," Report STL-89-25, Hewlett-Packard Laboratories, Palo Alto, California, 1989.

[Str86a]   B.J. Stroustrup, *The C++ Programming Language*, Addison-Wesley, Reading, Massachusetts, 1986.

[Wei88a]   A. Weinand, E. Gamma, and R. Marty, "ET++ — An Object-Oriented Application Framework in C++," *Proceedings OOPSLA 1989,* pp. 46-57, 1988.

A Comparative Study of Five Parallel Programming Languages

Henri E. Bal
Dept. of Mathematics and Computer Science
Vrije Universiteit
Amsterdam
bal@cs.vu.nl

Abstract

Many different paradigms for parallel programming exist, nearly each of which is employed in dozens of languages. Several researchers have tried to compare these languages and paradigms by examining the expressivity and flexibility of their constructs. Few attempts have been made, however, at practical studies based on actual programming experience with multiple languages. Such a study is the topic of this paper.*

We will look at five parallel languages, all based on different paradigms. The languages are: SR (based on message passing), Emerald (concurrent objects), Parlog (parallel Horn clause logic), Linda (Tuple Space), and Orca (logically shared data). We have implemented the same parallel programs in each language, using real parallel machines. The paper reports on our experiences in implementing three frequently occurring communication patterns: message passing through a mailbox, one-to-many communication, and access to replicated shared data.

1 Introduction

During the previous decade, a staggering number of languages for programming parallel and distributed systems has emerged [And83, Bal89]. These languages are based on widely different programming paradigms, such as message passing, concurrent objects, logic, and functional programming. Both within each paradigm and between paradigms, heated discussions are held about which approach is best [Car89b, Kah89, Sha89].

The intent of this paper is to cast new light on these discussions, using a practical approach. We have implemented a number of parallel applications in each of several parallel languages. Based on this experience, we will draw some conclusions about the relative advantages and disadvantages of each language. So, unlike most of the discussions in the literature, this paper is based on actual programming experience in several parallel languages on real parallel systems.

The languages studied in this paper obviously do not cover the whole spectrum of design choices. Still, they represent a significant subset of what we feel are the most important paradigms for parallel programming. We discuss only a single language for each paradigm, although other languages may exist within each paradigm that are significantly different.

The languages that have been selected for this study are: SR, Emerald, Parlog, Linda, and Orca (see Table 1). SR represents message passing languages. It provides a range of message sending and receiving constructs, rather than a single model. Emerald is an object-based

---

[*] This research was supported in part by the Netherlands Organization for Scientific Research (N.W.O.). A Preliminary version of the paper appeared in the *Proceedings of the PRISMA Workshop on Parallel Database Systems*, Noordwijk, The Netherlands, September 1990.

This paper was previously published in *Proceedings of EurOpen Spring '91 Conference*, 1991, Tromsø, Norway, and in *Future Generations Computer Systems*, Vol. 8, 1992, pp. 121-135.

language. Parlog is a concurrent logic language. Linda is a set of language primitives based on the Tuple Space model. Orca is representative of the Distributed Shared Memory model.

Table 1: Overview of the languages discussed in the paper

Language	Paradigm	Origin
SR	Message passing	University of Arizona
Emerald	Concurrent object-based language	University of Washington
Parlog	Concurrent logic language	Imperial College
Linda	Tuple space	Yale University
Orca	Distributed shared memory	Vrije Universiteit

We focus on languages for parallel applications, where the aim is to achieve a speedup on a single application. These applications can be run on either *multiprocessors* with shared memory or *distributed* systems without shared memory. We have selected only languages that are suitable for *both* architectures. So, we do not discuss shared-variable or monitor-based languages, since their usage is restricted to shared-memory multiprocessors. Functional languages are not discussed either. Most functional languages are intended for different parallel architectures, (e.g., dataflow or graph reduction machines) and often try to hide parallelism from the programmer. This makes an objective comparison with the other languages hard. We also do not deal with distributed languages based on atomic transactions (e.g., Argus [Lis88]), since these are primarily intended for fault-tolerant applications. The issue of fault-tolerant parallel programming is discussed in a separate paper [Bal92c].

The outline of the rest of this paper is as follows. In Section 2, we will briefly describe the applications we have used, focusing on their communication patterns. Next, in Sections 3 to 7, we will discuss each of the five languages, one language per section. Each section has the following structure:

- Background information on the language. (All languages have been described in a recent survey paper [Bal89], so we will be very brief here.)
- A description of our programming experience. We will comment on the ease of learning the language and on the effort needed to implement the communication patterns discussed in Section 2.
- Comments on the language implementation and its performance. Unfortunately, there is no single platform on which all the languages run, so we had to use many different platforms. The systems we used differ in the number of processors, processor type and speed, as well as in the way processors are interconnected. A fair comparison between the languages is therefore not possible, but the measurements do give some rough indication of the relative speedups that can be obtained.
- Conclusions on the language.

Finally, in Section 8, we will compare the approaches used for the different languages.

2 The applications and their communication patterns

There are many ways to compare parallel languages. One way is a theoretical study of the expressiveness of their primitives. This works well for languages using the same paradigm (e.g., message passing), but is more problematic for comparison between different paradigms. Comparing, say, remote procedure calls and shared logical variables is not a trivial task.

Distributed Open Systems

The approach taken in this paper is to implement a set of small, yet realistic, problems in each language, and compare the resulting programs. The example problems we have used include matrix multiplication, the All Pairs Shortest Paths problem, the Traveling Salesman Problem, alpha-beta search, and successive over relaxation.

The applications and the algorithms used for them are described in detail in [Bal90b]. For this paper, we will restrict ourselves to only two applications: the All Pairs Shortest Paths problem and the Traveling Salesman Problem. These applications will be described below. We will focus on the communication aspects of the applications, since, from a parallel programming point of view, these are most interesting.

2.1 The Traveling Salesman Problem (TSP)

The Traveling Salesman Problem computes the shortest route for a salesman among a given set of cities. The program uses a simple branch-and-bound algorithm and is based on replicated workers style parallelism [And91, Car86a]. The TSP program uses two interesting communication patterns: mailboxes and replicated shared data.

A *mailbox* (see Figure 1a) is a communication port with **send** (nonblocking) and **receive** operations [Bal89]. Mailboxes can be contrasted with direct message passing, in which the sender always specifies the destination process (receiver) of the message. With mailboxes, any process that can access the mailbox can receive a message sent to it. So, each message sent to a mailbox is handled by one process, but it is not determined in advance which process will accept the message.

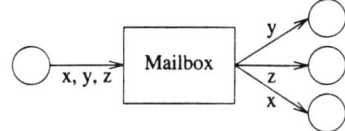

(a) **Message passing through a mailbox (used by TSP).**

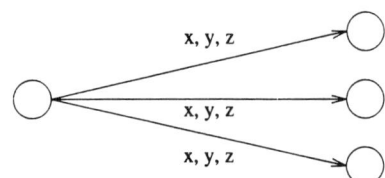

(b) **One-to-many communication (used by ASP).**

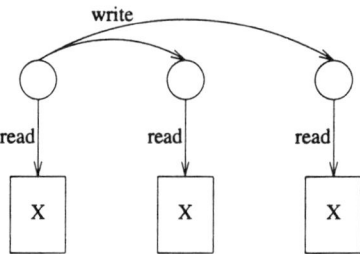

(c) **Communication through replicated shared data (used by TSP).**

Figure 1. Communication patterns used by the two applications discussed in the paper.

The TSP program uses a mailbox for distributing work. A process that has computed a new job (to be executed in parallel) sends it to a mailbox, where it will eventually be picked up by an idle worker process. Since it is not known in advance which worker process will accept the job, mailbox communication is required here, rather than direct message passing.

The second communication pattern used in the TSP program is *replicated shared data* (see Figure 1c). The branch-and-bound algorithm requires a global variable containing the length of the current best solution. This variable is used for pruning partial solutions whose initial paths are already longer than the current best full route.

In a distributed system, this global variable cannot be put in shared memory, since such systems lack shared memory. One solution is to store the variable on one processor and let other processors access it through remote operations. For TSP (and many other applications), however, a much more efficient solution is possible. The bound is usually changed (improved) only a few times, but may be used millions of times by each processor, so its read/write ratio is very high. Therefore, the variable can be implemented efficiently by *replicating* it in the local memories of the processors. Each processor can directly read the variable. Physical communication only occurs when the variable is written, which happens infrequently.

2.2 The All Pairs Shortest Paths problem (ASP)

The second application is the All Pairs Shortest Paths problem, which computes the lengths of the shortest paths between each pair of nodes in a given graph. ASP uses a parallel iterative algorithm. Each processor is assigned a fixed portion of the rows of the distances matrix. At the beginning of each iteration, one process sends a *pivot row* of the matrix to all the other processes. Each process then uses this pivot row to update its portion of the matrix.

The most important communication pattern of the ASP program thus is *one-to-many* communication (see Figure 1b). This pattern transmits data from one process to many others, *all* of which use these data. (In contrast, a message sent to a mailbox is used by only *one* process.)

Of course, this pattern can be simulated through multiple point-to-point messages, but frequently much better solutions are possible. Many networks have a *multicast* or *broadcast* capability, which can be used to speed up one-to-many communication significantly. So, there are two issues involved here: how one-to-many communication is *expressed* in a given language and how it is actually *implemented*. For ASP, it is very important that the implementation uses a real multicast. Otherwise, the communication costs may easily become a dominating factor.

3 Synchronizing Resources (SR)

SR [And86, And88] is a language for writing distributed programs, developed by Greg Andrews, Ron Olsson, and their colleagues at the University of Arizona and the University of California at Davis. The language supports a wide variety of (reliable) message passing constructs, including shared variables (for processes on the same node), asynchronous message passing, rendezvous, remote procedure call, and multicast.

3.1 Programming experience

Given its ambitious goal of supporting many communication models, it is not surprising that SR is a fairly large language. Yet, we found it reasonably easy to learn. With regard to the sequential parts, the syntax, type system, and module constructs are different from most other languages. Nevertheless, these were fairly easy to learn, although the type system is far from perfect [Bal92a].

SR tries to reduce the number of concepts for distributed and parallel programming by using an *orthogonal* design. There are two ways for sending messages (blocking and nonblocking) and two ways for accepting messages (explicit and implicit). These can be combined in all four ways, yielding four different communication mechanisms. We agree with the designers that this orthogonality principle simplifies SR's design. Unfortunately, there also are some less elegant design features. The concurrent-send (**co**) command, for example, is a rather *ad hoc* extension of the basic model, with specialized syntax rules.

Our programming experience indicates that, even within the restricted domain of parallel programming, nearly all facilities provided by SR are useful. We found uses for synchronous and asynchronous message invocation, explicit, implicit, conditional, and ordered message receipt, and multicast [Bal92a]. Below we will report on our experiences in implementing the three communication patterns of Figure 1 in SR.*

3.1.1 Mailbox communication

Despite its large number of features, SR does not directly support message passing through a mailbox. The receiver of a message is fully determined when the message is *sent*. With a mailbox, the destination process is not determined until the message is *accepted* (serviced).

In contrast with the sender of a message, the receiver need *not* specify the other party, so in this sense message passing in SR is asymmetric. This observation also implies a solution to the mailbox problem. We can simply add an intermediate *buffer* process between the sender and receivers, as shown in Figure 2. The sender sends its message to this buffer process, so the (initial) destination is fixed. The receivers ask the buffer process for a message, whenever they need one.

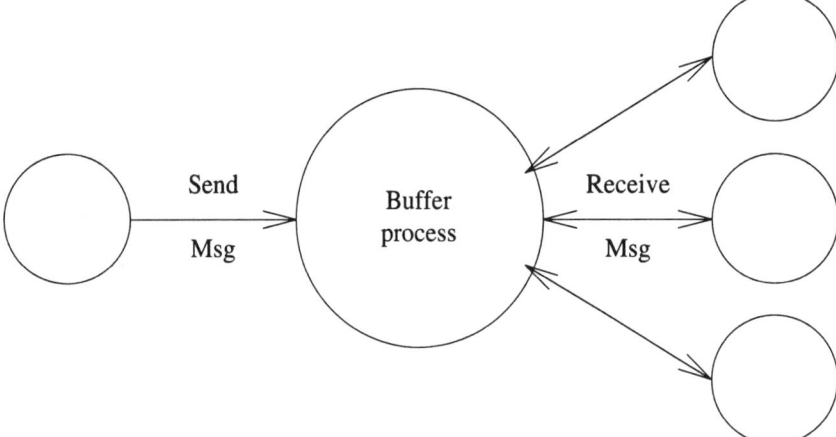

Figure 2. Simulating message passing through a mailbox in SR.

The buffer process accepts *SendMsg* and *ReceiveMsg* requests one at a time; if the buffer is empty, only *SendMsg* will be accepted. With this scheme, the destination of each message is fixed: it is sent to the buffer process. In this way, the asymmetry of message passing is worked around, at the overhead of implementing an extra process.

In applications where only one process is sending messages, a simpler solution can be used. When the sender wants to send a message, it blocks until a receiver asks for a message. In this case, the receiver can directly fetch a message from the sender, thus eliminating the need for a buffer process.

---

* The language used for this paper is referred to as SR Version 1.1. The SR designers are currently working on Version 2, in which many of the problems described here will be solved.

3.1.2 One-to-many communication

The second communication pattern, one-to-many communication, is supported in SR through a special language construct:

```
co (i := 1 to P)
  send receiver[i].SendMsg(msg)
oc
```

The **co** statement sends a message concurrently to several processes, as specified in the array *receiver*. This approach to multicasting has an important disadvantage, however. If two SR processes concurrently multicast two messages, these messages need not arrive in the same order everywhere. In other words, multicast in SR is not *indivisible*. If ordering matters, the applications must control it themselves.

3.1.3 Shared data

The third communication pattern, replicated shared data, is not supported by SR. Only processes running on the same node can share variables, other processes must communicate through message passing.

Of course, shared data can be simulated by storing them on one server process and having other processes send messages to this server. As stated before, however, we assume that the read/write ratio of the shared data is very high, in which case it is far more efficient to *replicate* the shared data in the local memories. Each processor keeps its own local copy, which is used for *reading*. Whenever the variable is *written*, all these copies are updated.

Concurrent updates of the shared data will have to be synchronized. For example, if two processes P and Q simultaneously write the shared data, all copies should be updated in a consistent way. It should never be the case that part of the copies are set to P's value while another part is set to Q's value. With message passing this requirement is difficult to realize, because messages are not globally ordered. In other words, the update messages sent by P and Q may arrive in different orders at different receivers.

The solution we have taken is to send update messages through a central manager process. This process orders the update messages and forwards them in a consistent order to all other processes. These update messages are accepted implicitly by each receiver, which means that the run time system will automatically create a new process for servicing such a message. This is important, since it is not known in advance when the update messages may arrive.

3.2 Implementation and performance

SR has been implemented on a range of multiprocessors (Encore, Sequent Balance, Sequent Symmetry) and distributed systems (homogeneous networks of VAXes, Sun-3s, Sun-4s, and others). The compiler and run time system are available from the University of Arizona.

We have done some initial performance measurements on a Sequent Symmetry with 6 CPUs. Although this machine has a shared memory, SR uses it only for implementing message passing, so the machine is not really used as a multiprocessor.

For the All Pairs Shortest Paths problem, we have measured a speedup of 4.08 (on 6 CPUs). The reason why this speedup is less than linear is the fact that the **co** statement currently is not implemented as a true (physical) multicast. The message is copied once for every receiver. The communication overhead of the ASP program therefore is high, which prevents a linear speedup.

For the Traveling Salesman Problem, we measured a maximum speedup of 5.87. The latter program uses the simplified solution for mailbox communication (i.e., the manager generates only one job at a time and blocks until this job has been accepted).

3.3 Conclusions on SR

Since SR provides so many communication primitives, it is a flexible language. SR is also more expressive than most other message passing languages. It can be argued, however, that message passing is a low level of abstraction. As we will see, for several applications other mechanisms than message passing are simpler to use. These higher-level mechanisms are frequently more expressive yet less flexible. In conclusion, SR is reasonably suited for virtually all applications. It is seldom spectacularly good or bad for any application.

4 Emerald

Emerald [Bla87, Jul88] is an object-based language, designed at the University of Washington by Andrew Black, Norman Hutchinson, Eric Jul, and Henry Levy. An object in Emerald encapsulates both static data and an active process. Objects communicate by invoking each other's operations. There can be multiple active invocations within one object, which synchronize through a *monitor*. The remote invocation mechanism is *location transparent*.

Central to Emerald's design is the concept of *object mobility*. An object may migrate from one processor to another, as initiated either by the programmer or the system. Emerald uses a novel parameter mode, *call-by-move*. This mode has similar semantics as call-by-reference, but additionally moves the object parameter to the node of the invoked object.

4.1 Programming experience

Emerald is reasonably easy to learn. Since it is an object-based language, it treats all entities as objects. Unlike object-*oriented* languages, it does not support inheritance. Notwithstanding its object-based nature, Emerald contains many constructs also found in procedural languages (e.g., nested scopes, functions, expressions, assignment and control statements). The type system is one of the more important contributions of the language. Although it is not easy to get used to, it is flexible and features static type checking and polymorphism.

Below, we will discuss how mailboxes, one-to-many communication, and shared data can be implemented in Emerald.

4.1.1 Mailbox communication

A message (or operation) in Emerald is always sent to a specific object, so mailbox-style communication is not provided. It is possible, however, to construct a mailbox *object*, which can be accessed by the senders and receivers. Such an object has the following user-defined polymorphic type:

```
type Mailbox
  operation AddMsg[eType]         % Add a message to the mailbox
  operation GetMsg -> [job: eType]% Fetch a message from the mailbox
end Mailbox
```

The object type is implemented using a queue of messages. To synchronize access to the queue, it is encapsulated in a monitor. The *AddMsg* and *GetMsg* operations are thus executed in a mutually exclusive way. Also, the *GetMsg* operation will block on a condition variable if the queue is empty; this condition variable will be signaled by an invocation of *AddMsg*.

This implementation of mailboxes is roughly similar to the SR version, except that a passive object rather than an active process is used for storing the message queue. Also, the synchronization of the queue operations is entirely different. In the SR version, the buffer process synchronizes the operations by accepting them one at a time and by delaying requests for messages when the buffer is empty. The Emerald version uses a monitor and a condition variable for synchronizing the operations.

4.1.2 One-to-many communication

Emerald does not support any form of one-to-many communication. To send data to multiple objects, a sequential **for** loop has to be used. A subtle problem arises here that does not occur in the other languages. Emerald provides a uniform parameter mechanism: all objects are passed by reference, no matter where the sender and receiver are located. With multicasting, however, each receiver should be given a *copy* of the data, not a remote reference to it. What is needed here is call-by-value semantics, which is not supported in Emerald.

Thus, the sender must copy the data explicitly and pass this copy as call-by-move parameter. A distinct copy must be made for every receiver. So a multicast is simulated as follows in Emerald:

for *all receivers r* **do**
   *r.send[***move*** copy[msg]]*

Here, *copy* is a user-defined procedure that copies a message.

The Emerald implementation of one-to-many communication is fairly complex. In addition, the solution is far from efficient. Not only does it refrain from using physical multicast, but it also forces the sender to copy the message once for every receiver, which may become a sequential bottleneck.

4.1.3 Shared data

Although Emerald supports a shared namespace for objects, this is not sufficient for implementing replicated shared data. If a shared variable were stored in a single object, nearly all accesses to the variable would require physical communication, including read-only operations. What is needed is a replicated object, which is not provided in Emerald.

The programmer therefore has to replicate data explicitly. A copy of the shared data is kept by each process needing the data. To update these copies, a similar scheme as for SR is used, based on implicitly received messages. The main difference with the SR solution is the usage of a monitor for synchronizing access to the local copy of the shared variable.

4.2 Implementation and performance

A prototype implementation of Emerald exists on networks of VAXes or Sun-3 workstations, connected by an Ethernet. The Emerald system is not yet available to other users. We have not been able to do any meaningful performance measurements on the prototype system.

4.3 Conclusions on Emerald

Support for parallel and distributed programming in Emerald is best understood using two levels of abstraction. At the highest level, we have concurrent objects that invoke each other's operations in a synchronous (blocking) way, certainly a nice and simple abstraction. To see what is really going on, we need to look at how invocations are implemented and synchronized. Here, we are at the level of *monitors*. Monitors are well understood, but are harder to program than most other mechanisms discussed in this paper. This clearly shows of in the implementation code: most of our Emerald programs are significantly longer than their counterparts in the other languages.

For parallel programming, Emerald is less flexible than SR. It provides only one form of interprocess communication: synchronous remote procedure calls that are accepted implicitly. The parameter mechanism is consistent (call-by-reference is used throughout), but copying parameters is a problem. In principle, call-by-value parameters could have been allowed for passive objects (not containing a process). This extension would have made the parameter mechanism less uniform, however, and would have created a distinction between active and passive objects.

Emerald probably is more suitable for distributed applications (e.g., electronic mail, name servers) than for parallel applications. For such distributed applications, features like object migration and location independent invocations are more beneficial and the need for copying objects (e.g., electronic mailboxes) will be less.

5 Parlog

We have chosen Parlog [Cla88, Cla86, Con89, Gre87] as representative for the large class of concurrent logic languages. Parlog has been developed at Imperial College, London, by Keith Clark, Steve Gregory, and their colleagues.

The language is based on AND/OR parallelism and committed-choice nondeterminism. The user can specify the order (parallel or sequential) in which clauses are to be evaluated. For this purpose, sequential and parallel conjunction and disjunction operators can be used.

5.1 Programming experience

The time needed for learning Parlog depends on one's background education in concurrent logic programming. The language itself is quite simple. In addition, there are certain programming idioms one should master, such as streams and objects built with shared logical variables.

5.1.1 Mailbox communication

As in most concurrent logic languages, processes in Parlog can communicate through message streams. Such streams can easily be built out of shared logical variables. Streams, however, have one disadvantage: the receiving end can *scan* over the stream, but it cannot *remove* items from it [Car89b]. Thus, mailbox-type communication cannot be expressed easily with streams.

Instead, we can use similar solutions as for SR, which means either adding a buffer process between the sender and receivers (see Figure 2), or blocking the sender of the message. For our TSP program [Bal91], we have chosen the latter option. There is only a single sender, which blocks when it wants to send a message. The sender takes a stream of incomplete messages of the form *getmsg(Msg)* as input. These messages are generated by the receivers. After receiving such a message, the sender instantiates the logical variable *Msg* to the next message it wants to send.

5.1.2 One-to-many communication

One-to-many communication is easy to express using shared logical variables. All that is needed is a stream of messages shared among the sender and the receivers. All receivers can scan this stream, thus receiving all the messages.

It depends on the language implementation whether physical multicast is used for this type of one-to-many communication. For example, multicast is used to some extent in the hypercube implementation of Flat Concurrent Prolog [Tay87]. The Parlog system we have used uses shared memory, which takes away the need for physical multicast.

Our Parlog ASP program uses an even simpler approach to one-to-many communication. Rather than creating a fixed number of long-living processes, it creates a new set of parallel processes for each iteration of the algorithm. The pivot row for the next iteration is passed as parameter to each of these processes. In other words, the program does not send a message to existing processes, but it creates new processes and passes the message as a parameter. This approach only works well because the Parlog system efficiently supports fine-grained parallelism. With the other languages discussed in this paper, the overhead of creating new processes for each iteration would be far too high.

5.1.3 Shared data

Parlog supports shared logical variables, but these variables can be assigned only once. Implementing mutable shared variables in Parlog is much more complicated. We represent such a variable as a stream of values, the last one of which is the current value of the variable. The predicate *current_value* scans the stream until the tail is an unbound variable, and returns the current last element of the stream as output value:

```
mode current_value(Stream?, Value^). % Stream is input, Value is output
current_value([V|Vs], Value) <- var(Vs): Value = V; % tail is unbound
current_value([_|Vs], Value) <- current_value(Vs, Value). % try next element
```

To update the variable, a new value is appended to the end of the stream. A process using the variable must periodically check for new values, by scanning the stream until the end. (This technique is also used by Huntbach [Hun89]).

An important issue is how often to check the stream. Since scanning streams is expensive, it cannot be done too often. On the other hand, if it is done infrequently, the process will usually have an old value of the shared variable. For branch-and-bound applications like TSP, this means pruning will become less efficient, so more nodes will be searched (the so-called *search overhead*).

This solution is somewhat similar to the SR and Emerald implementations described above. The stream representing the shared variable can be regarded as a stream of *update* messages. An important difference is the way these messages are accepted. In SR and Emerald, a new process is created when a message arrives, which will service the message immediately (i.e., the message is received implicitly). Parlog does not have implicit message receipt, so the receiver must explicitly look for new messages. Since it is not known in advance when update messages may arrive, there is a problem in deciding *when* to look for them.

5.2 Implementation and performance

An interpreter for Parlog has been implemented on several shared-memory multiprocessors (Sequent Balance and Symmetry, Butterfly). A commercially available subset of Parlog, called Strand, has also been implemented on distributed systems (hypercubes, networks). The Parlog system is available from Imperial College.

We have used a 6-CPU Sequent Balance for running some initial performance measurements. This implementation of Parlog relies on the presence of shared memory. Also, the implementation is based on an interpreter and runs on slow processors, so its absolute performance currently is one to two orders of magnitude less than that of the other languages described in this paper. These two issues taken together result in a relative communication overhead that is far less than what would be expected in a production-quality, distributed implementation.

We have measured a speedup of 5.33 for ASP and 4.98 for TSP, using 6 CPUs. The speedup for ASP is fairly high, due to the low communication overhead. For TSP, the speedup is not optimal, because the global bound is not kept up-to-date everywhere. The TSP program therefore suffers from a search overhead.

5.3 Conclusions on Parlog

The shared logical variable is at a higher level of abstraction than message passing. For some applications, it is spectacularly expressive. Our Parlog program for ASP, for example, is just as simple as the original *sequential* algorithm. The synchronization of the parallel tasks is done implicitly, using suspension on unbound logical variables. On the negative side, it is not clear whether the program will run efficiently on a realistic large-scale parallel system.

For other applications, shared logical variables are less suitable, but one can then fall back on message passing through streams. This form of message passing has some drawbacks, however, as discussed in [Car89b].

6 Linda

Linda is a set of language primitives developed by David Gelernter and colleagues at Yale University [Ahu86, Car89a, Car89b]. Linda is based on the Tuple Space model of communication. The Tuple Space is a global memory consisting of tuples (records) that are addressed associatively. Three atomic operations are defined on Tuple Space: **out** adds a tuple to TS; **read** reads a tuple contained in TS; **in** reads a tuple and also deletes it from TS, in one atomic action.

6.1 Programming experience

Of all five languages discussed in this paper, Linda undoubtedly is the simplest one to learn. It adds only a few primitives to an existing base language. Below, we will discuss how these primitives can be used to implement the three communication patterns.

6.1.1 Mailbox communication

The simulation of a mailbox in Linda is simple. A mailbox is represented as a distributed data structure [Car86a] in Tuple Space. To send a message to the mailbox, a new tuple containing the message is added to this data structure. To receive a message, a tuple is retrieved from Tuple Space and its contents are read.

To preserve the ordering of the messages, a sequence number field is added to each message tuple. The tuples are generated and retrieved in the same order. The next sequence number to generate and the sequence number of the next message to accept are also stored in tuples. They are initialized to zero, by the statements:

```
out("head", 0); # initialize tuple containing index of head of queue
out("tail", 0); # initialize tuple containing index of tail of queue
```

To send a message *msg* to a mailbox, the following code is executed:

```
in("tail", ? &tail);    # obtain next sequence number
out("tail", tail + 1);  # put back next sequence number
out("MB", msg, tail);   # put message with sequence number in TS
```

The **in** operation blocks until a matching tuple is found. Next, it assigns the formal parameters of the **in** (denoted by a "?") the corresponding values of the tuple. Finally, it deletes the tuple from Tuple Space. All of this is done atomically.

Receiving a message from a mailbox is implemented through the following code:

```
in( "head", ? &head);      # first obtain sequence number
out("head", head+1);       # put sequence-number tuple back in TS
in("MB", ? &msg, head);    # now fetch message with right sequence number
```

The tuples can be thought of as forming a distributed *queue* data structure, with pointers (indices) to the head and tail of the queue.

This example clearly illustrates the advantages and disadvantages of Linda. The mailbox implementation is very simple: it requires only a few lines of code. On the other hand, the operations used for accessing the mailbox are fairly low-level. For example, three Tuple Space operations are needed for sending or receiving a single message. It is far from trivial that this code is correct. Also, the implementation must do extensive optimization to make the send/receive operations efficient.

6.1.2 One-to-many communication

In Linda, data can be transferred from one process to all the others by putting the data in Tuple Space, where it can be read by everyone. So, expressing one-to-many communication in Linda is trivial; it just requires a single out statement:

```
out(msg);
```

A key question that remains, however, is what *really* happens. For efficiency, it makes considerable difference whether the data are transferred through a real multicast protocol or not.

There are many different implementations of Tuple Space to consider. The S/Net system replicates all tuples everywhere, using the S/Net broadcast capability [Car86b]. The hypercube and Transputer implementations of Linda, on the other hand, hash each tuple onto one specific processor and do not replicate tuples [Bjo89, Zen90]. In this case, the data in the message will not be multicast. Each receiver will have to fetch the data itself, using a **read** statement. The communication overhead will thus be linear to the number of receivers. In conclusion, expressing one-to-many communication is Linda is trivial, but the performance will be hard to predict.

6.1.3 Shared data

In theory, a shared variable can be simulated in Linda by storing it in Tuple Space. This solution makes heavy demands on the implementation of Tuple Space, however. If the variable is read very frequently (as is true in TSP), the overhead of reading it must be very low. So, for efficiency each processor should have a local copy of the tuple. Not all Tuple Space implementations have this property. The hypercube and Transputer implementations mentioned above, for example, store each tuple on only a single processor. An additional performance problem is the associative addressing of Tuple Space. Part of this overhead can be optimized away [Car87], but it is not clear whether it can be eliminated entirely. So, whether or not the above solution is practical, depends on the implementation.

6.2 Implementation and performance

Linda has been implemented on many parallel machines, both with and without shared memory, and has been used for numerous applications [Car89b]. The system is distributed as a commercial product. (The Linda system we have used for our performance measurements is not the most recent one; newer versions of the Linda software may obtain better performance.)

We have used a VME-bus based multiprocessor for some initial performance measurements. For the All Pairs Shortest Paths problem, we have measured a speedup of 7.4 on 8 CPUs. Since the implementation uses shared memory, the distribution of the pivot rows is efficient. Each new pivot row is put in a tuple in shared memory, where it can be read by all processors.

The Traveling Salesman Problem program obtains a speedup of 7.06 on 8 CPUs. The program stores the global bound in a tuple. In our Linda system, using this tuple for every read access is too expensive. Therefore, each processor also keeps a local copy of the variable. These copies are updated occasionally. So, this implementation is similar to the Parlog implementation, except that the bound is stored in a tuple rather than in a stream. Updating the local copies is relatively cheaper in the Linda version, so it can be done more frequently. As a result, the relative search overhead in the Linda program is less than that of the Parlog version.

6.3 Conclusions on Linda

Most of the criticism on Linda in the literature is related to efficiency. The associative addressing and global visibility of the Tuple Space have led many people to believe that Linda cannot be implemented efficiently. However, its implementors have made considerable progress during the past few years in optimizing the performance on several machines. The **in** operation, for example, hardly ever scans the entire Tuple Space, but typically uses hashing or something even more efficient. Just as with virtual memory, however, there will probably always remain cases where the easy-to-program approach will not be optimal. So, the performance of Linda programs may sometimes be hard to predict.

An important decision in Linda is to hide the physical distribution of data from the user. In contrast, Emerald gives the programmer control over the placement of data, by supporting user-initiated object migration. The Linda approach is simpler, but it makes heavier demands on the implementation. Again, the transparent approach will sometimes be less efficient, but it remains to be seen how big the differences in performance are for actual programs.

The concept of distributed data structures is probably one of the most important contributions of Linda. However, the way Linda implements distributed data structures — through a fixed number of operations on Tuple Space — is rather low-level, in our view [Kaa89].

7 Orca

Orca is a language for implementing parallel applications on distributed systems. Orca was designed at the Vrije Universiteit in Amsterdam [Bal88, Bal90a, Bal90b, Bal92b].

The programming model of Orca is based on logically shared data. The language hides the physical distribution of the memory and allows processes to share data even if they run on different nodes. In this way, Orca combines the advantages of distributed systems (good price/performance ratio and scalability) and shared-memory multiprocessors (ease of programming).

The entities shared among processes are data objects, which are variables of user-defined abstract data types. These data objects are replicated in the local memories, so each process can directly read its own copy, without doing any communication. The language run time system atomically updates all copies when an object is modified.

This model is similar to that of Distributed Shared Memory (DSM) systems [Li89]. In Orca, however, the unit of sharing is a logical (user-defined) object rather than a physical (system-defined) page, which has many advantages [Bal90b].

7.1 Programming experience

Orca is a new language rather than an extension to an existing sequential language. An important disadvantage of extending a base language is the difficulty of implementing pointers and global variables on systems lacking shared memory. These problems can more easily be avoided if the language is designed from scratch. Orca, for example, supports first-class *graph* variables rather than pointers. Unlike pointers, graphs can freely be moved or copied from one machine to another. Of course, this approach also implies that programmers have to learn a new language. The design of Orca has been kept as simple as possible, so this disadvantage should not be overestimated.

7.1.1 Mailbox communication

A mailbox can be implemented in Orca in a similar way as in Emerald, by using a shared mailbox object. The specification of a generic abstract data type *Mailbox* in Orca is shown below:

```
generic (type T)
object specification GenericMailbox;
  operation AddMsg(Msg: T);
  operation GetMsg(): T;
end generic;
```

The implementation of the mailbox is simpler than the one in Emerald, because operations in Orca are indivisible. In other words, mutual exclusion synchronization is done automatically in Orca, whereas Emerald requires the usage of a monitor construct for this purpose. Also, Orca provides a powerful mechanism for condition synchronization (based on guarded commands), so blocking the receivers when the mailbox is empty is easy to express.

7.1.2 One-to-many communication

Orca's shared data-objects can be used for expressing one-to-many communication. If one process applies a write-operation to an object, all other processes sharing the object can observe the effects. Our ASP program in Orca, for example, uses an object-type *RowCollection*, with the following operations:

```
object specification RowCollection;
   type RowType = array[integer] of integer;
   operation AddRow(iter: integer; R: RowType);
         # Add the row for the given iteration number
   operation AwaitRow(iter: integer): RowType;
         # Wait until the row for the given iteration is available,
         # then return it.
end;
```

The process that wants to send the pivot row applies the operation *AddRow* to the object. The run time system will then update all copies of this object by multicasting the operation [Bal92b]. A process requiring the pivot row invokes the operation *AwaitRow*, which blocks until the requested row has been added to the object and then returns this row. The latter operation is done locally, without needing any communication. So, the Orca solution is efficient, since it uses physical multicasting, if available.

7.1.3 Shared data

Orca has the support for logically shared data as a design goal, so it is no surprise that communication through shared data is easy to express in this language. The shared variable is put in a data object shared among all processes. The run time system automatically replicates the object in the local memories, so processes can directly read the value. Whenever the object is changed, all copies are updated immediately, by broadcasting the new value. Moreover, atomicity of the operations is already guaranteed by the language. This solution is both simple and efficient. The only overhead in reading the value is that of a local operation invocation. When the variable is changed, its new value is broadcast to all processors containing a copy.

7.2 Implementation and performance

Orca has been implemented on top of Amoeba [Tan90] as well as on a collection of MC68030s connected through an Ethernet. The latter implementation uses the physical multicast capability of the Ethernet. The Orca implementation is being distributed as part of the Amoeba system.

We have done many performance measurements on these systems, as described in detail elsewhere [Bal90b]. Here, we will present some recent results for the multicast system, using 16 CPUs.

The measured speedup for the All Pairs Shortest Paths problem on 16 CPUs is 15.9. This high speedup is mainly due to the efficient broadcast protocol, which is used for transmitting the pivot rows. For the Traveling Salesman Problem, the speedup on 16 CPUs is 14.44. Since all copies of the global bound are updated immediately, the search overhead is low.

7.3 Conclusions on Orca

Orca is *not* an object-based language; it merely provides abstract data types. It supports both active processes and passive data-objects. Since objects in Orca are purely passive, they can be replicated, which is a very important goal in the implementation.

An important difference with Linda is the support for user-defined, high-level operations on shared data [Kaa89]. Linda only provides a fixed number of built-in operations on tuples, but Orca allows programmers to construct their own atomic operations. Unlike Linda, Orca uses direct rather than associative addressing of shared data, and thus avoids any problems with associative addressing.

For some applications, Orca has important advantages over other languages. Programs that need logically shared data are easy to implement in Orca and are efficient. Orca also is one of the few languages that uses physical broadcasting in its implementation. As we have seen, for ASP this is of critical importance. On the other hand, there also are cases where the model is less efficient, for example when plain point-to-point message passing is required.

8 Discussion

In the previous three sections we have looked at how the five languages deal with three example communication patterns. The results of this study are summarized in Table 2. Below, we will compare the approaches taken for the different languages.

Table 2. Summary of the solutions taken for all five languages
to the three communication patterns

	Mailboxes	One-to-many communication	Replicated shared data
SR	Buffer process	Concurrent send	Messages with implicit receive
Emerald	Shared-object message queue	Point-to-point messages	Messages with implicit receive
Parlog	Buffer process	Shared stream (or solution with fine-grained parallelism)	Messages with explicit receive
Linda	Distr. data structure message queue	Shared data	Shared tuple (or m.p. with explicit receive)
Orca	Shared-object message queue	Shared data	Distributed shared memory

For communication through mailboxes, there are three different solutions. For Linda, we store a mailbox as a distributed data structure in Tuple Space. This solution requires only a few lines of code. For Emerald and Orca, a mailbox is represented as an abstract object, with operations to send and receive messages. This approach requires more code, especially for synchronizing access to the mailbox. On the other hand, the abstract operations on a mailbox object are higher level than the Linda operations on tuples. The third solution, used for SR and Parlog, is to add an extra buffer process between the sender and receivers.

For one-to-many communication, Parlog, Linda, and Orca provide the simplest solutions, all based on shared data. SR has a concurrent-send primitive built in, but it does not make any guarantees about the order in which messages are delivered. Emerald has no provision for one-to-many communication, so it must be simulated with multiple point-to-point messages, which are sent sequentially. An important issue is how one-to-many communication is implemented: as a physical multicast or not. Most language implementations do not use multicast, Orca and Linda being two notable exceptions.

The third communication pattern, replicated shared data, is simple to express in Orca and Linda, since these languages provide logically shared data. For Linda, the performance of the resulting programs is hard to predict, because many different strategies are used for distributing tuples. Orca, on the other hand, always tries to replicate shared objects wherever they are needed. For the other languages, we simulate shared data through message passing. Here, the ability to accept messages implicitly (i.e., by a newly created process) is very important. SR and Emerald both provide this facility. Parlog uses only explicit message receipt, which makes efficient updating of the copies of shared data harder.

Acknowledgments

The work on SR and Emerald was done while the author was visiting the University of Arizona, Department of Computer Science, Tucson, AZ. The work on Parlog was done while he was at Imperial College, Department of Computing, London. The author is grateful to both departments for receiving him as an academic visitor. Also, he would like to thank Nick Carriero, Greg Andrews, Dave Bakken, Gregg Townsend, Mike Coffin, Norman Hutchinson, Keith Clark, Jim Crammond, and Andrew Davison for the discussions on their languages. The work on Orca and Linda has been done in cooperation with Frans Kaashoek. Erik Baalbergen, Arnold Geels, Frans Kaashoek, and Andy Tanenbaum provided useful comments on an earlier version of the paper.

References

Ahu86. S. Ahuja, N. Carriero, and D. Gelernter, "Linda and Friends," *IEEE Computer* **19**(8), pp. 26-34 (Aug. 1986).

And83. G.R. Andrews and F.B. Schneider, "Concepts and Notations for Concurrent Programming," *ACM Computing Surveys* **15**(1), pp. 3-43 (March 1983).

And86. G.R. Andrews and R.A. Olsson, "The Evolution of the SR Programming Language," *Distributed Computing* **1**, pp. 133-149 (July 1986).

And88. G.R. Andrews, R.A. Olsson, M. Coffin, I. Elshoff, K. Nilsen, T. Purdin, and G. Townsend, "An Over-View of the SR Language and Implementation," *ACM Trans. Program. Lang. Syst.* **10**(1), pp. 51-86 (Jan. 1988).

And91. G.R. Andrews, "Paradigms for Process Interaction in Distributed Programs," *ACM Computing Surveys* **23**(1), pp. 49-90 (March 1991).

Bal88. H.E. Bal and A.S. Tanenbaum, "Distributed Programming with Shared Data," *Proc. IEEE CS 1988 Int'l Conf. on Computer Languages*, Miami, FL, pp. 82-91 (Oct. 1988).

Bal89. H.E. Bal, J.G. Steiner, and A.S. Tanenbaum, "Programming Languages for Distributed Computing Systems," *ACM Computing Surveys* **21**(3), pp. 261-322 (Sept. 1989).

Bal90a. H.E. Bal, M.F. Kaashoek, and A.S. Tanenbaum, "Experience with Distributed Programming in Orca," *Proc. IEEE CS 1990 Int'l Conf. on Computer Languages*, New Orleans, LA, pp. 79-89 (March 1990).

Bal90b. H.E. Bal, *Programming Distributed Systems,* Silicon Press, Summit, NJ (1990), (also published by Prentice Hall Int'l, 1991).

Bal91. H.E. Bal, "Heuristic Search in PARLOG Using Replicated Worker Style Parallelism," *Future Generations Computer Systems* **6**(4), pp. 303-315 (Sept. 1991).

Bal92a. H.E. Bal, "Parallel Programming in SR," *Proc. IEEE CS 1992 Int'l Conf. on Computer Languages*, Oakland, CA, pp. 310-319 (April 1992).

Bal92b. H.E. Bal, M.F. Kaashoek, and A.S. Tanenbaum, "Orca: A Language for Parallel Programming of Distributed Systems," *IEEE Transactions on Software Engineering* **18**(3), pp. 190-205 (March 1992).

Bal92c. H.E. Bal, "Fault-Tolerant Parallel Programming in Argus," *Concurrency: Practice and Experience* **4**(1), pp. 37-55 (Feb. 1992).

Bjo89. R. Bjornson, N. Carriero, and D. Gelernter, "The Implementation and Performance of Hypercube Linda," Report RR-690, Yale University, New Haven, CT (March 1989).

Bla87. A. Black, N. Hutchinson, E. Jul, H. Levy, and L. Carter, "Distribution and Abstract Types in Emerald," *IEEE Trans. Softw. Eng.* **SE-13**(1), pp. 65-76 (Jan. 1987).

Car86a. N. Carriero, D. Gelernter, and J. Leichter, "Distributed Data Structures in Linda," *Proc. 13th ACM Symp. Princ. Progr. Lang.*, St. Petersburg, FL, pp. 236-242 (Jan. 1986).

Car86b. N. Carriero and D. Gelernter, "The S/Net's Linda Kernel," *ACM Trans. Comp. Syst.* **4**(2), pp. 110-129 (May 1986).

Car87. N. Carriero, "The Implementation of Tuple Space Machines," Research Report 567 (Ph.D. dissertation), Yale University, New Haven, CT (Dec. 1987).

Car89a. N. Carriero and D. Gelernter, "How to Write Parallel Programs: A Guide to the Perplexed," *ACM Comp. Surveys* **21**(3), pp. 323-357 (Sept. 1989).

Car89b. N. Carriero and D. Gelernter, "Linda in Context," *Commun. ACM* **32**(4), pp. 444-458 (April 1989).

Cla86. K.L. Clark and S. Gregory, "PARLOG: Parallel Programming in Logic," *ACM Trans. Program. Lang. Syst.* **8**(1), pp. 1-49 (Jan. 1986).

Cla88. K.L. Clark, "PARLOG and Its Applications," *IEEE Trans. Softw. Eng.* **SE-14**(12), pp. 1792-1804 (Dec. 1988).

Con89. T. Conlon, *Programming in PARLOG*, Addison-Wesley, Wokingham, England (1989).

Gre87. S. Gregory, *Parallel Logic Programming in PARLOG*, Addison-Wesley, Wokingham, England (1987).

Hun89. M. Huntbach, *Combinatorial Search in PARLOG Using Speculative Computation*, Imperial College, London (May 1989).

Jul88. E. Jul, H. Levy, N. Hutchinson, and A. Black, "Fine-Grained Mobility in the Emerald System," *ACM Trans. Comp. Syst.* **6**(1), pp. 109-133 (Feb. 1988).

Kaa89. M.F. Kaashoek, H.E. Bal, and A.S. Tanenbaum, "Experience with the Distributed Data Structure Paradigm in Linda," *USENIX Workshop on Experiences with Building Distributed and Multiprocessor Systems*, Ft. Lauderdale, FL., pp. 175-191 (Oct. 1989).

Kah89. K.M. Kahn and M.S. Miller, "Technical Correspondence on "Linda in Context"," *Comm. ACM* **32**(10), pp. 1253-1255 (Oct. 1989).

Li89. K. Li and P. Hudak, "Memory Coherence in Shared Virtual Memory Systems," *ACM Trans. Computer Systems* **7**(4), pp. 321-359 (Nov. 1989).

Lis88. B. Liskov, "Distributed Programming in Argus," *Commun. ACM* **31**(3), pp. 300-312 (March 1988).

Sha89. E. Shapiro, "Technical Correspondence on "Linda in Context"," *Comm. ACM* **32**(10), pp. 1244-1249 (Oct. 1989).

Tan90. A.S. Tanenbaum, R. van Renesse, H. van Staveren, G.J. Sharp, S.J. Mullender, A.J. Jansen, and G. van Rossum, "Experiences with the Amoeba Distributed Operating System," *Comm. ACM* **33**(12), pp. 46-63 (Dec. 1990).

Tay87. S. Taylor, S. Safra, and E. Shapiro, "A Parallel Implementation of Flat Concurrent Prolog," *Int'l J. of Parallel Programming* **15**(3), pp. 245-275 (1987).

Zen90. S.E. Zenith, "Linda Coordination Language; Subsystem Kernel Architecture (on Transputers)," RR-794, Yale University, New Haven, CT (May 1990).

StormCast: Yet Another Exercise in Distributed Computing

Dag Johansen
Department of Computer Science
University of Tromsø
Tromsø, Norway
<dag@cs.uit.no>

Abstract

This paper presents an architecture for distributed monitoring applications. The architecture has been tested through prototype implementations in both local area and wide area network environments. The architecture suggests directions for the design and implementation of large-scale distributed applications monitoring weather and pollution parameters.

1 Introduction

The last 10 years have seen an increased interest in and evolution of distributed systems. However, we have not seen similar innovative changes in user applications, which still are often constructed on the basis of a monolithic approach that does not take advantage of the distributed nature of the underlying distributed system. A common approach is basically to run traditional sequential applications on one element in a distributed system, rather than to construct truly distributed applications in which computations can span several computers. Such a distributed application consists of a set of separate modules, or processes, cooperating to meet an overall application goal.

This paper focuses on the StormCast architecture as a framework for construction of large-scale distributed applications monitoring weather and pollution parameters. This architecture has provided the guidelines for the design and implementation of several advanced prototypes of the StormCast distributed application and its customized cousins [Joha88] [Hart88] [Hart90] [Joha91].

There are several reasons for this application focus. First, we intend to legitimize the existence of distributed applications as a means of monitoring certain parameters from larger geographical areas. Moreover, we intend to devise a general architecture for this type of monitoring application. Finally, we intend to evaluate various operating system services as a basis for the abstractions needed by a large-scale, wide area network-based distributed application. At present we are constructing our platform on top of UNIX.

The current approach is to develop StormCast applications in real environments to fully utilize the idea of a top-down approach. Currently, this is being done in cooperation with Norwegian industry in order to get it scaled to the proportions demanded by real users. Aspects such as functionality, performance, scalability, security, and fault tolerance of these distributed applications can then be evaluated.

The rest of this paper is organized as follows: Section 2 argues for the application sectors chosen for distributed processing. Section 3 describes the StormCast architecture. Sections 4 and 5 present designs and prototype implementations based on this architecture. Section 6 presents experiences and lessons learned from the architecture and its derived prototypes. Section 7 presents future plans, and Section 8 concludes the paper.

2 The weather and environment sectors

The sectors we have chosen for distributed processing purposes are outside the typical operating system sector. This decision is based on the recognition that real-life monitoring is distributed in its nature. This includes monitoring for industrial purposes, as, for example, a factory automation application monitoring the different stages in a production line or a defense application monitoring specific events occurring in a geographical area of interest.

We have chosen to investigate the weather and environment sectors. As argued in [Joha88], the weather sector is a candidate that lends itself naturally to distributed computing. The reasons for the choice of these sectors include the following:

(1) Monitoring of weather data is distributed in its nature. Weather data is monitored either from different points on the ground or at upper air installations, such as weather balloons or satellites. Typically, this includes such data as temperature, wind speed and wind directions, humidity, cloudiness, precipitation, brightness, and visibility. We intend to determine whether both monitoring and transmission of weather data can be fully automated.

(2) Use of weather data is already heavily based on computers where monitored weather data is input to complex numerical computations. This involves heavy computations requiring hours of mainframe processor time. We intend to determine if numerical weather models can take advantage of the parallel processing potential in distributed systems viewing the net of processors as a large parallel computer. We also intend to determine if alternative computational models can improve the process of predicting weather, either exclusively as separate computational models or together with existing numerical models.

(3) Applications exist in the weather domain monitoring data automatically or predicting weather through expert systems or numerical computations. To our knowledge, no weather application fully automates the process from weather monitoring to weather prediction. For instance, weather forecasts in Norway are produced by the Norwegian Meteorological Institute. Several times a day, it gets input from about 40 automatic weather stations and about 750 manual weather stations, most of which are located on the mainland. In addition, raw weather data input comes from weather balloons, weather satellites, weather-buoys, and a ship dedicated to weather monitoring. A CRAY Y-MP runs numerical weather computations to produce weather forecasts. These forecasts, as well as forecasts received from Reading, England, are combined with raw data input to manually produce the final weather forecast, which is distributed to users. We intend to automate as much of this process as possible and to combine input from different sources such as an automatic weather station and a weather satellite in one distributed application.

(4) The geographical area to monitor spans areas so large that wide area networking is commonplace. Consequently, the distributed application must operate in local area networks as well as in wide area network environments, including mobile computers and loggers using packet radio and satellites for communication. Research on distributed systems and distributed applications in this type of environment is rare. We intend to add to the knowledge in this particular field.

(5) Located next to a country where potential radioactive pollution sources are commonplace, we intend to expand the applicability of a weather-monitoring application. We

intend to enhance existing hardware and software built and installed for weather data monitoring so that it can also monitor pollution parameters.

(6) Last, but not least, there is a local interest in the weather domain because StormCast is intended to operate in the Arctic regions of the world. This is a geographical location where human activity often depends heavily on current and future weather conditions.

To summarize, we assume that the weather and environment sectors are proper candidates for the construction of realistic distributed applications.

3 The StormCast architecture

A primary objective of the StormCast project is the study of architectural issues of distributed applications monitoring environments which cannot be controlled in the short term. This is opposed to reactive systems, or applications, in which discovering specific behavior leads to certain actions to control the environment monitored. Monitoring and controlling a nuclear power plant is one such example; certain actions to control the plant are taken based on analysis of monitored data from the plant itself. Monitoring and controlling a robotic vehicle is another example [Payt91], as is monitoring and controlling distributed applications [Marz91].

There are several reasons for devising a new architecture. One is that architectures for reactive applications focus on small domains with hard real-time properties. "Hard real-time" [Lein80] [Stan85] implies that a computation fails entirely if timing constraints are not met. An example of a hard real-time application is one that monitors a nuclear power plant. Applications deduced from the StormCast architecture, on the other hand, are examples of soft real-time applications. "Soft real-time" implies that a computation does not as a rule fail if all timing constraints are not met. A consequence of missed deadlines can be a degradation in the quality of services provided.

The StormCast architecture is intended for applications operating in large geographical areas where hard real-time requirements can be difficult to meet due to technical limitations. Unstable wide area networks with low bandwidths cause some problems. Missing scheduler features in the operating system and the use of CSMA/CD-based local area networks make it even theoretically impossible to guarantee hard real-time properties. Hence, StormCast applications are built as soft real-time applications tolerating unpredictable response times.

Moreover, current monitoring approaches focus more on controlling the present situation immediately, while an important part of StormCast is prediction of longer term, future behavior. Storage of monitored data is a key in that respect.

The architecture also takes into account fault tolerance requirements to improve both reliability and availability. "Reliability" means to get correct data, and "availability" means to get data at the right time. This also includes situations where the different modules of a distributed application can be partitioned due to, for instance, network malfunctions. Approaches in which such disconnected operability is a major requirement are rare at the application level, but in the StormCast architecture, disconnected operability is important.

The StormCast architecture also allows for integration with other applications such as input of satellite pictures. Human input by those who are not regular users is also allowed, and this input is to be processed and evaluated. For instance, human-generated input as a weather forecast can be compared with similar predictions made by fully automated weather forecasting processes. The term "critic" is used for an application that examines and critiques human-generated solutions [Silv92].

The StormCast architecture has changed over the years based on experience with the architecture and its distributed applications [Joha88] [Hart88] [Hart90] [Joha91]. The identification of the flow of data and information has been vital in the progress toward the current StormCast architecture. Figure 1 shows the flow of data and information on which we base the StormCast architecture.

The three bottom layers observe, collect, and store raw data. The next two layers transform data to information and store the information. (*Data* is defined as a physical representation of human abstractions, and *information* is defined as the meanings we assign them [Hans73].) Finally, both raw data and information can be visualized. The flow of data is illustrated in Figure 1 with solid, vertical arrows while the flow of information is represented by dotted, vertical arrows.

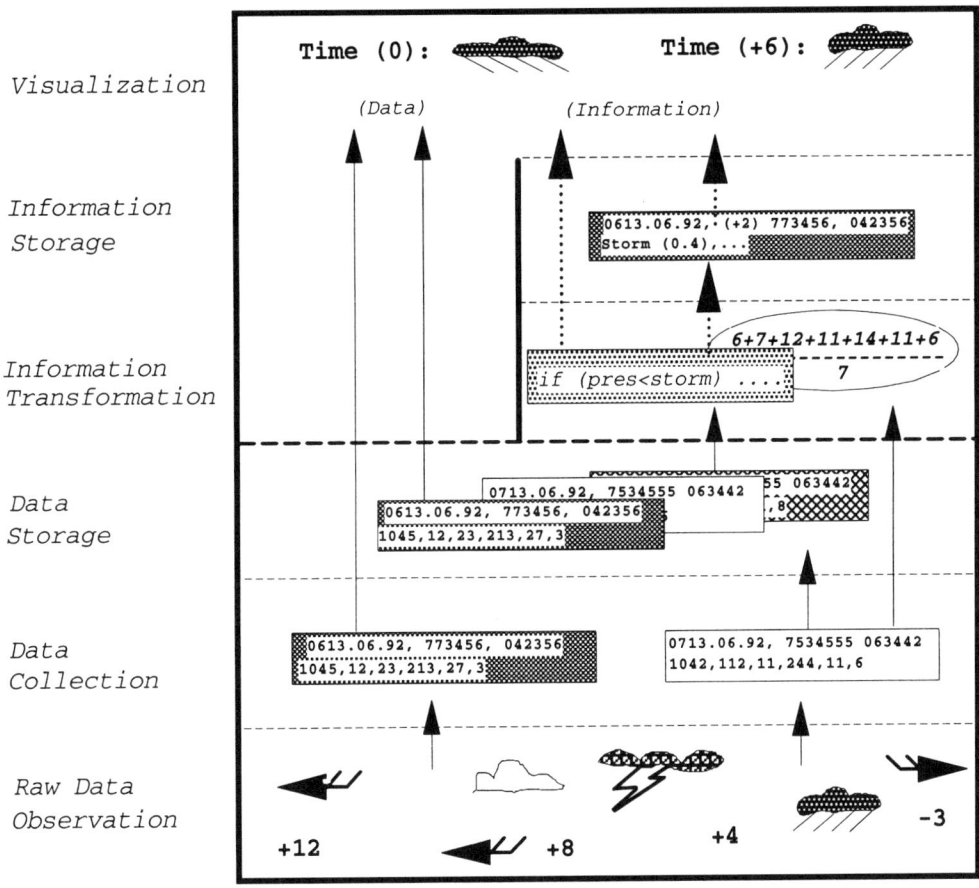

Figure 1. Interfaces for data and information flow.

The StormCast architecture for construction of large-scale, critic, soft real-time distributed monitoring applications consists of six layers. This is closely related to the flow and transformation of data and information as illustrated in Figure 1. The StormCast architecture is shown in Figure 2. It is important to note that several of the layers can be omitted if not needed in an application.

Distributed Open Systems

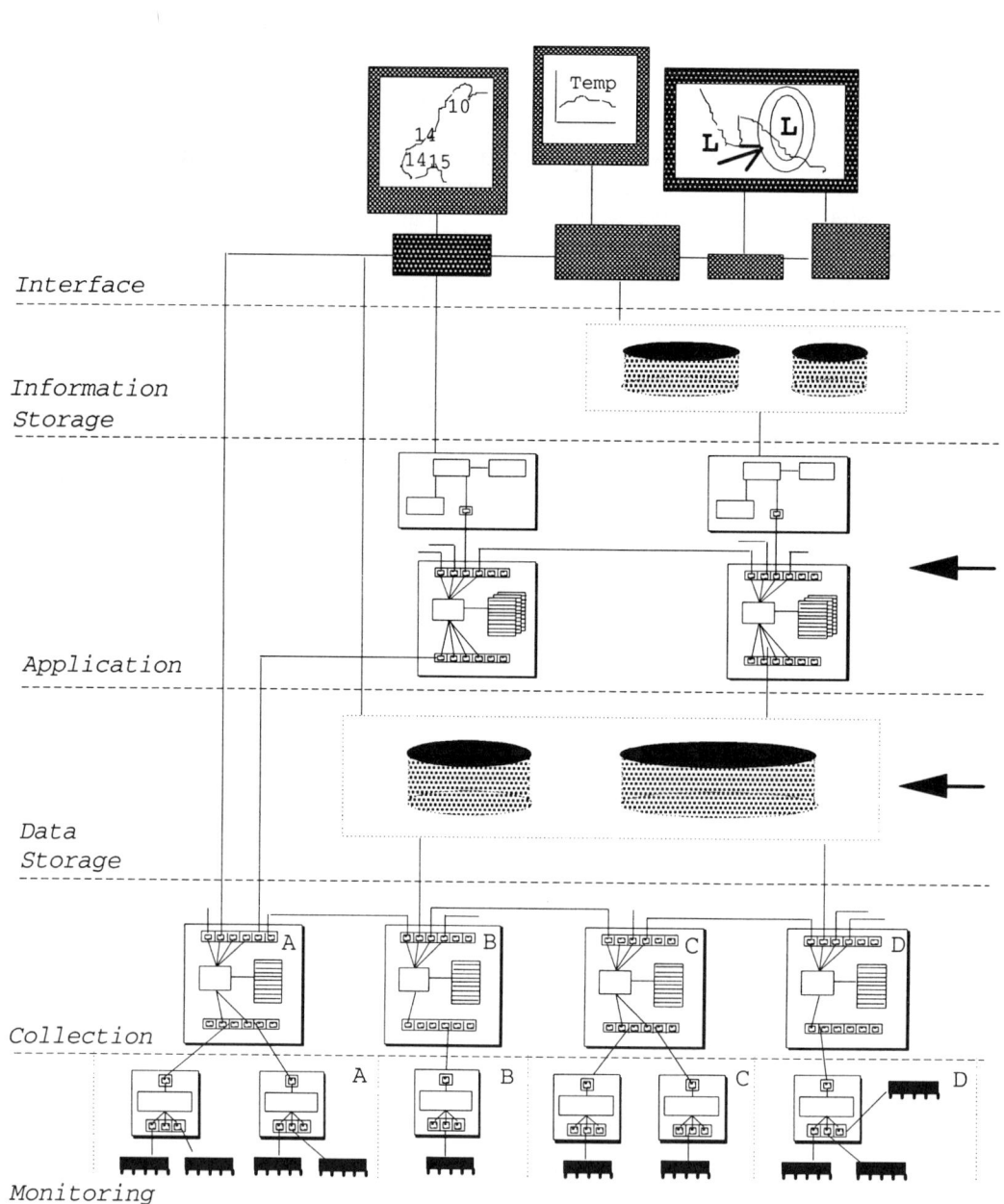

Figure 2. The StormCast architecture.

The calling pattern among the layers is essentially based on a request-reply relationship resembling the client-server model. Most requests for data or information go downward through the layers.

3.1 The monitoring layer

The monitoring layer is responsible for capturing the behavior of real events. Examples are monitoring of the air temperature or the wind direction by real sensors located in the area being monitored. The monitoring devices grouped together in one unit are called a monitoring station.

This is typically made up of seven or eight different hardware sensors being polled by a nearby logger station in the same layer. This logger station calibrates input from sensors and responds to requests from the collection layer. The architecture suggests that the first level of data storage should be supported by loggers at this bottom layer. This data is not permanently stored.

The bottom layer is also responsible for the reliability of the data monitored where hardware replication techniques can be used to achieve reliability. Depending on the functionality of the higher layers, this replication can be completely hidden by the loggers. If it is to be hidden, there is a distinction between a logical and a physical monitoring station. A physical monitoring station is the real monitoring hardware capturing actual events, and a logical monitoring station is an abstraction representing two or more physical monitoring stations in the same area. This replication is not visible outside the logger providing this abstraction. The architecture suggests no policy on how to respond when there is a discrepancy in the data sets from the different physical monitoring stations in one logical monitoring station. This might vary in the applications derived from this architecture.

The monitoring layer also checks monitored data against threshold values, triggering an alarm which can propagate up through the layers as soon as a threshold value is exceeded. Finally, this layer also stamps data with the current time and location. Location information can be more than a globally unique name as mobile sensors are allowed.

Figure 2 shows four different areas (A–D) being monitored. Area A is monitored by two logical monitoring stations, each consisting of two physical monitoring stations. Area B contains only one logical and one physical monitoring station.

3.2 The collection layer

The collection layer is responsible for collecting the monitored data from the bottom layer; it filters data to be transmitted higher up in the architecture. The layer consists of a set of collection modules, each responsible for the collection of raw data from one or several geographical areas. If higher layers request data from a certain area, the collection layer is responsible for carrying out this request.

The architecture allows for a structure of collection modules which can be either flat or hierarchical. The flat structure, illustrated in Figure 2, is recommended for applications that do not need to scale much. When data is being scaled, the collection modules should be structured as a tree hierarchy with a root node, subnodes, and leaves mapping existing real-world naming strategies. For instance, a real-world mapping can have the world as the root node, Europe as a subnode, Norway as a subnode in Europe, North-Norway as a subnode in Norway, and Tromsø as the end leaf of this branch. The root, each subnode, and each leaf are represented by a collection module. At the architectural level, this is not seen as a bottleneck.

Another feature of this layer is the temporary storage of data obtained from the bottom layer. The architecture suggests that data requested through a certain collection module is cached locally following a FIFO replacement strategy. If current data is impossible to obtain from the monitoring layer, old data cached at this layer can be returned as responses to requests from higher layers. A time stamp always follows the data, and it is the responsibility of higher layers to validate the data based on the time stamp.

3.3 The data storage layer

The data storage layer is the first layer that permanently stores data. No processing is done on the data and, once stored, the data never changes. This layer requests and stores data from certain areas at predefined frequencies, and it replies with retrieved data when it receives requests from higher layers.

The StormCast architecture allows for integration with both data and information from other sources. The horizontal arrow in the data storage layer in Figure 2 indicates that data can come from sources other than the collection layer. Applications derived from the architecture can, for instance, store data collected from a diverse set ranging from human beings to satellites.

3.4 The application layer

The application layer contains the services that convert raw data into information. The layer requests data from both the data storage layer and the collection layer. Input can also come from other sources, as indicated by a horizontal arrow in Figure 2. This can be information coming from sources ranging from human-based weather predictions to output from monolithic weather applications run on supercomputers and based on numerical weather models.

Different types of application modules can be located in this layer. One example is an application which provides statistics by working on data obtained from the data storage layer. Another application predicts future weather based on input from the collection layer, the data storage layer, and human experts in the field.

3.5 The information storage layer

A distinction is made between storage of raw data and processed data in the StormCast architecture. The information storage layer provides the same set of services as the data storage layer, but only processed data is stored at this layer. As with the data storage layer, information can be stored here based on processed data from certain areas at predefined frequencies.

3.6 The user interface layer

The user interface layer creates and manages the user dialogues. Typically, a client module is activated for each service requested. Each such client module interacts with one or several servers logically found in lower layers of the architecture. An intermediate structure called a service provider is involved in this process. Such a service provider extends the typical stub [Birr84] functionality.

A service provider represents a service on each node where a user interface is represented. It functions as a front end to servers typically found in the application layer. Hence, a client module interacts with the service provider. The service provider locates and communicates with the appropriate server or servers in lower layers of the architecture. Also, each service provider maintains a local cache to be used if the remotely implemented service fails. One extreme is that a user interface node might be fully disconnected from the rest of the application; then the content of the different caches can be used to provide a minimal functionality.

4 The design and implementation of StormCast 2.0

Based on the StormCast architecture, different distributed applications have been designed and prototyped [Joha88] [Hart88] [Hart90] [Joha91]. StormCast 2.0 is the latest in a series, and it is derived directly from the architecture described in the previous section. All six layers of the architecture have been further designed and implemented.

Running mainly on a set of 88 PA-RISC-based Hewlett-Packard 9000/7x0 workstations connected through a 10 Mbit/s Ethernet, this distributed application is mostly used for evaluation of operating system support needed. Each workstation is normally equipped with a 64-Mbyte RAM and an 850-Mbyte disk.

HP-UX Release 8.07, X Windows/Motif 1.1, TCP/IP, and the ISIS Toolkit 2.2.5 [Birm87] are used as a software platform for StormCast 2.0. Special-purpose interprocess communication protocols developed as part of the StormCast project are also used.

StormCast 2.0 consists of a set of communicating processes written in the C programming language augmented with library calls for interprocess communication. FORTH is used to program the loggers, and CommonLisp is used to implement a weather forecasting service in the application layer.

4.1 The monitoring layer

The earliest versions of the StormCast distributed application used software random generators to simulate weather data [Joha88] [Hart88]. StormCast 2.0 receives real data from physical monitoring stations, and this includes weather data from public weather-monitoring stations.

The monitoring layer consists of a set of loggers and monitoring stations. Sensors for a certain geographical area are clustered around a logger that manages the access to these input devices. A logger converts analog input from the sensors to digital values and calibrates the data to such physical quantities as are shown in Table 1. The logger also stamps the data with the current location and time values.

All data requested is cached in the logger. Additionally, a logger can request data at certain predefined intervals to store it in the cache. A logger always tries to return real data but responds with cached data if real data cannot be obtained from the sensors.

A logger is typically a dedicated computer such as a VXI HP 75000. We have also built our own special-purpose logger allowing for both modem-based and packet radio communication. Currently, this logger is enhanced with equipment for satellite communication as well. Workstations directly connected to sensors have also been used as loggers.

Not all potentially relevant data is detected, only the kind of data based on the sensor types used. Table 1 shows a sample of sensor data received. This is real data from a physical monitoring station on the roof of the department building at the University of Tromsø. The logger has requested data every 10 minutes.

Table 1. Sensor data from a monitoring station.

Name	Time	WiSp	WiDir	Pres	Tmp1	Tmp2	Sun
		m/sec	degr	mbar	Cel	Cel	mW/cm2
CS.UoT. Tos.No.	230492-10.20.08	3.7	72.7	1013.3	1.2	1.0	8.8
CS.UoT. Tos.No.	230492-10.30.08	2.5	57.7	1013.3	1.5	1.4	11.5
CS.UoT. Tos.No.	230492-10.40.06	1.9	64.0	1013.3	1.7	1.6	16.1
CS.UoT. Tos.No.	230492-10.50.07	3.1	61.5	1012.9	1.4	1.3	16.1
CS.UoT. Tos.No.	230492-11.00.08	3.5	48.6	1012.9	1.3	1.3	31.3

This logger also checks data approaching specified threshold values. If these are exceeded, an alarm will be activated as a prompt upward notification sent to higher layers. Alternatively, data could have been checked at higher layers. This alternative was not chosen due to its more centralized processing structure, something we consider a scaling bottleneck. This alternative would have required a continuous stream of data being sent upward to be checked. Data monitored at a physical monitoring station typically counts for about 100 byte. Sampled once a second, this means that over 8 Mbyte would be sent upward during a day.

4.2 The collection layer

The collection layer is designed as a two-dimensional array of servers with each server implemented as a process. One of the dimensions contains a set of servers sharing the work requested by higher layers. Altogether, this dimension collects data from any of the areas being monitored. We have used both a flat and a hierarchical organization of this set. Figure 3 shows an area A with two subareas B and C.

The other dimension is along a fault tolerance axis where a replicated set of servers can be responsible for the same geographical area in a primary site scheme. ISIS [Birm87] is used to manage each such group with one active collection server at a time, but with one or several stand-by reserves. Only one server actively serves a request. Using several active servers would have involved redundant requests to the monitoring layer. Another group member is activated to carry out a request if the primary fails. Fast recovery from failure is ensured by ISIS, which keeps the backups up-to-date with the current state. Figure 3 illustrates the two dimensions used to increase availability of the collection layer. Subarea B has two stand-by reserves; subarea C has one.

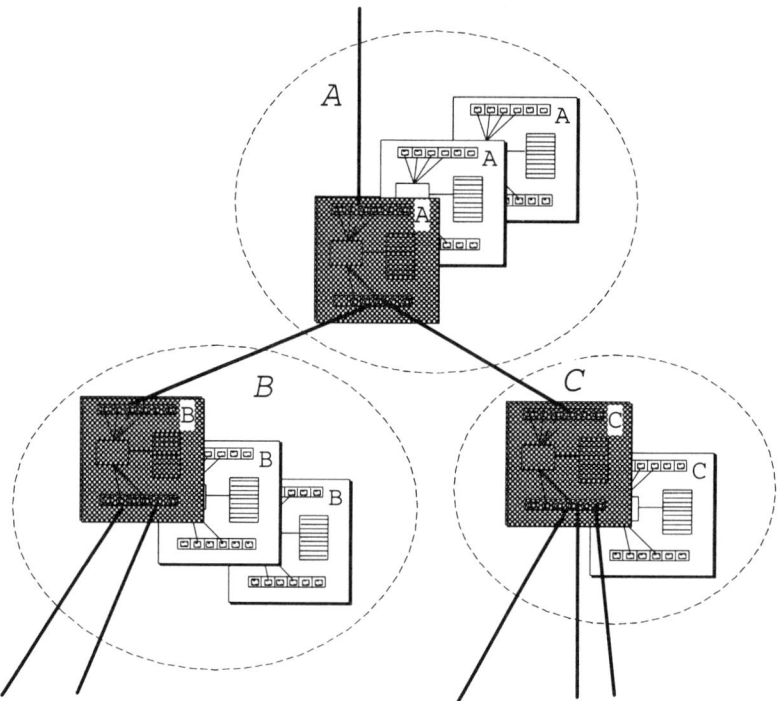

Figure 3. Replication at the collection layer.

All data requested through a collection module is temporarily cached by a collection server. Typically, if 1 Mbyte has been allocated for this purpose, about 10,000 data sets received from the monitoring layer can be cached. If more cached data is needed, this size is easily changed. How long the data remains in the cache depends entirely on the frequency of requests to the monitoring layer. Data from this cache is used whenever data cannot be obtained from the monitoring layer.

4.3 The data storage layer

An essential part of StormCast 2.0 is the ability to store raw data for later retrieval. Only important data exceeding certain thresholds or data sampled at certain frequencies is stored permanently. This is done by a storage service located at the data storage layer in the StormCast architecture. Data to be stored is normally requested by this storage service at certain predefined frequencies. For instance, once an hour weather data for a geographical area can be stored.

Once collected, data never changes, so it is stored as immutable files as in the Cedar File System [Giff88] or the Bullet File Server [Rene89]. Immutable files are files that can be read and deleted, but not modified. The storage service design in StormCast is motivated by fast and flexible retrieval of data, not by consistency requirements since multiple writes are not allowed.

Currently, we are designing and building several storage services for long-lived data, also called persistent data. One approach is based on flat UNIX files replicated on a set of servers. ISIS [Birm87] [Rene92] is used to get a group of servers to act as one. In contrast to the approach taken at the collection layer, each server in the group is actively storing data on separate disks. The different storage operations do not have to be synchronized since all data is time stamped. All that must be guaranteed is that a storage operation be carried out by all members of the group, an operation supported by ISIS; virtual synchrony, as provided by ISIS, is not needed.

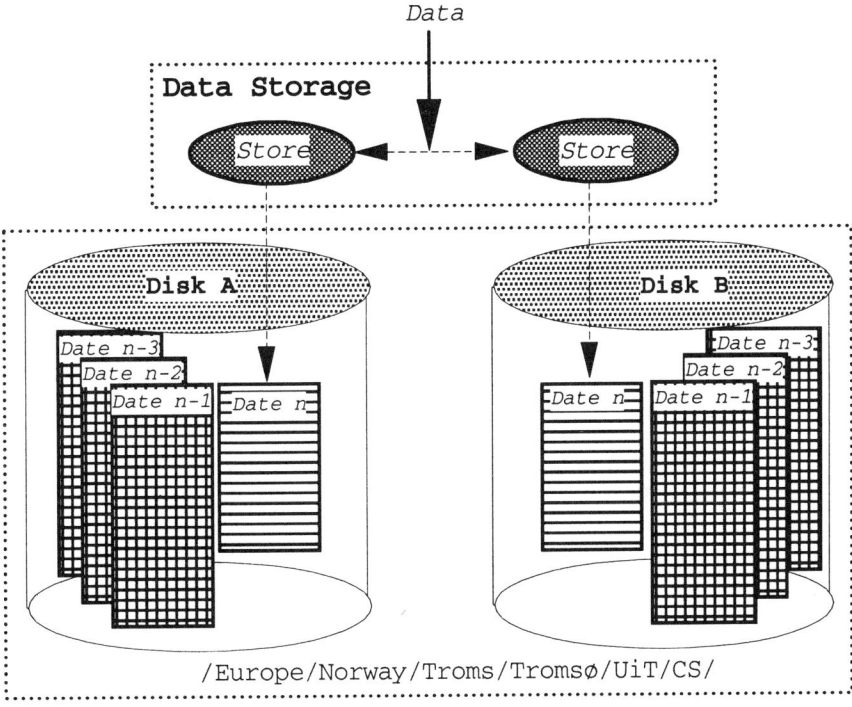

Figure 4. An ISIS-based approach for data storage.

Figure 4 illustrates a group with two members both storing the same data using immutable files. Optical disks have not yet been used, so a new version of a file is created when new data is appended to an existing file. Each area is represented with a separate set of files. Storing data every tenth minute means that 144 versions of a file can exist for a day. With each sample counting about 100 byte, this grows to approximately 14 Kbyte at the end of the day. Only the latest version of a file is stored permanently.

Retrieval of data is done by specifying a starting and stopping time and the location. Another approach is to single out certain patterns by specifying, for instance, requests for all weather data for an area with certain characteristics. This data is typically used by clients found in the application layer. It is also used to debug and improve the quality of the weather forecasting service by running maintained versions of this service on existing data sets.

4.4 The application layer

The application layer of StormCast 2.0 transforms data into information. One example is the service that provides weather statistics for a user. This service issues requests to the data storage service and produces various statistics.

Another service is the weather prediction service [Hart88] [Hart90]. This service is motivated by the fact that weather forecasters already base much of their work on output from computerized weather models, which are often complex numerical models running as monolithic processes on supercomputers. The weather prediction done in StormCast 2.0 is based on an alternative model in which a set of expert systems predicts weather forecasts. To simplify the actual weather forecasting problem, we restrict the weather forecasting process to severe-storm forecasting. We see the practical expert system approach as a supplement to traditional numerical model-based forecasts. This means that StormCast is intended to produce microforecasts, that is, highly detailed forecasts of conditions over relatively limited areas. This focus is motivated by the fact that very local storms can appear in the Arctic within very short time intervals.

The expert module in each domain regularly produces storm forecasts based on locally monitored data. However, storm forecasts are multicast to neighboring domains to aid in the prediction process in those other domains. For example, consider two domains, North and South. Domain South might have a storm prediction indicating that the probability of a storm in this region is 0.3. If an upcoming storm center is located in domain North heading south, the local storm prediction in domain North might be 0.9. If domain North multicasts this prediction to its neighbors, including domain South, domain South can use this information to give a more accurate microforecast for itself.

Communication of information is handled by a set of blackboards [Nii86]. The blackboards' main function is to offload communication processing from the weather forecasting modules and provide a globally shared memory of weather predictions. Each blackboard is directly related to an expert module, and each multicasts to its neighbors any local prediction received from the related expert module. Each blackboard is also member of a group together with its neighbors.

4.5 The information storage layer

Information can be stored at the information storage layer using the same approach as on the data storage layer. Indexed UNIX files (NDBM) and an SQL database (Ingres) have also been candidates for this layer. These provide more functionality in retrieving information, but the trade-off with performance is too high. The performance difference between a sequential UNIX file and the SQL approach is typically on the order of a factor of 80 for 10-byte data sets.

The amount and type of information stored depend largely on the users. Data stored in lower layers of StormCast 2.0 has more rigid requirements when it comes to amount and frequency. The reason for this choice is that data represents a real value while information depends on the type of service used to transform the real data to information.

One example of information stored at this layer is weather forecasts received from the Norwegian Meteorological Institute. This is output from a numerical weather application run on a CRAY Y-MP predicting weather in certain areas at certain times. These computations are based on input from up to 9,000 monitoring stations worldwide. Typically, the output is received and stored on files which average about 2 Mbyte.

4.6 The user interface layer

The graphical user interface of StormCast 2.0 is based on X and OSF/Motif 1.1 [OSF91]. Figure 5 illustrates the main user interface of StormCast 2.0.

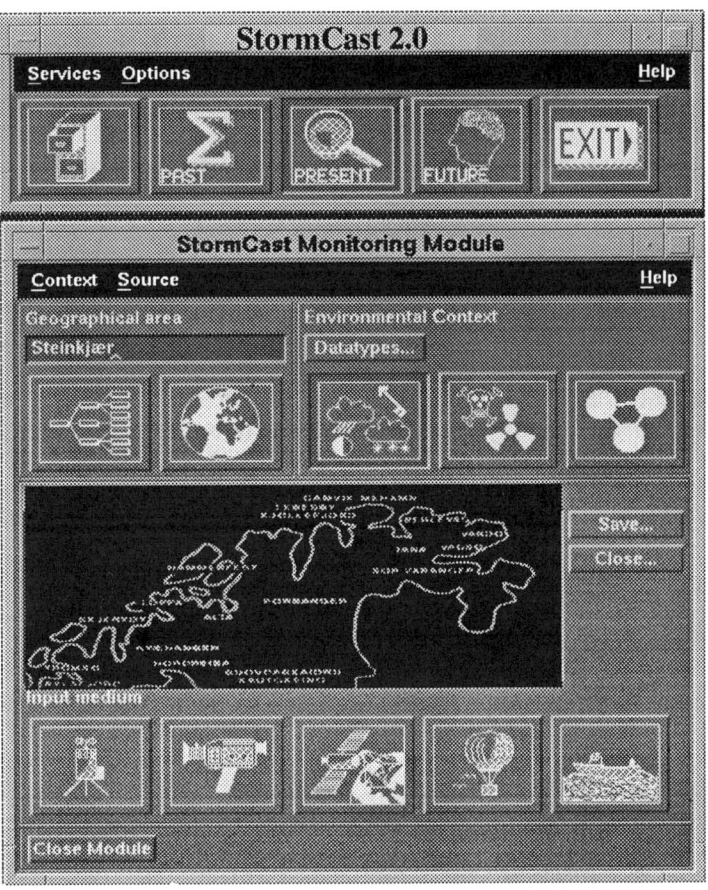

Figure 5. The StormCast 2.0 main user interface display.

The user interface layer handles all user interaction. A user acts as a client selecting a service or a set of services. Services that can be directly accessed by users are represented in this layer by separate service providers. Each service provider locates the appropriate server implementing the service and carries out the requested operations. Each service provider also caches data and information in case of network partitionings or servers not responding.

One example of such a service is the display of weather information for a selected area. A user typically selects an area by real-world names or by marking an area on a map. The service provider obtains the data needed from the collection layer and displays it.

Another example displays animation sequences of satellite pictures. Satellite pictures are received and stored for this purpose. Typically, each such picture takes up about 300 Kbyte.

Color is a very useful and efficient technique for transferring information to a user. Also, visualization is possible through volume rendering techniques. For instance, weather predictions received from the Norwegian Meteorological Institute as output from a CRAY Y-MP can be presented in three dimensions. A fourth dimension, time, can be implemented as a set of 3D ray traced images shown in animation sequences.

This is supported by several nodes in parallel; one possibility is to work in parallel on separate parts of each image, the other possibility is to work in parallel with different images.

5 Customized StormCast applications

For evaluation of architecture and design choices, several customized StormCast applications have been developed. Reuse of both design and implementations from the StormCast 2.0 distributed application has been possible to a large extent by using the same overall architecture. The following applications are built out of necessity and in real domains in cooperation with industry.

5.1 Weather monitoring of a small area — AirCast

A distributed application monitoring weather at an airport area was the first customized distributed application derived from the StormCast architecture and previous research prototypes. This application is called AirCast. The objective of AirCast is to predict potential dramatic weather situations when planes are about to land or leave. Located near the North Pole, small airports in the northern part of Norway are subject to turbulent weather conditions during the winter.

A similar approach is taken at the Mission Control Center in Houston [Mura90]. Selection of runways for a landing space shuttle is based on winds. Wind speed and wind directions from the landing areas are monitored automatically; crosswind components are computed; and an expert system applies flight rules to determine whether winds are within limits. The flight director makes the final decision based on this output.

The development of AirCast is done in four separate phases. Each phase begins with the development and validation of a prototype by the StormCast project; this prototype is then fully developed by industry. Phase one is finished with the monitoring layer, the collection layer, the data storage layer, and the interface layer developed. The functionality of AirCast Phase 1 is to visualize the current weather situation around the airport. Prior to AirCast, data was monitored automatically, but appeared as pure ASCII output on a printer.

Phase 2 is to connect different airports and to receive weather forecasts. AirCast Phase 2 is developed and prototyped, and we are now working with the prototype to AirCast Phase 3. This prototype will have more services found in the application layer. For instance, a local weather prediction module predicting dramatic weather situations and potential slippery runways is being developed. Phase 4, the final phase, will get the interface part of AirCast up and running in the planes. Consequently, the user interface of AirCast aspires to simulate instruments pilots normally use.

5.2 StormCast Arctic sea monitoring — SeaCast

A second customized StormCast application monitors offshore weather and pollution parameters. This distributed application is called SeaCast and is developed along the same lines as AirCast.

An important motivation for SeaCast is that fishermen and sailors in the Arctic region are very dependent on the weather. Human beings in these areas can be faced with dramatic and unpredicted storms without proper warning. One reason for this is that meteorological predictions received from the mainland are based on numerical computations that do not have proper input of real weather data from these huge areas. A quick look at a map over the Arctic gives an indication of the huge areas of water with little regular weather monitoring to base predictions on. Consequently, we have been motivated to build a StormCast version running on boats operating in the Arctic.

A second motivation is the potential pollution of radioactivity in these areas. Unfortunately, there are potential sources of very high radioactive pollution in neighboring Russia. Experience shows that accidents happen at both military and civil installations. It is also a matter of time until polluted leftovers from the nuclear industry influence the water basins connected with the Arctic sea. We intend to use the weather-monitoring infrastructure to monitor radioactivity parameters as well.

SeaCast is intended to be run on board ships in the Arctic. Initially, 16 boats have been running a prototype receiving weather forecasts from the Norwegian Meteorological Institute through the Inmarsat.c satellite running X.25. The extension we have devised is to add a monitoring layer and a collection layer on board these ships. Weather data can then be sent back to the mainland to be used as input in the weather computations running on supercomputers. The monitoring layer will also be enhanced to automatically monitor radioactivity levels in the sea around the boat.

The SeaCast distributed application also takes full advantage of the idea to use an expert system approach to predict severe storms. Based on locally monitored data and weather forecasts received from neighboring domains, local predictions will be done. Each boat running SeaCast will propagate local weather forecasts to its neighbors and receive forecasts in return. This weather forecast is also compared with the forecast received from the mainland.

The number of cooperating expert modules is also important. The application is designed to be able to operate totally isolated, with total local control. The decision process will be clearly weakened in this disconnected mode, but still operational.

5.3 StormCast water monitoring — WaterCast

The third distributed application based on the same StormCast architecture monitors a river. This application is called WaterCast, and the first version was based on real data monitored and collected from Akerselva, the main river in the capital city of Norway.

The rationale behind WaterCast is to be able to detect possible pollution and trace the sources of the pollution. This is possible by having a set of monitoring stations located along the river. The more stations, the easier it is to pinpoint the area the pollution comes from. WaterCast can also be used to verify the quality of water being used by human beings.

WaterCast is based on the monitoring, collection, data storage, and interface layers in the StormCast architecture. A service providing statistics is the only application found in the application layer.

Parameters including temperature, connectivity, acidity, and water level are monitored at regular frequencies. This data is stored for later statistical use. Threshold values are set for each parameter triggering an alarm if exceeded. A user might also get the current situation of the river monitored.

Currently, we are extending the functionality of WaterCast in other geographical areas. One version monitors a municipal sewage system and its sewage plant. Another WaterCast version allows more human-based input due to lack of appropriate sensor technology. This version was built for the border river between Norway and Russia.

Distributed Open Systems

6 Experiences and lessons

An objective of the StormCast project is to validate a certain application domain and its suitability for distributed computing. The area chosen is the monitoring of weather and environment parameters in real geographical areas. Another objective is to develop a general architecture and resulting distributed applications for this type of monitoring. A final objective is to construct an appropriate platform for distributed applications of tomorrow through a top-down approach. A number of lessons have been learned as we have met these objectives.

6.1 Distributed computing in the weather and environment domain

Section 2 argues for the weather and environment sectors as proper application domains for distributed computing. Experience clearly shows that this type of monitoring is distributed in nature. The monitoring is distributed since the area to be monitored is large. In addition, the amount of data monitored can be huge. A centralized solution would have required a high frequency of data received to be able to capture sudden changes. Distributing the processing close to the source of the data can reduce this frequency.

Potential users are not centralized, with fishermen out in the Arctic Sea as an example. Consequently, more than the monitoring part of an application in this domain should be distributed. For instance, a service such as the weather forecasting service can be distributed.

The first implementations of the customized applications described in Section 5 are operational. This serves as proof that a distributed application approach in this application domain is a good concept.

6.2 The StormCast architecture and its applications

Experience with StormCast implementations has taught us several lessons about the architecture devised and the different design alternatives. Layering of the architecture, interaction between modules, scalability, reliability, and availability issues will be discussed in the following subsection.

6.2.1 The layers of the StormCast architecture

The layering of the StormCast architecture is not randomly picked, but is a result of architecture proposals, applications developed based on the different architectures, and evaluations. Several StormCast architectures have previously existed, but never a centralized one.

The current StormCast architecture consists of six layers. Initially, we had a three-layer architecture [Joha88] with a bottom layer responsible for monitoring raw data, a middle layer responsible for collection of data, and a top layer displaying the data. The middle layer cached data on disk, but no permanent storage was provided. This StormCast architecture provided no layer to transform raw data into information.

Added functionality required storage of data for later retrieval by, for instance, expert system modules predicting future weather conditions. This meant devising a four-layer architecture [Hart88] [Hart90] with an application layer as the extra one.

Need for more permanent storage of data and information added two layers to this architecture. One alternative would have been to extend the caching functionality already present in the collection layer to allow permanent storage. A main reason for rejecting this was that we considered collection of data and storage of data as two separate tasks. The splitting of data and information has the same motivation.

Integration of weather predictions from other numerical computations as well as human interactions gave StormCast a critic [Silv92] functionality which the first architectures did not support. Our current architecture is a result of these developments.

Splitting data acquisition and application processing is considered important in a hard real-time environment, as at the Mission Control Center [Mura90]. Otherwise, increased application load can prevent the data acquisition from meeting the hard real-time constraints. Even if hard real-time constraints do not exist in StormCast 2.0, this separation is important. One reason is that these two tasks are separated in functionality; another is that this separation makes scaling easier. Different replication techniques can also be applied to different parts. For instance, pure hardware replication can be used in the monitoring layer, whereas a primary site approach can be used higher up in the layers.

The StormCast architecture is also comparable to the mediator architecture [Wied92]. The mediator architecture has a mediator layer between a user layer and a base layer. The user layer contains independent applications, and the base layer contains multiple databases getting input from a variety of sources. The mediator layer contains multiple mediators, which are software modules that exploit encoded knowledge about certain sets or subsets of data to create information for a higher layer of applications.

Several distributed applications have been developed based on the same StormCast architecture. Consequently, reuse of both design and implementations has been possible. It makes little difference whether it is water temperature or air temperature that is collected, stored, processed or visualized. The main difference can be found in the monitoring layer, which requires different sensors, and in the application layer, but even in the application layer reuse is possible to a large extent.

6.2.2 Interactions between modules

Client-server interactions dominate in StormCast, where a client issues a request for some data provided by one or a number of servers. Normally, a request goes from a higher layer to a lower layer in the architecture. An alternative would have been the other way around, but this is used only when, for instance, an alarm goes off in one of the lowest layers and has to propagate up the layers as soon as possible. Having the lower layer sending other data to higher layers was also considered, but not chosen. A main reason for this was that the interaction would be too rigid and too much based on a priori knowledge. With a user pattern of many requests for current data, the frequency of sending data up the layers would also have to be high to meet availability requirements. Another problem would be where to send all this data; one extreme would be to send all data to all potential users. Clearly, more network bandwidth would have been used with this approach, and available network bandwidth is still a problem in these environments.

Figure 6 illustrates main interaction patterns as found in StormCast applications. The patterns A–G described are all useful in real applications. All but the interaction pattern C are considered special instances of the client-server model. Interaction scheme C is based on multicasts to a group where no reply is required. This multicast is not atomic because this communication scheme is mainly used between a set of expert system modules in the SeaCast application. For instance, a local prediction from a weather forecasting module can be multicast to several other weather forecasting modules. Interconnection technology is unstable in the environments where SeaCast operates. This often implies that some members of a group do not receive the multicast. Of course, the multicast information will still be important for the rest of the group.

A, B, and E are used in all StormCast applications; D and F are used when replication techniques are employed. Interaction A illustrates a client-server interaction in which a client at the user interface layer requests a server in the information storage layer. B is a similar interaction, but illustrates that communication can be within the same layer. Interaction E illustrates a nested client-server relationship in which a client issues a request to a server in the layer below. This server acts as a client in a client-server relationship with a second server one layer further down.

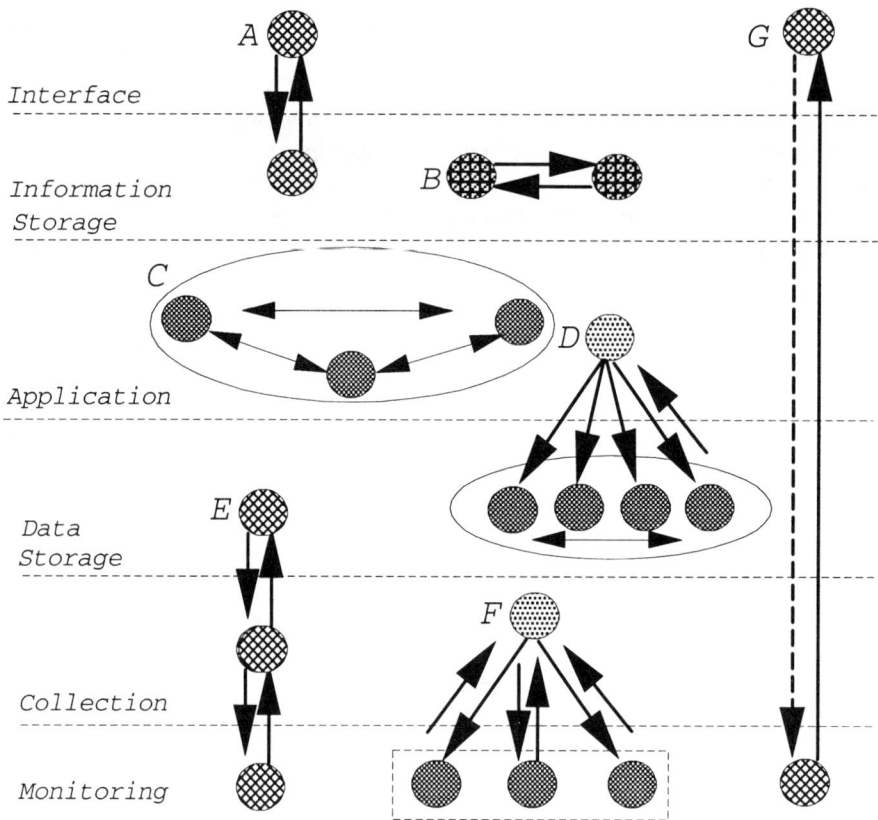

Figure 6. Interactions in StormCast.

Group communication is also a useful paradigm. Interaction scheme C is one example of group communication; another is sending a request to a group of servers. We consider group communication involving requests and replies as a special instance of the client-server model. Depending on the functionality chosen, one or several of the servers can reply. Interaction D illustrates that a client sends a request to a group of servers, and the group sends back one reply. For instance, a request for stored data can be sent to a group of data storage servers, but only one reply is sent back. Interaction F requires all servers to respond. In this interaction, only the client views the servers as a group. The servers in the group are not aware of each other. This interaction scheme is found at the lowest layers in the StormCast architecture, where a collection module obtains data from several subdomains in parallel.

Interaction G is a special instance of a client-server relationship. A client sends a request to a server asking for a reply when a certain event occurs at the server side. For instance, this is used to warn users about exceeded threshold values in the monitoring layer. These threshold values are adaptive, meaning that they are specified at higher layers and can vary from client to client. Interaction scheme C has also been used for alarm notifications to a group.

6.2.3 Scalability

Ability to scale well is an important characteristic of a distributed application. Scaling in StormCast applications is motivated by the need to add extra users and domains, not to scale to meet overall performance requirements from a single computation. StormCast applications have to be up and running over time and in very large scale to quantify and establish the scaling properties. A scaling of StormCast 2.0 using at most 88 workstations does not give more than indications. However, we estimate how well this scales by identifying how easily new users are added, how easily new geographical areas are added, and how well different parts of it behave when the frequency and the amount of data transmitted are increased.

Previous versions of StormCast [Joha88] [Hart90] did not scale well. In particular, the collection layer with its flat structure could be a bottleneck. StormCast 2.0 scales much better due to a hierarchical structure in the collection layer combined with replication techniques where needed.

Added users or areas to be monitored might introduce bottlenecks at nodes or in networks. Such bottlenecks are typical for centralized applications running on centralized hardware. Our approach avoids centralization as much as possible. For instance, the different services are provided by a replicated set of servers; more replicas might remove potential bottlenecks. Generally, it might be argued that too many replicas will introduce new problems with, for instance, mutual updates and synchronization between many replicas. Using immutable data reduces this type of problem to a question of which server responds to a request for a particular service.

The primary site approach used when replicating collection modules might, however, be a scaling bottleneck. Typically, requests to a group of collection servers responsible for the same area are carried out by one of the servers, and another server is activated only when this fails. ISIS [Birm87] is used for this purpose, and multithreading in ISIS [Rene92] can be used to handle several requests. This parallelism is only obtained at a single node, however.

The hierarchical structure in the collection layer is also important. This hierarchy is directly related to the real-world hierarchy. A new area added to StormCast will therefore find its natural place in this hierarchy.

Distributing processing normally done at a centralized node is one approach to achieving scalability. Another is the filtering of data, possibly done close to the source of data, reducing by selection the amount of data to be transmitted. This is done in StormCast applications. A centralized approach would have required much more network bandwidth to be able to extract the correct information.

Increased frequency of requests combined with larger data sets to transfer over networks might also be a scaling impediment. This is basically a technology and cost problem. The StormCast 2.0 already reduces these potential scaling bottlenecks by requesting data only when needed. Sending data at prearranged intervals would have caused scaling problems as more data would have to be sent to more locations. Controlling monitored data against threshold values as close to its source also eases scaling. Without this control, more data would have to propagate higher up in the layers increasing network traffic.

6.2.4 Reliability efforts close to the source of data

We define reliable data as correct data. Reliability requirements have influenced the StormCast architecture and its derived applications. The objective is to have the monitored data be correct and remain correct.

Reliability must be ensured when data is monitored if reliability is a requirement. Hardware replication of physical monitoring stations is then used to get more correct data at its source. The connecting logger might then mask errors transparently or reply with data from the different replicas. As Table 1 shows, data from two different temperature sensors is monitored. Monitored data close to a potential pollution area should especially be as reliable as possible since it is important to base an alarm on reliable data.

Sensors are also treated as a major source of errors by the Mission Control Center [Mura90], which uses a different approach to solve the problem: Noise-filtering techniques minimize the effects of incorrect data. Replication of sensors is used in StormCast. The former approach might be useful in an environment where data is acquired at very high frequencies under hard real-time constraints. The latter approach does not obtain data at high frequencies and cannot check several consecutive data sets and control them if they vary too much. Issuing a new request when erroneous data is discovered higher up in the layers might also be too time-consuming. This might, for instance, involve wide area network traffic, which can cause too long a delay for the intended operations relying on the correct data.

Replication techniques can be a source of unreliable data in a distributed application. Replication is often used to survive partial failures or to increase performance and availability by having local copies of data. This can cause consistency problems because updates on copies or on the original data are not always made visible at all potential locations. Problems with inconsistency are entirely avoided in StormCast 2.0. Immutable data remains the same over time, so it is up to the user of time-stamped data to decide whether the data is useful or not. Consequently, any data that is reliable when monitored will remain reliable.

6.2.5 Availability efforts throughout the application

Availability of a service means that it is carried out within the expected time. For instance, when the average response time of a service is less than a second, a response time of several minutes is not acceptable. StormCast 2.0 is designed and implemented to increase availability of its services. Again, replication is used for this purpose. If one server fails to carry out a request, another server providing the same service can take over the responsibility.

Distributing work among a set of servers also ensures availability. For instance, the user interface layer in StormCast 2.0 contains a set of service providers. Each is carrying out a separate task. A user can request several services more or less simultaneously, and they are carried out by each associated service provider. If several of these service providers have pending requests at the same time carried out at several other nodes, real parallel processing is achieved. This increases the availability of the entire application.

One availability extreme is to ensure that a request is carried out even if servers normally used to carry out this service cannot be requested. Typically, this is a situation caused by network partitioning. Mobile computers, as found in SeaCast, the customized StormCast application on board ships in the Arctic, will also need such functionality. The present geostationary satellite used is not sufficient for continuous communication in the very far north. An alternative is polar orbit satellites, but the current one being tested for this purpose passes an area once every 100 minutes. Hence, temporary partitioning of SeaCast nodes is not an exceptional case.

The approach taken in the StormCast architecture and the derived applications is to cache and store important data and information throughout the applications. In disconnected mode, imprecise results or old data can often be used. One extreme is that the user interface modules become partitioned from the rest of the application. Then the service providers have cached the latest data and information received from previous requests.

Experience shows that partitioning problems usually occur at the lowest layer in the architecture. For instance, the modem connection to a logger can fail. Higher up in the layers, replication of servers might solve such problems since another replica at another node might be contacted. There is a limit, however, on replication, especially when it comes to replication of hardware loggers in all areas to monitor. Consequently, the caching done at the collection layer is important. Alternative communication paths and networks also help to solve such network problems. The current logger built in the StormCast project uses modems and packet radio for communication. A routing protocol is developed using packet radio to communicate with neighboring loggers. These neighbors might then be used to forward requests and replies. This protocol runs at both 300 and 1200 baud, with 300 preferred. The error rate on 1200 baud is too high because the transceivers used are constructed for voice transfer. A third routing path will be through satellite communication as our current logger is extended with an interface for satellite communication. This possibility already exists on board the boats receiving weather forecasts from the mainland.

Disconnected operability must also be addressed when configuring a distributed application. For instance, different replicas of servers should be located at different nodes in case of hardware problems. More controlled partitioning caused by mobility also requires configuration support. Mobile nodes must be configured with the part of a distributed application needed for provision of important services while disconnected. For instance, all nodes running SeaCast should have at least servers found in the interface layer, the application layer, the collection layer, and the monitoring layer. Stored data might become unavailable, but current data can be monitored locally since both the user and the physical monitoring station are on board the same ship. Caching in both the logger and the collection layer provides historic data to some extent. Information about the latest weather forecast from the mainland is also cached in the user interface layer. Altogether, this enables a node to be fully disconnected over time. In addition, this approach assumes that every node has enough operating system support for disconnected operability. This excludes, for instance, operating system solutions where diskless workstations have to page over a network.

7 Present status and future plans

There are several main directions in which the StormCast project is progressing. First, StormCast 2.0 should be revised and rebuilt into a multimedia application. Currently, we work with integration of digital video and audio.

StormCast applications are not secure enough. The different workstations running processes in disjunct address spaces provide a minimal level of security. Proper authentication and authorization mechanisms have to get more attention. Cryptography of sensitive data is also a user requirement in StormCast applications.

More customized distributed applications should be developed to give new insights to the StormCast architecture. Currently, we are concentrating on monitoring air pollution, including radioactivity parameters. This is also done in cooperation with our external partners, and we concentrate on the border area with Russia.

The other ongoing customizing projects are also carried through. This allows our ideas to be incorporated into daily use, providing important feedback.

Finally, we are interested in operating system issues. The first prototype of StormCast was running on an Amoeba [Tane90] platform in wide area network environments [Rene88] [Joha88]. This was basically an exercise in distributed computing, stressing few real application aspects. Such aspects have been taken more and more into consideration as new versions have been built. More application focus also required a platform found in more than a few laboratories, and pragmatic decisions made UNIX the platform choice. Nevertheless, having used Amoeba as a first platform, we had certain expectations of a platform for distributed applications. ISIS has been used to fill the gap between a UNIX-based platform and a distributed system platform. Currently, we are using our experience with these platforms to build our own platform for this type of environment. Basically, a multi-RPC protocol as found in [Saty90] has been implemented, allowing a client to request several servers at the same time. A reply can typically be based on the first reply or the average reply from each of the servers requested. Based on UDP, a 10-Mbit/s Ethernet and Hewlett-Packard 9000/730 workstations, a null multi-RPC takes 1.1 msec between a client and one server at different nodes. A null multi-RPC involving 48 servers typically takes 30 msec.

A group abstraction still needs to be implemented on top of this multi-RPC to implement the subset of ISIS that we found most useful. This must allow groups to be partitioned, but with each of the subgroups operational. Our current ISIS version does not support such fragmentation well enough, especially when these subgroups are to join again to form the initial group. This is a typical situation with mobile users linked with unstable communication technology, as in SeaCast.

8 Conclusions

The StormCast architecture and its application derivatives have been presented. Currently, we are achieving the goals set for the StormCast project. The first goal was to legitimize distributed computing in the weather and environment domains. Real distributed applications meeting user requirements in this particular domain serve as more than an indication.

A general architecture for soft real-time distributed applications monitoring real-world events has been devised. This architecture has been developed and has matured over several years of experience. Currently, it consists of six layers, with the bottom layers capturing, collecting, and storing real-world events. The next two layers transform this raw data into information, and the highest layer interacts with users. Human-generated weather forecasts can also be input to the application layer that critiques these solutions.

Several distributed applications have been designed and implemented based on this architecture. Ensured fault tolerance is a basic design requirement, and replication techniques have improved both reliability and availability of the StormCast distributed applications. This includes improved disconnected operability of the distributed applications. Caching is heavily used in these applications, and cache consistency problems are avoided with immutable data.

A third objective of the StormCast project is the study of support requirements needed for distributed applications. Distributed applications have been run on different platforms, and a distributed system clearly provides, for instance, the naming, addressing, and location mechanisms that make this type of platform preferable. In retrospect, pragmatic requirements moved StormCast to a UNIX platform, a step back in functionality. Moving to an ISIS platform was a step forward again.

The basic assumption in the StormCast project is that several application sectors exist that lend themselves naturally to distributed computing. Experience also shows that a distributed system provides a convenient platform for distributed applications. Nevertheless, distributed applications are still rare. The problem might be that application engineers still consider applications in terms of monolithic structures. The opposite approach, as taken in the StormCast project, should be useful in other domains as well.

Acknowledgments

The author would like to thank all members of the StormCast project for their contributions. The StormCast project is a team effort in which Gunnar Hartvigsen plays a key role. Rolf Dahl and his StormCast crew at Norwegian Information Technology also play a vital role in customizing StormCast applications in real habitats.

Overcoming personal incompetence is important in an interdisciplinary project. In that respect, input from staff at the Norwegian Meteorological Institute has been indispensable. We would also like to thank Ken Birman, Robbert van Renesse, and Mike Schroeder for their helpful discussions and comments on earlier drafts of this paper.

References

Birm87 K.P. Birman and T.A. Joseph, "Exploiting Virtual Synchrony in Distributed Systems," *Proc. 11th ACM Symp. on Operating Systems Principles*, Austin, TX, Nov. 1987, pp. 123-138.

Birr84 A.D. Birrell and B.J. Nelson, "Implementing Remote Procedure Calls," *ACM Trans. Comput. Systems*, Vol. 2, Feb. 1984, pp. 39-59.

Giff88 D.K. Gifford, R.M. Needham, and M.D. Schroeder, "The Cedar File System," *Comm. ACM*, Vol. 31, No. 3, Mar. 1988, pp. 288-298.

Hans73 P.B. Hansen, *Operating System Principles*, Prentice Hall, Englewood Cliffs, N.J., 1973.

Hart88 G. Hartvigsen and D. Johansen, "StormCast — A Distributed Artificial Intelligence Application for Severe Storm Forecasting," *Proc. IFAC DCCS '88*, Pergamon, Elmsford, N.Y., 1988, pp. 99-102.

Hart90 G. Hartvigsen and D. Johansen, "Cooperation in a Distributed Artificial Intelligence Environment — The StormCast Approach," *Eng. Appli. AI*, Sept. 1990, pp. 229-238.

Joha88 D. Johansen, "Weather Forecasting — Distributed in Nature," *Proc. IFIP TC6/TC8 Open Symp. on Net. Info. Proc. Sys.*, North-Holland, May 1988, pp. 197-203.

Joha91 D. Johansen and G. Hartvigsen, "StormCast — A Distributed Application," *Proc. EurOpen Autumn '91*, Sept. 1991, pp. 273-286.

Lein80 D.W. Leinbaugh, "Guaranteed Response Times in a Hard Real-Time Computer System," *IEEE Trans. Software Eng.*, Vol. SE-6, Jan. 1980, pp. 85-91.

Marz91 K. Marzullo et al., "Tools for Distributed Application Management," *IEEE Computer*, Vol. 24, No. 8, Aug. 1991, pp. 42-51.

Mura90 J.F. Muratore et al., "Real-Time Data and Acquisition at Mission Control," *Comm. ACM*, Vol. 33, No. 12, Dec. 1990, pp. 19-31.

Nii86 H.P. Nii, "Blackboard Systems: The Blackboard Model of Problem Solving and the Evolution of Blackboard Architectures," *AI Mag.* (Summer), 1986, pp. 38-53.

OSF91 Open Software Foundation, *OSF Motif Style Guide Revision 1.1*, Prentice Hall, Englewood Cliffs, N.J., 1991.

Payt91 D.W. Payton and T.E. Bihari, "Intelligent Real-Time Control of Robotic Vehicles," *Comm. ACM*, Vol. 34, No. 8, Aug. 1991, pp. 49-63.

Rene88 R. van Renesse et al., "MANDIS/Amoeba: A Widely Dispersed Object-Oriented Operating System," *Proc. EUTECO '88 on Research into Networks and Distributed Applications*, North-Holland, Apr. 1988, pp. 823-831.

Rene89 R. van Renesse, A.S. Tanenbaum, and A. Wilschut, "The Design of a High-Performance File Server," *Proc. Ninth Int'l Conf. on Dist. Comp. Syst.*, IEEE, 1989, pp. 22-27.

Rene92 R. van Renesse et al., "Reliable Multicast between Microkernels," *Proc. USENIX Workshop on Micro-Kernels and Other Kernel Architectures*, Seattle, Washington, Apr. 1992, pp. 269-283.

Saty90 M. Satyanarayanan and E.H. Siegel, "Parallel Communication in a Large Distributed Environment," *IEEE Trans. Computers*, Vol. 39, No. 3, Mar. 1990, pp. 328-348.

Silv92 B.G. Silverman, "Survey of Expert Critiquing Systems: Practical and Theoretical Frontiers," *Comm. ACM*, Vol. 35, No. 4, Apr. 1992, pp. 107-127.

Stan85 J.A. Stankovic, K. Ramamritham, and S. Cheng, "Evaluation of a Flexible Task Scheduling Algorithm for Distributed Hard Real-Time Systems," *IEEE Trans. Computers*, Vol. C-34, No. 12, Dec. 1985, pp. 1130-1143.

Tane90 A. Tanenbaum et al., "Experiences with the Amoeba Distributed Operating System," *Comm. ACM*, Vol. 33, No. 12, Dec. 1990, pp. 46-63.

Wied92 G. Wiederhold, "Mediators in the Architecture of Future Information Systems," *IEEE Computer*, Vol. 25, No. 3, Mar. 1992, pp. 38-49.

Distributed Systems in Perspective

Dag Johansen
Dept. of Computer Science
University of Tromsø
Tromsø, Norway
<dag@cs.uit.no>

Robbert van Renesse
Dept. of Computer Science
Cornell University
Ithaca, NY, USA
<rvr@cs.cornell.edu>

Abstract

This paper summarizes benefits of distributed systems briefly. These are illustrated with systems discussed previously.

1 Introduction

A distributed system is an alternative approach to centralized computer systems and networking-based systems. The main difference between the distributed and the centralized approach is that, in the distributed case, software modules can be distributed over different nodes; the similarity is in the interface. Generally, both should look as though they were centralized. The main difference with a networked system is that the networked system does not appear as a single computer. For instance, a user of a networked system explicitly has to do a remote login to a certain node, or a user explicitly has to transfer a file from one node to another. The similarity between a distributed system and a networked system is the distribution of both hardware and software components.

Real applications already run on both centralized systems and networked systems. The move to another platform as provided by a distributed system must be legitimized. Several advantages of distributed systems have been put forward by the distributed systems community for this purpose. These include location transparency of networked resources, scalability, customization of operating system platforms, fault tolerance, and sharing of resources, as well as suitability for distributed applications.

In this last chapter we will summarize the benefits of distributed systems briefly, and illustrate these with the systems discussed in this book. For your convenience, Table 1 gives a brief overview of these systems. In the following sections we will discuss location transparency, scaling, customization, fault tolerance, resource sharing, and distributed applications.

Table 1. Overview of the different distributed systems.

	Amoeba	Mach/OSF	Plan 9	Chorus	ISIS
Architecture	Centralized processor pool	Symmetric	Centralized processor pool	Symmetric	Symmetric
Model	Object-based	? (configurable)	File-based	Object-based	Process groups
Communication	RPC + multicast	Message + RPC	Streams + file system interface	Message + RPC + unreliable multicast	Multicast + point-to-point
Naming	Capabilities + directory service	Port rights + naming service	File name space (directories)	Capabilities	Addresses
Protection	Capabilities	Port rights Kerberos	rwx bits like UNIX	Capabilities	Public key
Light-weight processes	Yes, kernel-scheduled	Yes	No	Yes	Yes
UNIX support	Slow source emulation	Yes	Almost exactly like UNIX	Yes	Not applicable
Distributed applications (across net)	Good support (ORCA)	OK	Not really	OK	Good support
Multiprocessor support	Yes	Good	Especially for UMA	Yes	Not yet
Virtual memory	Segments	Paging	Paging	Paging	N/A
Fault tolerance	Replicated services	No explicit support	Nice backups	Dynamic reconfiguration	Good support

2 Location-transparent environments

An important advantage of a distributed system is the potential hiding of networking details, especially in a local-area network environment. In a client-server relationship, this means that a client accesses a server without any knowledge of the actual location of the server. This is called location transparency. Implicit in this concept is that all servers present the same interface. The challenge is to build a distributed system that hides the physical distribution of both hardware and software components. Disjoint address spaces, lack of globally shared memory, absence of a global time frame, insecure communication, unpredictable communication delays, and nondeterministic behavior of communicating sequential processes complicate the provision of location transparency.

Location transparency can be provided different ways. For instance, a distributed system based on the Mach microkernel [Acce86] needs to provide location transparency at higher layers, because the Mach microkernel does not provide location transparency itself. In contrast, a distributed system such as Amoeba [Tane90] provides location transparency at the kernel layer.

3 Scaling properties

Cost considerations are always important when implementing real computer systems. A good price/performance ratio is often claimed to be one of the motivations for building distributed systems. The idea is to build distributed systems based on cheap components, so that the overall performance and functionality outperforms what is provided by more expensive monolithic approaches. Distributed systems should be able to scale to hundreds or even thousands of nodes depending on the changing user requirements.

There are two basic approaches to achieve better performance. One is to upgrade existing components. This is a relatively expensive approach. The other approach is to add extra resources to the existing computer system. This scaling does not increase the capacity of the individual nodes, but increases the overall capacity. The hope is to provide supercomputing performance at a fraction of the cost of a supercomputer.

Unfortunately, there are still few parallel applications, little scheduling support for sharing the processor load over the network of nodes, high communication costs, and overhead in moving processes around. We must distinguish between the scaling properties of a distributed system executing a single task on several nodes and a set of tasks on several nodes. The problem of utilizing the accumulated computing power is simpler when there are many users with lots of computations to run.

4 Customized environments

A distributed system can be classified as either a special purpose system or a general purpose system. A special purpose system is customized to meet special requirements, often implementing a specific application together with necessary operating system support. For instance, the monitoring of a nuclear power plant is implemented as a special purpose system not allowing other applications to coexist.

A general purpose system must be able to meet requirements for a diverse set of users. Amoeba, Chorus [Rozi88], Mach, and Plan 9 [Pres91] are all examples of platforms built to execute in an environment with coexisting applications, meeting a wide range of user requirements.

A distributed system can adapt to changing environments. This is simplified by microkernel technology and the idea of providing operating system services outside the kernels. Such services are implemented as servers running on one or several nodes, but not necessarily on all nodes in the distributed system. Through a network-transparent interface, these servers can be accessed from any location in the distributed system.

5 Improved fault tolerance

Even if methods to increase the quality of software exist, failure of applications at run-time occur. Such failures can cause economic disaster and even the loss of lives. We have become critically dependent on sophisticated applications. Because of this, fault tolerance is an important objective of a distributed system. This means that one or several failures should not halt the entire system. A single point of failure will often halt a centralized computer system, but a distributed system can be built to tolerate partial failures. ISIS [Birm87] [Birm91] is one such approach.

Fault tolerance is usually based on redundancy techniques, which have been adopted from the real world. One example is found in sports, where a team has backup players who can be used when needed. Another example is a firm which has trained several people to do the same job. Fault tolerance requires mechanisms for detecting faults and their sources, masking faults, and fixing the sources of the faults.

6 Sharing of resources

Since resources can be accessed at remote nodes in a distributed system, there is less need for replication of all resources at all nodes. Resources of the distributed system can be shared by users at different locations. There are two aspects to this. The first is sharing of common resources; the second is to utilize resources when they are not used by others. Having several users sharing the same resources avoids replication of all the resources at every node and improves cooperation.

Each user of a networked system can have accounts at several nodes in the system, allowing remote login and remote execution at non-local nodes. In a distributed system, this utilization of other nodes should be transparent. Additionally, when several nodes in a distributed system are heavily loaded while others are idle or lightly loaded, some sort of automatic job redistribution should be provided.

7 Distributed applications

Transparent or not, there are applications that would like to make explicit use of the multiple resources in a distributed system. Such applications come in two kinds: applications that want to exploit parallelism, and applications that need to use the physical distribution of the underlying resources.

The motivation for parallel applications is to achieve computational speedup. For example, a parallel version of the UNIX make program [Baal88] can achieve significant speedup for the compilation of large programs. Other application domains exist with inherent potential for parallel execution. The idea is to parallelize large applications into a set of processes which can be executed more or less independently. On one extreme processes have no interaction with each other; on the other extreme a lot of synchronization through inter-process communication is involved. Synchronization may result in a lot of overhead, so should be avoided.

The other kind of distributed applications are applications that are aware of the physical location of the resources, and use this information in the computation of their results. StormCast [Joha91] and Meta [Marz91] are examples of such applications. Such applications run well on networked systems, and it is important that sufficient support is given on distributed systems as well.

8 Summary

Ordinary users do not run operating systems, but applications. An operating system is just an intermediate software layer hiding hardware details and managing resources of the system. The less a regular user has to know about the internals of an operating system, the better. Although a distributed system interface appears as a centralized one like, for instance, the UNIX interface, the implementation of the distributed system is completely different. A distributed system is often a compromise within a set of conflicting goals. Clearly, technical limitations exist in meeting all objectives, especially where they must be accomplished simultaneously.

References

Acce86   M. Accetta, R. Baron, W. Bolosky, D. Golub, R. Rashid, A. Tevanian, and M. Young, "Mach: A New Kernel Foundation for UNIX Development," *Proc. USENIX 1986 Summer Conference*, pp. 93-113, Jul. 1986.

Baal88   E.H. Baalberge, "Design and Implementation of Parallel Make," *Comp. Syst.*, Vol. 1, No. 2, pp. 135-158, Spring 1988.

Birm87   K.P. Birman, and T.A. Joseph, "Exploiting Virtual Synchrony in Distributed Systems, *Proc. of the 11th ACM Symp. on Operating Systems Principles*, Austin, TX, pp. 123-138, Nov. 1987.

Birm91   K. Birman, and R. Cooper, "The ISIS Project: Real Experience with a Fault Tolerant Programming System," *Operating Systems Review*, pp. 103-107, Apr. 1991.

Joha91   D. Johansen, and G. Hartvigsen, "StormCast — A Distributed Application," *Proc. EurOpen Autumn '91*, pp. 273-286, Sep. 1991.

Marz91   K. Marzullo, R. Cooper, M. Wood, and K. Birman, "Tools for Distributed Application Management," *IEEE Computer*, Vol. 24, No. 8, pp. 42-51, Aug. 1991.

Pres91   D. Presotto, R. Pike, K. Thompson, and H. Trickey, "Plan 9, A Distributed System," *Proc. EurOpen Spring '91* (Tromsø, Norway), pp. 43-50, May 1991.

Rozi88   M. Rozier, V. Abrossimov, F. Armand, I. Boule, M. Gien, M. Guillemont, F. Herrmann, C. Kaiser, S. Langlois, P. Leonard, and W. Neuhauser, "CHORUS Distributed Operating Systems," *Computing Systems Journal* (The USENIX Association), Vol. 1, No. 4, pp. 305-370, Dec. 1988.

Tane90   A.S. Tanenbaum, R. van Renesse, H. van Staveren, G.J. Sharp, S.J. Mullender, A.J. Jansen, and G. van Rossum, "Experiences with the Amoeba Distributed Operating System", *Comm. ACM*, Vol. 33, No. 12, pp. 46-63, Dec. 1990.

About the Authors

Frances Brazier

Frances is a professor in the Department of Computer Science at the Vrije Universiteit in Amsterdam. Her main interests in distributed systems relate primarily to usability, both in theory and in practice.

Dag Johansen

Dag is a professor in the Department of Computer Science at the University of Tromsø, Norway. His research interests include most aspects of distributed systems and distributed applications. Currently, he is on sabbatical leave at Cornell University.

IEEE Computer Society Press

Press Activities Board

Vice President: Ronald G. Hoelzeman, University of Pittsburgh
Mario R. Barbacci, Carnegie Mellon University
Jon T. Butler, Naval Postgraduate School
J.T. Cain, University of Pittsburgh
Bill D. Carroll, University of Texas
Doris L. Carver, Louisiana State University
James J. Farrell III, VLSI Technology Inc.
Lansing Hatfield, Lawrence Livermore National Laboratory
Gene F. Hoffnagle, IBM Corporation
Barry W. Johnson, University of Virginia
Duncan H. Lawrie, University of Illinois
Michael C. Mulder, University of S.W. Louisiana
Yale N. Patt, University of Michigan
Murali R. Varanasi, University of South Florida
Ben Wah, University of Illinois
Ronald Waxman, University of Virginia

Editorial Board

Editor-in-Chief: Jon T. Butler, Naval Postgraduate School
Assoc. EIC/Acquisitions: Pradip K. Srimani, Colorado State University
Dharma P. Agrawal, North Carolina State University
Oscar N. Garcia, The George Washington University
Uma G. Gupta, University of Central Florida
A.R. Hurson, Pennsylvania State University
Yutaka Kanayama, Naval Postgraduate School
Frederick E. Petry, Tulane University
Dhiraj K. Pradhan, University of Massachusetts
Sudha Ram, University of Arizona
David Rine, George Mason University
A.R.K. Sastry, Rockwell International Science Center
Ajit Singh, Siemens Corporate Research
Mukesh Singhal, Ohio State University
Murali R. Varanasi, University of South Florida
Ronald D. Williams, University of Virginia

Press Staff

T. Michael Elliott, Executive Director
True Seaborn, Publisher
Catherine Harris, Managing Editor
Mary E. Kavanaugh, Production Editor
Lisa O'Conner, Production Editor
Regina Spencer Sipple, Production Editor
Penny Storms, Production Editor
Edna Straub, Production Editor
Robert Werner, Production Editor
Perri Cline, Electronic Publishing Manager
Frieda Koester, Marketing/Sales Manager
Thomas Fink, Advertising/Promotions Manager

Offices of the IEEE Computer Society

Headquarters Office
1730 Massachusetts Avenue, N.W.
Washington, DC 20036-1903
Phone: (202) 371-0101 — Fax: (202) 728-9614

Publications Office
P.O. Box 3014
10662 Los Vaqueros Circle
Los Alamitos, CA 90720-1264
Membership and General Information: (714) 821-8380
Publication Orders: (800) 272-6657 — Fax: (714) 821-4010

European Office
13, avenue de l'Aquilon
B-1200 Brussels, BELGIUM
Phone: 32-2-770-21-98 — Fax: 32-3-770-85-05

Asian Office
Ooshima Building
2-19-1 Minami-Aoyama, Minato-ku
Tokyo 107, JAPAN
Phone: 81-3-408-3118 — Fax: 81-3-408-3553

IEEE Computer Society

IEEE Computer Society Press Publications

Monographs: A monograph is an authored book consisting of 100-percent original material.

Tutorials: A tutorial is a collection of original materials prepared by the editors and reprints of the best articles published in a subject area. Tutorials must contain at least five percent of original material (although we recommend 15 to 20 percent of original material).

Reprint collections: A reprint collection contains reprints (divided into sections) with a preface, table of contents, and section introductions discussing the reprints and why they were selected. Collections contain less than five percent of original material.

Technology series: Each technology series is a brief reprint collection — approximately 126-136 pages and containing 12 to 13 papers, each paper focusing on a subset of a specific discipline, such as networks, architecture, software, or robotics.

Submission of proposals: For guidelines on preparing CS Press books, write the Managing Editor, IEEE Computer Society Press, PO Box 3014, 10662 Los Vaqueros Circle, Los Alamitos, CA 90720-1264, or telephone (714) 821-8380.

Purpose

The IEEE Computer Society advances the theory and practice of computer science and engineering, promotes the exchange of technical information among 100,000 members worldwide, and provides a wide range of services to members and nonmembers.

Membership

All members receive the acclaimed monthly magazine *Computer*, discounts, and opportunities to serve (all activities are led by volunteer members). Membership is open to all IEEE members, affiliate society members, and others seriously interested in the computer field.

Publications and Activities

Computer **magazine:** An authoritative, easy-to-read magazine containing tutorials and in-depth articles on topics across the computer field, plus news, conference reports, book reviews, calendars, calls for papers, interviews, and new products.

Periodicals: The society publishes six magazines and five research transactions. For more details, refer to our membership application or request information as noted above.

Conference proceedings, tutorial texts, and standards documents: The IEEE Computer Society Press publishes more than 100 titles every year.

Standards working groups: Over 100 of these groups produce IEEE standards used throughout the industrial world.

Technical committees: Over 30 TCs publish newsletters, provide interaction with peers in specialty areas, and directly influence standards, conferences, and education.

Conferences/Education: The society holds about 100 conferences each year and sponsors many educational activities, including computing science accreditation.

Chapters: Regular and student chapters worldwide provide the opportunity to interact with colleagues, hear technical experts, and serve the local professional community.